WINCHELL

WINCHELL

His Life and Times

Herman Klurfeld

PRAEGER PUBLISHERS · New York

Published in the United States of America in 1976
by Praeger Publishers, Inc.
111 Fourth Avenue, New York, N.Y. 10003

Library of Congress Cataloging in Publication Data
Klurfeld, Herman.
    Winchell, his life and times.
    Includes index.
    1.   Winchell, Walter, 1897–1972.   I.   Title
PN4874.W67K4   070'.92'4   [B]   74-29358
ISBN 0-275-33720-0

Printed in the United States of America

To

My Mother and Father

Contents

Acknowledgments

The book could not have been written without the love of my wife, Jeanette—a once-in-a-lifetime love that has given me the time of my life. I am grateful to my gifted son Jim Klurfeld, the inheritor of the family typewriter, and his wife, Judy, for their constant affection. My brilliant researcher, Jennifer Jason, merits a note of thanks.

I am also indebted to Jeffrey Lee Berkowitz, the prominent Miami attorney, and his lovely wife, Elaine, for their research covering the Miami Beach section of the Winchell story.

I am further indebted to my brother Sam Klurfeld for recalling significant episodes of the Winchell years. Typing and other assistance were provided by Ruth and Scott Klurfeld, as well as Rebecca and George Hellman.

My thank-you list would be incomplete without mention of the editing suggestions by Gladys Topkis, Léon King, and Vincent A. D'Arrigo.

And a special thanks to Arnold Forster, my old friend and comrade-in-arms.

WINCHELL

=1=
The Harlem Kid

On a crisp winter afternoon in the 1900s, the streets of Harlem were filled with people moving briskly among the rows of tenements and the litter. A confetti of sounds was in the air: the voices of conversations, the tinkling of a piano, the rumble of horse-drawn vehicles crossing the trolley tracks at Lenox Avenue and 116th Street, the occasional screech of a motor car, and the shrill cries of boys running, jumping, and gliding on their sleds.

Suddenly one sledder skidded into a horse-car, leaving him sprawled across the gutter, bleeding and terrified. Many years later, when the boy had became a man and was prowling the streets of Harlem in his car sniffing for excitement he pointed to the exact spot where he had been hit.

"That's where Mr. and Mrs. America almost lost their favorite newsboy," he said smiling.

The boy's injuries were minor, and within ten day he was playing on the streets again. But several local dailies reported the accident, marking the first appearance of Walter Winchell's name in the papers.

"I still have nightmares about it," Walter once told me. "I'll never forget how my mother and grandma cried and cried."

Walter's mother, Janet, a prematurely gray woman with lively blue eyes, had more than one reason for tears. She and her husband, Jacob Winchel, had migrated from Russia in 1893, lured by the glittering vision of America. Their disenchantment was cruelly swift. They settled in a tiny three-room apartment in Harlem, in a neighborhood mushrooming with Jewish, Italian, and one or two Negro families whose melancholy biographies were printed on their unpaid bills. "The devil came in the form of the landlord," Walter later recalled. On April 7, 1897, four years after Janet and Jacob's arrival in America, their first child was born. They named him Walter. Three years later, they had a second son, whom they named Albert.

Ill-equipped to enter the arts or the professions, Jacob Winchel, like many Eastern and Central European immigrants, tried to make a living by going into business for himself. He opened and closed several small shops on upper Broadway, mostly hole-in-the-wall emporiums where he sold silk piece goods, laces, and other sewing notions—little things for poor people. The struggle to make ends meet was brutal and at first Jacob fought bravely, but then he retreated and eventually surrendered. His annihilation was complete, and he exiled himself to the quiet shuffle of pinochle games with other defeated men in the neighborhood. "My pop," Winchell recalled, "wasn't much of a businessman, but he was a helluva pinochle player."

With Jacob lost in the world of pinochle, the burden of supporting the family fell to Walter's mother. Janet, a realistic, resourceful woman, went to work as a seamstress and took other odd jobs to keep the family afloat. But with only her earnings to live on, it was inevitable that tension should develop between her and Jacob. Beset by frustration and failure, they clawed at each other, and their bickering became more and more destructive. Eventually, after a succession of separations and reconciliations, Jacob deserted his wife and children. All alone now, Janet continued to provide for the boys as best she could. One way or another, she saw to it that they were always fed and housed, often boarding them out with strangers or sending them to stay with their grandmother, who operated a candy store nearby. Whenever they could, other relatives, aunts and uncles, pitched in to help her take care of the boys.

Janet Winchel had an alert and inquiring mind and considerable personal charm. "My mother," Walter recalled, "read books and tried to impress her sons with the value of formal education. I didn't listen, but my brother, Al, who was smarter in school than I was, eventually went to college and became an accountant. My big problem was math. I never knew anything about long division. I know that I disappointed my mother when I was a kid. But my grandma, who ran a candy store a few blocks from where we lived (117th Street and

Madison Avenue), was always understanding. She fed me chocolate twists and told me not to worry. She reassured me and comforted me with Yiddish proverbs, about being a good boy and things like that. I remember how beautiful it was to see my grandma light candles on Friday nights and say the traditional prayers."

At a very early age, Walter enlisted in the struggle for survival in the tough Harlem streets. Juvenile fights were a way of life, and kids huddled together in block gangs for security. Walter, as aware of his neighborhood as a tiger of his jungle habitat, became an aggressive leader of the young gang members. By the time he was ten he had begun to channel his energies not only into gang fights but also into a series of money-making chores. He sold papers, peddled magazine subscriptions, and waited with an umbrella near subway entrances on rainy days to escort people home for a nickel or a dime. Even at that age he was always on the watch for the big chance. A handsome lad with a lost-puppy smile, he knew even then how to manipulate people to get what he wanted. A tangled family life had deprived him and his brother of a warmth that he would miss all through his days, but the demanding fight for existence kept his mind clear and street-smart.

Being street-smart, however, did not win high marks at Harlem's Public School 184. "I was the school's prize dunce," Walter admitted in the *Journal American* in 1964. The succession of unfamiliar beds, the shattering image of a father's failure, and the need to scurry for odd jobs undoubtedly dulled the youngster's interest in classwork. and homework. Boredom bred rebellion. On one occasion Walter fled the school in tears after being censured by a teacher. In time he began to seek escape from the tedium of the classroom.

He found it in the city around him. In the 1900s New York's cosmopolitanism was speckled with provincial communities. Daily existence was generally confined to one's neighborhood, and the journey from the Bronx to Brooklyn was a great adventure. When Walter explored the "darkest Bronx," he found a dusty hamlet of elegant homes and trees where rabbits skittered at the sound of footsteps. Once or twice he and other truants went on an expedition in the other direction, as far as Brooklyn and even to Coney Island. A great deal more frequently (when he earned the price of admission), young Walter would skip school and head for the nickelodeon or a vaudeville show. Slouched in a darkened theater, with its gay tinkly sounds, he could shut out the harsh realities of home, the streets, and P.S. 184.

Walter would hike from Harlem to the newly rechristened Times Square (formerly Longacre) to see its fiery challenge to the night. ("New York is an electric city," reported the *Tribune* on September 22, 1906. "It is probably the most brilliantly illuminated city in the world. The most remarkable tract of night illumination lies in Broadway from 34th Street to 46th Street. The glittering trail along upper Broadway, the 'Great White Way,' is celebrated all over the world.")

He enjoyed watching the well-groomed folk sweeping in and out of such posh restaurants as Rector's and the Metropole, and on occasion he caught sight of show-business royalty of the period—the Floradora Sextette, Otis Skinner, Maude Adams, Ethel Barrymore. One night he slipped through the side door of a theater and saw the Weber and Fields act. Very impressed, he memorized their flippancies and later regaled his schoolmates with their routines. Four decades later, he still remembered snatches of the old-time songs and patter.

During the first decade of the century New York was the stage for another dazzling show. Daily newspapers engaged in no-holds-barred battles for circulation, and the winner was the first to deliver a kick in the groin. When James Gordon Bennett's *New York Herald Tribune* attacked William Randolph Hearst's moral and political character, Hearst returned the compliment. Bennett's paper was directed to a relatively sophisticated audience; however, prostitutes used its "personals" columns to advertise their fleshly lures in laundered phrases. Newspapermen called these lucrative columns "The Whores' Daily Guide." Hearst assigned one of his reporters to expose their sinful traffic. As a result, Bennett was eventually convicted of sending obscene matter through the mails and fined $25,000.

Joseph Pulitzer's *World* was the first paper to earn the epithet "yellow press," but Hearst's *Journal* outdid its competition with front-page stories of personal scandals headlined in big black letters. The *New York Times* shunned the hoopla of its rivals and adopted the air of informed dignity that was to become its trademark.

Young Walter's interest in journalism at this time was confined to hawking papers. He walked the streets of Harlem bellowing out headlines. Years later, he would shout them on the radio for $1,500 a minute, but at the age of eleven he was satisfied with two dollars a week. His earnings enabled him to contribute to the family's support. No less important, they made it possible for him to indulge with increasing frequency in his favorite escape: vaudeville shows.

In school, there was no music or applause, nor were there bright visions. The classroom environment, never a joy, became a daily torment for young Walter. At twelve he was the oldest student in the sixth grade, having been left back twice. More and more he replaced school—his gray reality—with the multihued dreams of the stage. He took on the style and accoutrements of a vaudevillian. With sharp-pronged iron strips hammered into the toes and heels of his shoes, he spent hours at home practicing the ratatat of tap dances on the white-tiled bathroom floor, humming the songs of the day. Eventually his tapping brought complaints from the neighbors and his mother forbade him to dance in the house. Walter then transferred his performances to school, where, during his infrequent visits, he would dance and sing for the other kids. A failure as a pupil, he was something of a success as the class entertainer. He never forgot his early triumphs and forty years later he would say, "I can still remember the way I felt when the other kids watched me dancing. It was a kind of exciting, breathless feeling. And it was more fun than playing cops and robbers."

One of the neighborhood kids impressed by Walter's hoofing was George Jessel, who lived with his widowed mother and grandparents at 118th Street and Lenox Avenue. Mrs. Jessel, the ticket-taker at the local Imperial Theater, got her George and Walter jobs as ushers at the theater. Walter was thrilled. And, a little later, when he and George Jessel were asked to entertain during intermissions, he was beside himself with joy.

The youngsters put all they had into singing old and new ditties, from "Swanee River" to "Pony Boy," the hit of the moment, the lyrics being flashed on the screen so that the audience could sing along. The $4 a week they earned as ushers was not increased when they became singers, but, for Walter at least, the spattering of applause was payment enough. They did their duets from the orchestra pit because they were too young to appear on the stage, but that didn't bother Walter. He was in show business and all his mother's finger-waving arguments couldn't stop him. He was a celebrity on his block.

When a lad named Jack Weiner joined Walter and George, they became the Imperial Trio. Later Walter conjured up a deluxe tag for them: "Lawrence, Stanley, and McKinley." The names, otherwise meaningless, they thought, "had the connotation of class." The trio was billed as "The Little Men with the Big Voices." "Little men" they were, but "big voices" was a typical billboard exaggeration.

Weiner had almost no singing ability, and Jessel's voice even then had virtually no range. Walter, whose tenor was at least adequate, provided the harmony for the trio. But as far as the young performers were concerned, they were the archetype of the big-time vaudeville act. And, for about three months, they made up for their lack of talent with vigor and enthusiasm.

Once he had become famous, magazine profiles of Winchell invariably included this anecdote: One afternoon Walter neglected to come to the theater. When Weiner and Jessel raised ragged voices, there ensued a series of vibrations that had little or no relation to music. The audience responded with a shower of fruit and vegetables. The house lights were turned on. And there, in the back row, was the missing Walter, smooching with a girl. When I asked Walter about the anecdote, he smiled and said, "It's a good story, but it never happened. I missed the performance because I was sore at my partners about something or other. Maybe I was too busy selling papers."

Eventually "Lawrence, Stanley, and McKinley" were dismissed from the Imperial, but the trio, especially Walter, continued rehearsing and dreaming. His first taste of mass approval had fortified his vision of the stage as a safer and happier playground than the streets. The feeling was intensified by his increasing difficulties at P.S. 184. At the end of the school year, he learned that he had been left back for the third time.

A week later, the Imperial Trio was auditioned by Gus Edwards, a small-time vaudeville producer-performer. Edwards liked their act and asked them to join his troupe. This was the escape hatch Walter had been looking for. At last he would be able to put behind him the shame of school and the disappointments of family life. When he was twelve years old, going on thirteen, Walter, with more relief than remorse, left home.

After he became Walter Winchell, the columnist, the harsher realities of his childhood faded.

Once I accompanied him on a sentimental journey to Harlem. He parked his car at 120th Street and Lenox Avenue, stepped out, and beckoned me to follow. A few hours earlier he had conducted his weekly monologue for Mr. and Mrs. America, heard by an estimated 30 million people. But here, at 5 A.M. in the streets of Harlem, we were alone.

Walter moved quickly along the street. Head turning and eyes roving, he seemed responsive to a thousand external and internal influences. From time to time he would stop and make a comment. "When I was a kid there was a kosher butcher shop there," he murmured, pointing to a hardware store. "I used to run errands. Deliver the chickens and get a penny or a nickel tip. When things were dull I swept the place and wiped the blood off the hooks. It wasn't Miami Beach!" As we walked he remembered the candy store of the area: "My first Stork Club." He recalled it as the hangout of neighborhood kids, the place where they would meet to argue and wrestle and gossip. We continued our tour. Pointing to an apartment building, he whispered, "That's where Ruthie Rosenberg lived. She was my girl." Then he suddenly remembered: "Y'know, I never told Ruthie I planned to leave home. And I didn't tell my mother. After my third straight flop in the sixth grade, I decided to go someplace else, anyplace else."

As we drove from the Harlem streets, I inquired, "What kind of kid were you?"

"I just received a letter from my fifth-grade teacher," he said. "Her name is Mary Petrey. She says she remembers me as a boy with perfect manners. She remembers how I always doffed my hat, the only boy in the school of fifteen hundred kids who didn't wear a cap."

"It's hard for me to image you in a Lord Fauntleroy role," I chuckled.

"When I had to be tough, I was tough. Tough as hell. On the streets, where you had to be tough."

"But kids learn courtesy from their parents," I observed.

"My mother and grandma taught me how to be a good little boy. Don't forget, my grandpa had been a rabbi and a cantor.

"Yes," he continued, "my mother and father went to *shool* on the High Holy Days. But they weren't orthodox, although we had kosher foods in the house."

He laughed. "Now when I tell my mother about all the great food on the Stork Club menu, she says, 'What's wrong with a corned beef sandwich?'

"For me it's baloney and eggs," Walter sighed. "The trouble with poverty is that it's so damn boring."

Suddenly he reminded himself, "You know, my mother loved to go to vaudeville shows when she could afford it in the Harlem days. When she got home she repeated the acts practically word for word. Maybe that's where I got my taste for show business."

He was silent for a moment or two and then repeated a thought I had often heard him express: "The tough life is not so tough. Harlem gave me something money can't buy. It cost me a lot, but I learned plenty. It wasn't all bad. Not bad at all."

=2=
The Song-and-Dance Days

In 1910, vaudeville was at the height of its katzenjammer period. All across the nation, from big city palaces to provincial bistros, hypnotists, one-legged dancers, ventriloquists, comics, dramatic actors, singers, wirewalkers, contortionists, female impersonators, and other assorted acts with more courage than talent provided thrills for Mr. and Mrs. America. Except for a tiny elite, the vaudevillians found neither fame nor riches. But they were hooked on "show biz."

As homeless as clouds, they wandered from place to place. Each day added to their store of anguish and humiliation, but they never stopped hoping. Sporting flashy clothes and big imitation diamonds, they were always prepared for trades with pawnshops when bookings were scarce. They lived in the same boarding houses, spoke a special language, and had similar hopes and fears. Children joined their parents onstage and took bows. When they grew up, they went into vaudeville and the pattern was repeated.

What vaudevillians called "kid acts" were usually a pretty sure thing. They were cheap and they always got a good response from the audience. That was why Gus Edwards had recruited not only Walter, George Jessel, and Jack Weiner but also Eddie Cantor, George Price, and Lila Lee. He called the group the "Newsboy Sextette" and opened it at a theater in Union Hill, New Jersey. The theater was more like a rabbit hutch than anything else, but for thirteen-year-old Walter and the others it was a pleasure dome.

Eyes popping, arms windmilling, the ragamuffins dashed onstage and performed a series of demonic exercises. With flapping shirts, long trousers, and huge rainbow-splashed ties they zigzagged around chattering nonsense while Walter ran from one kid to another clubbing him with a rolled-up newspaper and yammering, "Shaddup!" It wasn't art, but Walter made $15 a week. Later, when he took on the duties of handling and caring for the props, he was raised to a lavish $25.

After several months of touring, Gus Edwards sold the act to Roy Mack, a former vaudevillian turned booking agent. Mack renamed it "Gus Edwards' School Days," increased the cast to ten teenagers and choreographed their routine for a dizzying pace.

The act would open with the entire company bellowing the song "School Days"; then all the kids would begin dashing hither and thither. The teacher, played by Dorothy Mack, would calm the bedlam by rapping a hickory stick on her desk, but as soon as she did another brushfire of insubordination would flare up. Wearing a stiff white collar and spectacles, with his cheeks rouged, Roy Mack was the focus of the taunts of the rambunctious pupils, who slapped, teased, and pelted him. He played the part of the execution victim resigned to his fate. He accepted the boys' indignities with bland resignation, gaining sympathy laughs by suffering in silence. Pouting and shrugging, he faced the malevolent universe, which had singled him out for siege, with his shoulders hunched for self-protection. The act was a monument to the "Unknown Chump." The eternal patsy that is in every man and every kid.

Walter portrayed a bad boy, a leering nogoodnik. Garbed in a turtleneck sweater, cap yanked down over his left eye, face frozen in a scowl, he roamed the room belting random victims with his standard prop—a rolled-up newspaper. Using a newspaper as a weapon was in the shape of things to come for Walter. The act raced to a finish, with the entire gang singing a medley of pop tunes. The chanting kids, emitting joy as if they were anticipating candy, won the admiration of the audience. The act was a successful one. It toured for more than four years.

For Walter, the vaudeville circuit was a new world. A snapshot taken during these years was inscribed, "Hello, Ma, here I am in San Diego!" On others he penciled in the names of towns and cities he visited with the vaudeville vagabonds. In some of the photos he wears a cap at a rakish angle. He was in a perpetual state of discovery. Everything excited his curiosity—a new dance step or gag, some odd fact about the towns he toured. His occasional letters to his mother were highlighted with impressions of people and places. Once, in response to my questioning, he said, "I don't remember being home-sick during those years. In the first year or two I was too excited about what was going to happen tomorrow."

The excitement was combined with hard work. Walter "never knew when to quit," said Eddie Cantor. "While the rest of us were fooling around, he was occupied with some project or other. I hardly ever remember seeing him relax. He didn't have any definite direction, but he was all motion."

After a year of swatting heads with a newspaper, he began to watch and study other acts. One that fascinated him particularly was the sand dance. In that routine, the performer ambled onstage with a cardboard box half filled with sand. To the sound of soft music, the performer would cavort in an imitation ballet while sprinkling the stage with sand. Then he would hand the container to someone in the wings and go into a series of slides, shifts, and shuffles augmented by a light tap. It seemed an effortless routine, but actually it was quite difficult. Walter learned it well enough to beguile performers back-stage with his own version of it. He wasn't really good, but he was energetic.

Whenever vaudevillians got together offstage they talked shop. Communicating in their own jargon, they frequently discussed audiences, but mostly they talked about one another, their acts, their families, their gay and melancholy experiences on the road. Their backstage conversations were often peppered with talk about sex. This was gossip pure and simple, sometimes tangy, sometimes malicious, but always a continuous gabble. Whether or not he knew it, Walter was developing a taste for gossip communicated in breezy, direct language.

Vaudevillians, like most professionals, were extremely status-conscious. In their rigid caste system, billing determined status, and there was a marked difference between headliners and small-timers. Walter learned to divide people into those who had "class" and those who didn't. The people with class were generally successful or famous. A goggle-eyed adoration of stars characterized Walter all his life. Stars had class.

Walter's education, as he later remarked, came from "meeting people everywhere and reading newspapers in every city. I read the editorial page to find out what the news and happenings meant. I became interested in the world around me." This was undoubtedly true.

But his more enduring education came from vaudeville. In myriad playhouses, he learned from audience reactions, getting the feel of crowds, to know what people wanted, what excited them, and what trick or style manipulated them. Almost by osmosis he learned about the mob, the public—the conglomeration of humanity he was later to enthrall. He learned how to quicken the imagination, developing a subtle and mysterious power that can come under the heading of "showmanship."

Still, he was a standoffish, complex youngster who puzzled those around him. The crises of his early life made him, at heart, something of a loner and left him with a frosty edge. There was always some part of Walter that was secret. Perhaps the fear of losing himself in the motley family of vaudeville forced him to isolate himself. In any event, his human relationships were never wholly satisfactory. Sometimes he seemed to crave attention. At other times he pulled away from any participation in social relationships. A "quite good-looking kid, he talked very little about himself. He didn't engage in the usual roughhousing. He seemed very alone and aloof," recalled one of his companions during his vaudeville era.

Eddie Cantor, who was older and more mature than the other youngsters in the troupe, once said to Walter, "In this business you'll meet the most beautiful girls in the world. But you must remember that your career comes first. Don't waste your time with the other nonsense." Walter relished the nonsense, however, and when he was sixteen he fell madly in love with a taffy-haired girl he met on a train. He wrote her poems and passionate letters, but she never replied. "I've had trouble with girls since I was sixteen," he once sighed.

This remark has no basis in reality unless you consider having too many girls a problem. Walter was always popular with girls, but when he was on the brink of seventeen he was more concerned about his career than anything else. If he remained with the Schooldays act another year or two he would outgrow the act and find himself a full-fledged failure at eighteen or nineteen. He had to find a way out. The most obvious out was an act of his own. Walter began spending hours in boarding-house bathrooms outlining a song-and-dance turn spiced with patter. He wrote in the bathroom because it was the "only place I could get peace and quiet." After several months of preparation he decided it was time to leave. About this time, the marquee at a Chicago theater misspelled his name, adding a second "l." Walter liked the way it looked, and from that time on he was Winchell.

In December 1914, in Detroit, Walter said good-bye to the School-days act. The break was not easy. "When the time came to leave, I was more than a little afraid," Walter remembered. "I was leaving home again. After I made my decision, I wasn't sure it was the right thing to do. But I had done it and that was that. I sure as hell remember I couldn't sleep that night. But I wasn't alone. One of the dolls in the show kept me company."

Those first four years in vaudeville were more significant in Walter's development than any comparable period of his life. Thanks to a vast amount of sheer nerve, the skinny, good-looking youngster had become enormously self-sufficient. His contacts with new people and new experiences were exhilarating as well as educational. Most important, vaudeville gave him a feel for life and eventually a choice of career.

Unfortunately, there was a human penalty for the rewards of the vaudeville experience. Difficult as it is for most people to put the pieces of their life together, it was especially arduous for Walter. He never really had an opportunity to know his mother, father, and brother. There was no time for a normal relationship. After all, he was only about six years old when he went to work after school, a bare thirteen when he departed. He was out of the house and into the world before he could form mature relationships with his family. Throughout his years in vaudeville, Walter's family remained a series of distant figures. He was never able to reach out to it.

Yet he adored his mother and eventually showered her with material goods. But the man who communicated with millions was unable to communicate with his mother. When he was with her, he talked about his triumphs as a columnist and newscaster, which probably bored her after a while, although she was proud of him. "When I'm with my mom," Walter complained, "she talks about her aches and pains and sick relatives." Whether it was his mother, his wife, or his children, he had little time and less patience for ordinary family obligations.

Some of Winchell's thornier critics later portrayed Walter the vaudevillian as a glacial, calculating young man of meager talents. A kindlier portrait was drawn by surviving vaudevillians who had been impressed with his energy and single-minded will to succeed. Always infectiously and throbbingly alive, he had a sense of drama about himself and his destiny.

=3=
A Taste of Failure—and the
Smell of Newsprint

Back in New York, Walter moved into a small hotel on West 44th Street and began making the rounds of agents. But with little to offer except furious dancing and borrowed jokes, all he could get were sporadic bookings—split weeks at broken-down theaters in the boon-docks.

Now that he was on his own, it seemed that he would become a failure before he got started. But he wouldn't give up. He would sit for hours on end with other small-timers in shabby Broadway restaurants, bemoaning the frustrations and indignities of vaudeville and asking veteran performers about gimmicks he might use to make his act unique. One suggested, perhaps in jest, that he dance on roller skates. Walter bought a pair of skates and spent weeks trying to learn to dance on them. But he gave it up when he saw an act with a roller-skating chimpanzee as its chief attraction.

In 1915, America was swept by patriotic fervor, and vaudeville was quick to realize that flag-waving spectaculars would be good box office. Such titles as "For Your Country and My Country," "You've Got to Be an American to Feel That Way," "Let's All Be Americans Now," and "Liberty Bell, It's Time to Ring Again" began to appear on bill-boards and programs. Comics would peer down at the orchestra pit and blandly inquire, "How are you boys down there in the trenches?" Walter wrote a song called "The Land I Love" and spaced his hoofing with a fiery patriotic oration complete with a quavering finish. He took the act on the road and had fairly steady bookings. But everyone jumped on the bandwagon, and before long patriotic acts were a dime a dozen. Managers again demanded something new. So after six months of small-time success, Walter was again an unemployed vaude-villian.

He returned to New York. In the mornings he would once again make the dreary rounds of agents' offices, but at noon he would station himself in front of the Palace with other players who were "at liberty." "I often stood in front of the Palace for hours swapping lies," he re-called. "There were always jobs we turned down because the agents were either too stupid to appreciate us or unable to meet our price. I used to wait at the Palace hoping to meet a friend rich enough to in-vite me to join him across the street for a cup of coffee and a sandwich. It was all so damn frustrating and humiliating. The strange part of it was that none of us ever thought about trying another job or getting into another field. It was like a religion. We were in show business, and we intended remaining in it even if it meant we had to starve to death. There is something about the pride of actors that is hard to understand. I guess you have to be an actor to understand it. It cer-tainly isn't anything rational."

When Walter recalled this experience, it was with a sort of ironic jocularity. To him it gave harsh relevance to his opportunistic methods and his oft rendered admonition "Save your money while you're hot—you stay cold a long time."

Despite the rebuffs and layoffs, Walter continued trying to find some-thing unique to impress agents and managers. For a while he thought of forming his own "Schooldays" act, but by then there were more than sixty such acts on the boards, including one featuring the Marx brothers. He beseeched act writers for something new and went to vaudeville shows in and around New York whenever he could to pick up new ideas. While doing so, he frequently dated girls in the com-panies he went to see. One of his dates was a dancer named Rita Greene, who had been George Jessel's partner. Trim and saucy, Rita was as ambitious as she was talented. On dates she and Walter swapped ideas for improving their acts and eventually decided to form Winchell and Greene, which played for the first time in 1916.

Walter gave me a vivid description of the act one evening after a newscast in June 1942. Three or four of us were sitting in the studio. Walter was relaxed and, as happened now and then, he began talking about his vaudeville days. Suddenly he leaped from the chair facing the microphone, nodded toward an invisible orchestra, and said, "If you please, professor, bring me on with 'Give My Regards to Broadway' with lots of brass."

"I danced out with my cane, straw skimmer, and white flannels," he said.

His feet swished against the carpeted floor in a shorthand version of a time-step.

"I waited for the opening applause. It wasn't always there. The second curtain parted, and my partner, Rita Greene, sat on a replica of a wall, gazing soulfully at the sky. She looks my way and then we duet —a love song for the act which I named 'Spooneyville.' "

Winchell gazed upward as if searching for the balcony's reaction.

"Then we danced together for a short time, a bit of cakewalk, continuing to give out with the romantic duet. And don't forget that blue spotlight. Oh, how I waited for the sound of applause. If it came, it was something grand. After the duet, my partner exits. I take the stage solo."

With a passing genuflection to the honor of the stage solo, Walter continued, "I then sang a war song, just to get the chill out of their bones. I wrote the lyrics." He glided from one side of the studio to the other, miming a song. "Then my partner returned to the stage for her solo dance. A twirly-whirly. When she was finished, she pretended she was breathless. The hard breathing was a popular bit. It helped milk applause."

Walter flapped his arms. "Then I bounced back onstage for an exchange of gags with my partner. Oh, those jokes! They were such dandies as 'Are oysters healthy?' 'I never heard them complain.' 'Yocky-yockyyock.' Then there was 'You can drive a horse to drink, but a pencil must be lead.' And listen to this: 'I sent my wife to the Thousand Islands for a vacation. Why the Thousand Islands? A week on each island.' "

A quick jig and another swish-swish-swish on the carpet.

"After each joke the band would hit a crescendo, to whip up applause or make it impossible for us to hear the lack of it. Then I went into my topical humor: 'Walter,' she asked, 'what's your idea of a good time?' My punchline: 'Watching a shipload of second lieutenants sinking!' Then came the musical thunder.

"The act finished with a double bit of wild tapping." Winchell leaned over and moved his feet and arms briskly in an effort to recall the mounting intensity.

"Segue into two choruses of 'Swanee River' pizzicato and pianissimo

—until the last four bars. Then bring it up fast and forte to the exit and the bows."

Then he commanded with harsh emphasis, "Applaud, you bastards, applaud!"

The audience of two or three dutifully applauded while Winchell took bow after bow.

Winchell and Greene worked steadily for almost a year. They played the Sun Circuit, a chain of eight theaters in the Midwest owned by Gus Sun, the leading impresario of vaudeville's lower depths; the Sullivan-Considine Chain in Washington, Oregon, and Vancouver; and the Pantages Circuit, which included a half-dozen theaters on the West Coast. The money, between $50 and $75 a week, was no great shakes by movie-star standards, but it was better than average for lesser vaudevillians. Besides, for Walter there were other compensations. He had an independent act for the first time, and it was well received by managers, audiences, and his fellow vaudevillians. "It wasn't sensational, but it was pretty good," remembered Emmett Callahan, one of Walter's contemporaries. "It had good potential. Walter was a cocky kid. And many of us believed he was going places."

But just when it looked as though Winchell and Greene were on their way, "the war came along and everything went blooey," Walter recollected. With the country's entry into World War I, military service shriveled the ranks of performers as well as audiences. Many show people who were not in uniform volunteered their talents to entertain the troops at home and abroad. An evening blackout was ordered for Broadway and other entertainment centers, and theaters were closed on Tuesdays to conserve fuel. The box-office problem was compounded when the nation was hit with a flu epidemic. For many weeks, Walter and Rita discussed what they should do. Finally, Walter returned to New York and enlisted in the Navy. "I decided to enlist because I thought it was the right thing to do. Politics or philosophy had nothing to do with it. It was just an emotional thing. And I was damn proud."

He was assigned to the New York City customs house as a receptionist for Rear Admiral Marbury Johnson. In his more imaginative moments, Walter later described his military function as that of a "courier," giving the impression that he was engaged in some sort of cloak-and-dagger work. Actually his duties consisted of handling, stamping, mailing, and applying sealing wax to envelopes. In other words, he was a uniformed office boy.

One day, while using a candle to spread sealing wax, Walter leaned forward to eavesdrop on Admiral Johnson's conversation with other officers and burned his nose. This story, one of Walter's favorites, became a staple in magazine interviews, but when I casually mentioned to him that it sounded too pat, he grinned and said, "Never spoil a good story by trying to verify it."

For many people the war was a time of loneliness and introspection. And so it was for Walter. When he was off duty, he would seek out fellow vaudevillians to discuss the news and to gossip. He planned to return to the stage once he got out of the navy, but he felt a nagging yen to do something else. He and Rita exchanged torrid love letters. Whenever she came to New York, they discussed their future. In the back of his mind, Walter wondered what kind of future they would have if he remained in vaudeville. But vaudeville was the only game he knew.

Shortly after the Armistice was signed, Walter and Rita were married in a civil ceremony in New York. Having decided to revive the "Spooneyville" act, they spent their honeymoon playing the Pantages Circuit. A time bomb had been placed under acts like theirs in the form of the new movie industry, but Walter and Rita were oblivious to the threat to their career. "We were always hoping and planning, striving to improve," he recalled. "Other acts might go from nowhere to somewhere, and we thought it might happen to us."

It almost did. In March 1919, Winchell and Greene appeared at the American Roof in New York. The *Variety* critic described it as a "likable act" and hailed the singing and dancing but was unimpressed with some of their lyrics. He concluded, "The turn isn't one to bring forth any volume of applause, but it's pleasant." For their appearance at the American Roof, Winchell and Greene received $100 a week. The act never rose above the number-two spot. In the vaudeville hierarchy this was one step above the opening turn, which was generally an animal act. As the months passed, hopes of upgrading the act's billing became more and more remote. Walter and Rita then took their repartee, songs, and footwork to the stages of the Midwest and the Far West. Lightning didn't strike, but at least they had steady work.

It could have been the culmination of a chain of events, or it could have been a sudden whim. In any case, while playing a Chicago theater, Walter pinned on the backstage bulletin board a typewritten sheet that he called "Newsense." An informal guide for vaudevillians, peppered with human interest, jokes, and plugs for restaurants popular with performers, it was an instant hit. Walter could hardly believe it.

He brought out other issues of the sheet from time to time, gradually adding tidbits regarding births, deaths, and marriages among show people. Soon "Newsense" expanded to two typewritten pages spiced with romantic items, and Walter found that his behind-the-scenes billing was suddenly elevated. Onstage, he was a "deuce act," practically a second-class citizen; backstage, he was becoming an admired chronicler.

There were exceptions, of course. One member of an acrobatic act was so incensed by an item in "Newsense" that he threatened to punch Walter in the nose. But such reactions were rare. The popularity of Walter's sheet spread beyond the backstages, and one day while playing a theater in Chicago he was asked by an acquaintance on the *Herald and Examiner* to cover the arrivals and departures of well-known people at the Illinois Central Station. Walter promptly tagged himself the *Herald and Examiner*'s traveling reporter."

When the "traveling reporter" left Chicago, he returned to his backstage beat. With considerable relish, Walter would spend several hours a day drumming with two fingers on the keys of a borrowed typewriter. Turning out "Newsense" became almost an obsession with him. The one-man paper began to take on a life of its own, an exciting life that enlivened Walter's otherwise routine existence as a small-time vaudevillian. Slowly his interests were being diverted. The mirage of vaudeville stardom began to give way to the vision of himself as a newspaperman. By the end of 1919, Walter had begun submitting items to various trade papers. Most of them spurned his material, but *Billboard* accepted some of his submissions and published them under the heading "Stage Whispers." Signed "W.W.," they were mostly about the comings and goings of vaudeville acts. There was no such thing as a gossip column then, and Walter's efforts were rather tame and dull. Occasionally, however, there was an item with a touch of piquancy: "Seen outside of a Cleveland movie theater: Geraldine Farrar supported for the first time by her husband." His initial *Billboard* check was for $6.90, and he literally jumped for joy. "Imagine being paid for something you would do for nothing. I later received fancier paychecks, but no reward, not even the five-figure fees I received for a single broadcast, gave me the glorious feeling I had then. It was just great."

Another paper to which Walter sent contributions was the *New York Vaudeville News,* a propaganda sheet launched by Edward F. Albee, the vaudeville tycoon, to "put *Variety* out of business." *Variety,* a sprightly, independent show-business weekly, had dared to criticize

Albee's dictatorial methods and express its support for the actors' union known as the White Rats—"star" spelled backwards. The union had been organized to break Albee's grip on vaudeville. Albee immediately inserted in all his contracts a clause that read, "The Actor hereby guarantees that he is not a member of the White Rats Actors Union and that he is a member in good standing of the National Vaudeville Artists. In the event that either of these statements be found untrue this contract is automatically canceled." The National Vaudeville Artists was a company union, and the *New York Vaudeville News* was its organ. In 1919, when the White Rats became the first actors' union to obtain a charter from the AF of L, the struggle against the Keith-Albee empire intensified. The White Rats struck against Albee, who responded by using his own acts as strikebreakers and bribed and intimidated others to works in his theaters. Sime Silverman, the publisher of *Variety,* made the White Rats' cause his own. It was a David-and-Goliath struggle, but in the end the mighty Albee was forced to give his performers better salaries and better working conditions.

Walter's association with the organ of Albee's National Vaudeville Aritsts was not, as some of his later critics claimed, a reflection of his antilabor bias. At the time, he was a struggling vaudevillian with no deep convictions about the dispute. If he thought about it at all, his sympathies probably lay with the White Rats. Then, as later, however, he was primarily pro-Winchell, and his chief concern was his budding writing career.

Conditions may have improved somewhat for vaudevillians in general, but for Winchell and Greene the going was downhill. They seemed to be frozen in the number-two spot, and long hours in day coaches, plus the monotony of small-time theaters, were taking their toll in the Winchells' personal and professional lives. While they were playing Birmingham, Alabama, their act was suddenly canceled in the middle of the week, leaving them with just enough money for one of them to take the train home. Walter gave all their money to Rita. His own passage, on a railroad car that was transporting chickens, he earned by feeding the birds en route. "For years afterwards," he recalled, "I hated to eat chickens. Boy, how they stunk."

When he returned to New York, he no longer had visions of making it big in vaudeville. He asked Glenn Condon, editor of the *New York Vaudeville News*, for a permanent job on the paper. Finally, on November 1, 1920, Condon made him an offer. Walter wrote to Howard Langford, a vaudeville friend:

> My dear Howard:
> I am writing you again to tell you what a wonderful proposition has been made to me from the Keith Exchange to be assistant editor of the *Vaudeville News*. I have accepted believing that the future of such a proposition holds remarkable things for me (if I show 'em what I'm made of) and has unlimited possibilities.
> You no doubt don't blame me, because you have heard me mention that I would love to become a figure in the world, preferably the news game. I have always had an inclination toward it, and at last have had my wish granted.
> Of course, the money is not a helluva lot, and I know I cannot save, but the fact is that any day may bring more wonderful things, on the connection itself with such a wonderful organization as the B. F. Keith Exchange can give.
> I also realize that when I tire of this (if I do) I can always go back to being an ordinary actor, can't I?

Walter's departure from vaudeville was an act of surrender. According to George Jessel, his failure was due to his inability to enjoy either his audiences or his work. A more realistic appraisal is simply this: Audience resistance to Walter's talent had become insurmountable. Any lack of affection Walter felt for his audiences was merely a response to their lukewarm reception of his efforts. All his life, he craved affection and attention, and if there had been any enthusiasm for his act, he certainly would have returned the sentiment. What Walter disliked, with spitting distaste, was failure. Period.

By the end of 1920, Walter had cut his ties with Rita. Their marriage had been built on their youthful dreams of success, and when those illusions were shattered the marriage was doomed. Years later, newspaper and magazine writers working on stories about Walter tried to interview Rita. She always turned them down. For years she worked as a typist in a law office while Walter continued to pay her alimony. In 1940, it was reported that she was writing a book about her early days with Walter, but it never materialized. Rumor had it that Winchell had paid her to suppress the book, but Walter always denied the story.

In 1950, Walter and Rita had a chilly reunion in Walter's office at the *Daily Mirror* to discuss an increase in alimony payments. As the day of the meeting approached, Walter grew skittish. "How do you act with an ex-wife you haven't seen for years? What do you say? How will she look to me? How will I look to her?" Afterward, Walter was morose. "I could see how old I was getting by looking at her," he said. It had been thirty years since he had crossed the threshold of the world of the 1920s, a world that would nourish him and give him wings.

=4=
The Byline Opiate

When Walter got his first regular job on a newspaper in 1920, tabloids were becoming common in America. It had taken almost two decades for them to spread to this country from Britain, where, at the turn of the century, Alfred Harmsworth had started a "halfpenny illustrated" called the *London Daily Mail*. The low-priced "busy man's newspaper," with its capsule news and lively features, was a howling success, and in time Harmsworth started another paper, the *Daily Mirror,* which splashed pictures all over its pages and instigated bizarre promotional stunts such as an expedition to the Arctic. Its circulation rocketed to more than a million, and before long the *Mirror* had two imitators—the *London Daily Sketch* and *The Daily Graphic*—and Harmsworth had become Lord Northcliffe. On a visit to the United States he urged Joseph Pulitzer to publish an edition of the *World* in tabloid form. Pulitzer published a single issue, and it added one hundred thousand to the *World's* circulation, but he shrugged it off as a mere curiosity and promptly forgot about the new format.

In 1919, Joseph Patterson, publisher of the *Chicago Tribune,* with his cousin Robert R. McCormick, visited Lord Northcliffe in England. Impatient with the reluctance of Americans to begin publishing tabloids, Northcliffe told Patterson, "New York's got to have a picture tabloid. If the rest of you don't see the light soon, I'll start one myself." Patterson, the son of a wealthy and influential family, had long ago abandoned his flirtation with socialism, but he retained an intuitive awareness of the preferences of masses. Perhaps he sensed that the swift expansion of cities and the quickened pace of life in the previous

23

decades had made the American public hungry for newspapers that could be read quickly and digested easily. He knew that soaring production costs had forced publishers into a circulation battle with an increase in the number of sensational stories and entertainment features. Moreover, shocking war pictures had created a mounting interest in news photos.

Patterson returned from Britain and made arrangements to use the *New York Evening Mail*'s plant to publish a tabloid to be called the *Illustrated Daily News*. Simultaneously, William Randolph Hearst equipped a tabloid plant at 55 Frankfort Street in New York City and waited to see how Patterson's experiment would turn out. The *Illustrated Daily News* credo was published in the paper's first issue:

WHO WE ARE

The Illustrated Daily News is going to be your newspaper. Its interests will be your interests. . . . It is not an experiment, for the appeal of news pictures and brief, well-told stories will be as apparent to you as it has been to millions of readers in European cities.

We shall give you every day the best and newest pictures of the interesting things that are happening in the world. . . . The story that is told by a picture can be grasped instantly. Ten thousand words of description cannot convey to you the impression you receive when you look at Millet's painting 'The Angelus.' . . .

No story will be continued to another page—that is to save you trouble. You can read it without eye strain.

The policy of the *Illustrated Daily News* will be your policy. It will be aggressively for America and for the people of New York. . . . It will have no entangling alliance with any class whatever. . . .

Because the doings of the very fortunate are always of interest we shall print them as interestingly as possible in our society column. Because fiction will always be appealing we shall print the best and newest that is to be had. We shall print the best features that are to be found.

Advertising in the *New York Times,* the *Daily News* invited the public to "SEE NEW YORK'S MOST BEAUTIFUL GIRLS EVERY MORNING IN THE ILLUSTRATED DAILY NEWS." Within six months the *News* had a circulation of four hundred thousand—more than any other paper in New York. Journalism had entered a new era. The stage was set for Walter Winchell.

Bursting with ideas and, as his boss, Glenn Condon, recalled, "always talking," Walter lost no time in attracting attention at the *Vaudeville News*. At twenty-three, he already had traces of gray in his hair, but his burning eyes and lean, handsome face gave him an electric presence. He showed uncanny resourcefulness as he went around town picking up quips and items for columns he called "Merciless Truth" and "Broadway Hearsay." He was constantly looking for ways to supplement his $25 weekly salary. The paper had been distributed as a throwaway, but two months after Walter joined the staff he persuaded Condon to charge a nickel for it and make him advertising manager with a commission of 20 percent of the gross. As both columnist and advertising salesman, he often earned more than $100 a week, though he averaged half of that. By an unwritten agreement, he gave favorable mention in his column to actors or restaurants who bought advertising space in the paper. Occasionally, however, he would toss in an item critical of an advertiser, just to assert his independence.

Quips, comments, and superficial notes were the stuff of Walter's early columns. His material was rather bland, but occasionally there was a whiff of something new, a turn of phrase, a unique spelling, or a hint of gossip. To compensate for his lack of formal education and his limited vocabulary, Walter invented words. Many of them were difficult to understand, but some of them had imaginative and humorous qualities that immediately conveyed their meaning. Walter was like a clumsy juggler, but gradually he gained control. With each column he became more nimble.

He wrote, for example, "One of the Vanderbilts is about to be Renovated [divorced]. . . . The A. K. Rowans of the Vaudeville Set are expecting a baby-joy. . . . Are the Jerome Astors of High Sassiety tossing it out the window? . . . A blondiful sextress is asking for trouble. Fooling around with married men. Are there any other men? Hehehheh."

I once asked Walter how he created his three-dot style to . . . separate . . . items. He explained: "I originally used dashes when I was writing 'Newsense.' But the dash key got stuck, so I used three dots. I don't know why it was three. It just looked right, I guess."

The columns sent out ripples in all directions. Among his early fans were newspapermen, politicians, gangsters, and, above all, show people, whose press agents began submitting material to him. Walter was quick to judge the ability of these people to help him, to feed his column. Years later, he would say, "Doing a column is a tough job. I think I'm appreciative of the people who help me. When they help me, I try to return the compliment. Everything else is a waste of time. The truth is that any time spent without any value to the column is a waste of time. A bore." The roots of that philosophy went back to Walter's very first months on the *Vaudeville News*.

Prohibition had just spawned the speakeasies. The best of them were the nightclubs run by Texas Guinan, Harry Richman, Helen Morgan, and a few others, most of them financed by beer barons and mobsters. From midnight to dawn, show people, politicians, gangsters, high-society types, and other celebrities hobnobbed in the clubs, where they conducted their business deals and their amours. Their table talk was grist for Walter's mill. He began making the rounds of the clubs, and before long he had cultivated a wide circle of contacts and created a network of news sources that would be of inestimable help to him. One of the people he met during his rounds was Mark Hellinger, the *Daily News* Broadway reporter, who introduced him to Texas Guinan, hostess of the most popular speakeasy in town. Born in Waco, Texas, Mary Louise Cecilia Guinan, came to New York in 1922. She earned her Broadway stripes as a chorus girl and fell in love with a married mobster who gave her the opportunity to manage one of his clubs. Soon she was the raucous darling of the speakeasy habitues. Her "Hello, suckers!" welcome to patrons, and the nude dancers she featured, made her nightclub one of the more fashionable watering places of the Prohibition era.

By the time Walter had been on the *Vaudeville News* for a little more than a year, he was a minor celebrity in his own right and the star of the paper. He was becoming the "folksinger of show business," Glenn Condon later recalled. Show people talked more about his items than about Albee's ponderous editorials.

In the spring of 1923, Condon gave Walter an assignment that would change his life. The editor had received a tip about a jobless girl who had taken in a homeless infant and was struggling to survive and support the child. "It sounds like a good human-interest yarn," he said. Walter listened and nodded.

He walked out of the *Vaudeville News* office and over to the small hotel on West Forty-sixth Street where the girl was supposed to be staying. He knocked on her door. No answer. He knocked again. Still no answer. "I was about to leave," Walter recalled, "when something made me knock again." A woman's voice from behind the door asked who he was. Walter explained that he was a *Vaudeville News* reporter. Silence. Walter explained again. This time the voice said, "Go away, I have nothing to say. Peddle your papers elsewhere."

Walter then said he had heard that the young woman was jobless and caring for someone else's baby. "Is the story true?" he bellowed.

The young woman replied that she was temporarily caring for a friend's child.

Satisfied with the explanation, Walter wheeled and walked away from the door. Then, suddenly, he made an about-face. "I fell in love with her voice," he said later. He returned to the young girl's door and knocked again, announcing, "This is Walter Winchell." The young woman unlocked her door.

As they stood facing each other, Walter was unusually silent. He gave her a long look and was promptly enthralled.

"I'd like to call on you tomorrow," he stammered.

"Go ahead," she said calmly as she closed the door.

June Magee was a blue-eyed, titian-haired beauty who had left her native Mississippi to become part of a girl dance team called Hill and Aster. The act's success, or lack of it, matched that of Winchell and Greene. June's experience on the battlefield of small-time vaudeville and a broken marriage had made her shrewd, down-to-earth, and realistic. She was more detached, more reflective, and in some ways tougher than Walter.

After their first date, Walter gave June his version of a romantic token: a free photo of her dance team on the inside cover of the *Vaudeville News*. It was his equivalent of caviar and orchids. Three weeks after they met, Walter and June married and moved into a two-room apartment on West 46th Street, a few doors down from the hotel where they had met. For a while, June accompanied Walter on his nightly rounds of the clubs, but she soon tired of night life and exiled herself from the spurious wonderland. In later years, it was rare for her to join him.

The year Walter and June married, Patterson's *Daily News* zoomed to a circulation of half a million, topping Hearst's *American*. A zany circulation war began. The *American* started a lottery with a grand prize of $1,000 and many other cash awards. Mob scenes accompanied the distribution of numbered coupons in Manhattan, and the *American*'s circulation soared. The *Daily News* countered with its own lottery for a top prize of $2,500. The next day, the *American* raised its top prize to $5,000. From then on, it was no holds barred. Every other day, one paper or the other increased the amount of its grand prize, and news about the contest crowded out the news of the day. When the *Daily News* raised the ante to $25,000 and the *American* matched it, Patterson's paper announced that it would double any prize offered by the *American*. On hearing this latest bit of one-upmanship, Victor Watson, the *American*'s editor, literally fainted. The circulation war lasted for another month, until both publishers decided it was too costly. The *Daily News* came out of it with an edge it never relinquished.

The success of the *Daily News* in appealing to the masses paved the way for two papers that seemed to be made for Walter. In 1923, Hearst decided to storm the tabloid fortress with the *New York Daily Mirror*. At the same time Bernarr Macfadden and Fulton Oursler were planning a tabloid called the *New York Evening Graphic*.

Macfadden had amassed a fortune with raw carrots and sex. He had built a multimillion-dollar empire with his two magazines, *Physical Culture* and *True Story,* and "he reasoned that if a million readers paid a quarter each to palpitate with a good woman who kept her virtue despite temptation, countless readers would pay two cents a day to read the same story with names, addresses, and pictures of the leading characters," one of his staff members later recalled.

The first issue of the *New York Evening Graphic* appeared on September 15, 1924, with an editorial proclaiming:

> We intend to interest you mightily. We intend to dramatize and sensationalize the news and some stories that are not new.
>
> But we do not want a single dull line to appear in this newspaper. If you read it from first to last and find anything therein that does not interest you, we want you to write and tell us about it.
>
> We want this newspaper to be human, first, last and all the time. We want to throb with those life forces that fill life with joyous delight.
>
> We want to show our readers how to live 100 percent.
>
> Don't be a dead one! Gird up your loins. Make ready to fight for the thing that you want in life and if you read the

GRAPHIC with sufficient regularity you can be assured of worth-
while assistance.

The loins-girdling, life-forces throb was exemplified by a page-
one heading: "SHE GAVE UP ART FOR A BARONET." Page two was
emblazoned with "MY FRIENDS DRAGGED ME INTO THE GUTTER,"
detailing the sad story of a minor motion-picture actress who had
fallen on hard times. Another column on the same page was headlined, "BROADWAY GOLD-PAVED FOR WALTER WINCHELL." Walter
had joined the *Graphic.*

Through Norman Prescott, a vaudeville friend, Walter had met
Fulton Oursler, cofounder with Macfadden of the *Graphic.* Oursler
was a reader of the *Vaudeville News* and had even submitted some
verse, which Walter had rejected. When they met, Oursler told Walter
that the rejection showed good editorial judgment. Right then and
there, Walter pitched for a job. Oursler promised to think it over.
Always impatient, Walter awakened Oursler at two the next morning
with a phone call: "Have you made up your mind about me?" Oursler,
barely awake, succumbed and hired him. Years later Oursler said to
me, "The funny thing is that I hired him because I believed he would
be a good source of stories for the *Graphic.* The column was secondary.
Originally, the *Graphic* wasn't column-minded. Its big attraction was
human interest."

Walter started at $100 a week plus a percentage of the revenue
from the advertising he solicited. Eventually he held down five jobs
for the *Graphic*: amusement editor, drama editor, drama critic, amuse-
ment-advertising manager, and Broadway columnist. He launched his
career on the *Graphic,* however, as a once-a-week columnist, appearing
on Mondays. His pieces were headed "Broadway Hearsay" and "Your
Broadway and Mine."

The gossip was tame. Most of the space in the columns was given
to reports of the casting activities of Broadway shows, plus verse and
gags. Winchell led off his first *Graphic* column with a syrupy poem
entitled, "A Newspaper Poet's Love." The column also revealed his
penchant for verbal fornication. More and more words were mated—
"cinemagic," "playbore." They gave his column a verve and style
that became his hallmarks.

One day Winchell heard that a male musical-comedy star and a
chorine were sailing for Europe in adjoining staterooms. Winchell
noted the rumor in his column. The city editor deleted the item, saying

that it was "not news." Winchell fumed. Several days later he defied
his superiors by printing the following:

> Helen Edy Brooks, widow of William Rock, has been plung-
> ing in Miami real estate. . . . It's a girl at the Carter de
> Havens. . . . Lenore Ulric paid $7.00 income tax. . . . Fannie
> Brice is betting on the horses at Belmont. . . . S. Jay Kaufman
> sails on the 16th via the *Berengaria* to be hitched to a Hun-
> garian. . . . Reports have it that Lillian Lorraine has taken a
> husband again.

Several hours after the paper hit the stand, his managing editor,
Emile Gauvreau, called him. Instead of administering the expected
rebuke, the editor conceded that the items were interesting and urged
Winchell "to write more of the stuff." Thus the modern gossip column
was born.

Within two months after Walter joined the *Graphic,* his column
became its biggest mail-puller. Soon he was allowed to write several
columns a week and was given a $65 raise.

As his popularity mounted, Winchell began spicing his column
with startling intimacies. He promptly ran into opposition from
Gauvreau. For the *Graphic* editor to frown on gossipy tidbits was a bit
incongruous. Morally, it was the equivalent of a prostitute's closing
her ears to profanity. The blue-pencil slashing surprised and infuriated
Winchell. Twenty years later, the incident still rankled. "This was my
first contact with stupid censorship," he fumed. "It was so damn ridiculous, it made me punching mad."

The Gauvreau-Winchell tussle became a daily exchange. The editor,
one of the leading newspapermen of the period, obviously resented
the up-and-coming Winchell. Gauvreau's critics said he had an over-
bearing power drive. Because Winchell's hunger for power was almost
insatiable, the collision was inevitable. Moreover, the cat-and-mouse
game was intensified by a basic personality clash.

At a time when the *Graphic* editor objected to Winchell's reports
of imminent divorces and other scandals, the paper's headlines tended
to feature rape, murder, and suicide. But Gauvreau had made his
decision, and for a time Winchell submitted his items only to have
them fired into a wastebasket. "I was giving them hot news," Winchell
recalled, "and the dumb bastards were throwing them on the floor.
Sometimes they didn't even bother to read them."

Gauvreau was later to inscribe his impressions of Winchell in a book:

> In a corner sat a hunched figure with a white lean face of decep-
> tive humility, looking up occasionally, startled. He pecked a type-
> writer nervously, with a frenzied determination, but from the
> machine, a form of gossip was beginning to appear which he
> himself never dreamed could be accorded the benediction of
> print in a daily paper. When his column, "Your Broadway and
> Mine," became the talk of the town, no vestige of humility
> remained in him.
>
> He was known as Walter Winchell, a vaudeville "hoofer"
> who had been introduced to me by Fulton Oursler. . . . No
> stranger phenomenon has yet appeared in the newspaper busi-
> ness. Gossip acquired such a tangibility, such a grip on his
> life, chiefly from the bare nucleus of a slim fact that, many
> times, he was more often cleverly wrong than monotonously
> correct. . . . That he could convey as much implication in a
> line as could be safely expressed in a column undoubtedly
> accounted for the fact that, some fifteen years later, his tech-
> nique had helped him to "salt away two million smackers."

Winchell's income-tax returns indicate that this statement might approach at least 60 percent in accuracy.

Gauvreau continued:

> His lack of newspaper experience, when I began to handle
> his copy; his refreshing insouciance about the difference be-
> tween a subject and a predicate, became an ironical asset which
> preserved his personality and may have had the virtue of saving
> him years of learning to be like everyone else. In his pate
> rattled more than a grain of genius which was to produce a
> "slanguage" often too puzzling for the venerable gentlemen
> of the courts who were not permitted to go beyond old man
> Webster.
>
> "Blessed events" were no longer confined to official bulletins
> from royal households, and disintegrating marriages appeared
> in print long before the judges heard their painful details.
> Making an innocent interrogation serve the purpose, at times,
> of damning affirmation had as much to do with the rash of
> intimate columns now spread over the land as Winchell's
> diaper drolleries. For more than a decade I was to be held to

the task of "legalizing" his output. Our mutual relationship was never boring. No paper but Macfadden's tabloid could have nursed such a prodigy who, by some form of self-hypnosis, came to feel himself the center of his time.

But Winchell wasn't selling syntax. Grammatical and other niceties were picayune considerations. Nor was he engaged in a moral crusade. He was writing what he considered news, and to hell with anything else. His gossip was Rabelaisian and earthy. Of course, it was occasionally tasteless, malicious, and inaccurate—but it was always readable. If the column material had a stink to it, at least it was the aroma of humankind. For Gauvreau, the editor of an anything-goes paper, to place an ethical yardstick against Winchell's column was pure hypocrisy.

What was often damned as the early Winchell's weakness was his strength. He was a primitive, and he took his work as seriously as any master of the high Renaissance. Winchell reacted almost physically to gossip and seemed to purr with delight when he had a particularly juicy item. While on a news-gathering foray, he would approach potential sources and impudently inquire, "Got an item for me? Have you heard a new joke?" He was as fascinated and unself-conscious as a four-year-old gravely making mudpies. As it turned out, the things that fascinated Walter also mesmerized millions of others. For better or worse, Winchell was doing something new and catchy in journalism.

The ban on Winchell's gossip was temporary. With an assist from Fulton Oursler, the Winchell column became Winchelly again. When the *Graphic*'s circulation then increased dramatically, Gauvreau renounced his objections and enthusiastically acknowledged the worth of gossip. In newspaperdom, circulation is the name of the game.

Thirty years later, *Time* magazine rehashed the Gauvreau-Winchell tangle. The news weekly wrote, "Gauvreau's most durable contribution to U.S. journalism was a vaudeville hoofer named Walter Winchell, whom he launched as a daily columnist. It was a contribution he bitterly regretted: He soon loathed Winchell, once threw a bust of Napoleon at him."

Winchell responded: "(1) Fulton Oursler was the one who launched me on a daily newspaper. But Gauvreau always stole the bows. . . . (2) I soon despised him for reasons that are unpublishable. . . . (3) He flung a bust of Napoleon at me??? It was I who did the flinging. I flung him down a flight of stairs after he took advantage of his game leg and threatened to hit me with a weapon."

Over the years, Winchell's relations with editors, with several exceptions, were taut and tense. Because he was as fiercely independent as an emperor and was the principal actor in all of his own performances, he resented what he considered to be intrusion in his domain. During his peak years, when he was sure of his power, Winchell goaded and teased editors and made them his unwilling servants. If, in his judgment, an editor had tinkered with his column, he ordered the syndicate to immediately stop servicing the offending paper with his column. "For the first time in history," he once crowed, "a reporter fired a publisher."

Some of the more portentous significance-spotters in later years, including the *New Yorker* magazine, were to label Winchell's free-wheeling gossip in the *Graphic* as the start of a journalistic revolution. But at the time he was unaware of his journalistic implications, social significance, or psychological repercussions. As a reporter, he was covering Broadway in inventive fashion and was interested solely in the pragmatic alliance of money and power. As a scholar, his subject was biology, Broadway style.

Winchell of the *Graphic* was a young man in a hurry. The purity of his ambition and his uncomplicated attitude toward the value of his work gave him the proper spirit to achieve success. He was engaged in an unsparing struggle for excellence in his field. If some purists objected to his rat-a-tat-tattling, there were many other people who were impressed with his style and success.

While the column's primary throb was derived from gossip, more than half of its space was devoted to verse, gags, and vignettes. In many respects, this branch of his column-writing was an echo of "The Conning Tower," the column by F.P.A. (Franklin Pierce Adams) in the *New York World.* Incidentally, one of F.P.A.'s features consisted of spotlighting grammatical boners in other columns. Winchell, a frequent victim, never forgave F.P.A. for citing his. Thirty years later, when he learned that the aged and ailing F.P.A. was in a nursing home, Winchell coldly commented, "Too bad about him. But he wasn't a very nice man. He once made a young man named Winchell very sick with his petty copyreading, holding up my mistakes for everybody to see."

In his second year with the *Graphic,* Winchell's Broadway trivia column was having an impact that exceeded his own compulsive ambitions. It had become the most talked-about newspaper feature.

The *Daily News* kept pace with Mark Hellinger's Broadway column.
Winchell and the tabloids—the dirty-faced boys of journalism—were
smudging some of the well-groomed papers. The *New York Times*
devoted more space to the sensational Hall-Mills murder case than the
Mirror and *Graphic* did. Readers gaped at the sideshow, and circula-
tion-hungry papers were quick to produce tawdry spectaculars. In this
respect, Winchell and the tabloids were putting on the best acts.

The "gee-whizzer" of 1927 was the brainchild of Broadway producer Earl Carroll. He had made a happy splash in the tabloids with a
party that inspired the headline-catching word "orgy." Carroll invited
Broadway luminaries, including Winchell, to the wingding. He
had one of his chesty chorines, Joyce Hawley, dunking happily in a
bathtub fizzing with champagne. As Miss Hawley giggled and
swished in the jolly carbonation, the assembled guests stared and
wahooed and filled their glasses with the bathtub champagne. As the
champagne was consumed, more and more of Miss Hawley's natural
charms became visible. In the end she showed all of what pretty
girls are made of—and the gurgling shingdig ended with the cheers
of goggle-eyed guests.

The tabloids joyfully covered what Miss Hawley uncovered. A
police investigation followed, and Winchell was eventually summoned
to be a witness in court. When he mounted the stand, the judge
urged him to identify some of the people at the party. The columnist
testified, "Among those at the party was Senator . . ." The judge's
gavel promptly came down, and Winchell was excused from offering
further testimony before he could utter the name. *L'affaire* Hawley had
a three-day tabloid spin and was forgotten.

Much to his delight and surprise, Winchell was acquiring an aura
of respectability. He was befriended, encouraged, and hailed by
some of the towering literary newspaper figures of the day. Heywood
Broun publicly embraced him by writing that "Winchell was the
only thing worth reading in the *Graphic*." Alexander Woollcott turned
out a magazine piece in praise of Winchell. An exception was Damon
Runyon, who was unimpressed. He considered gossip "strictly for
women" and failed to savvy the dither Winchell created. Nevertheless,
periodicals catering to the bookish crowd, among them *Vanity Fair*
and the *Bookman,* ran articles bylined with Winchell's name. Simon
and Schuster signed him to write a book entitled, *The Private Papers
of Walter Winchell.* He hobnobbed with the Algonquin's famed
Round Table, whose members detected an unusual literary quality in

Winchell's boyish mischief and analyzed it out of all proportion. His early columns were vaudeville baroque, and those who made literary evaluations were really only fishing for whales in a shallow stream. Nevertheless, the attention he received elevated his status and gave him a tinge of distinction he dearly loved. Throughout his career he glowed when he received attention or admiration from those he considered "real writers." Deep within him was a sense of inferiority and shame about the playpen items he inscribed, and he felt that the support of those he respected gave him a sort of ethical sanction. But the only practical effect of his contacts with the prime newspaper stock of the 1920s was to extend the chain of his news sources. He could not be weaned from his attraction to gossip and his penchant for outrageous puns and coined words. But the unquenchable thirst for respectability and renown remained.

By far, Winchell's greatest single asset in his *Graphic* days was the support of Sime Silverman. The editor and founder of *Variety* became friendly with Walter during his first year on the *Graphic*. Silverman was a beloved titan in show business. A fiercely independent individual, he created an honest, informative weekly written with a slangy artistry that remains unmatched. *Variety* was later dubbed the "Bible of show business."

Silverman took a paternal interest in Winchell. He lent the columnist money, conuseled him ("There's nothing new, Walter, but try to write it differently"), and helped him in many other ways.

Silverman's major assist to Winchell was a transfusion of news. At the *Variety* office on West 46th Street, there was a cracker-barrel informality. Stars of show business and journalism dropped in to exchange news, ideas, and hopes. It offered a juicy source of material for Winchell. Among the people Silverman introduced to Winchell was Walter Kingsley, the Keith press agent, who made a significant contribution to Winchell's columns at that time. Silverman also made gifts to Winchell of news gathered by himself and members of his staff. Winchell ran exclusive items that *Variety* later confirmed. No newspaperman has ever done more for another. Silverman's largesse was pure gold.

Happy, grateful, and probably startled by Silverman's profligacy with news, Winchell once asked for an explanation. The *Variety* editor smiled. "Walter, I give you tips to use so that I can jack up my staff for being scooped."

Unfortunately, their friendship later cooled. Occasionally in 1926,

items twitting Winchell appeared in *Variety*. They were written by
staffers but Silverman allowed them to pass. These items inspired
Winchell to write to Silverman, "I don't know what's happened, but
whatever it is they told you, it's a lie. If you don't believe me, just
write 'Nuts' across this whole letter and return it."

The response was another brief item: "*Variety* heard Winchell was
slandering it, but Winchell denies it, so the thing remains a standoff."

Silverman also sent Winchell a letter: "Forget it. People are getting
to know you. You're now news. And *Variety*'s business is printing the
news. That's your business, too. When you feel like it, print what you
like about us."

One can detect in Silverman's letter a disenchantment with the
rising young columnist. Winchell was characteristically unable to
establish close and enduring relationships. He liked the help people
gave him more than he liked people. Friendship was a business ex-
pedient. He held it gently, like raspberries in the hand, while he
needed it. When it had lost its usefulness, he squeezed hard, and the
dead friendship ran blood red.

The Winchell-Jessel case history exemplifies the emotionally impoverished foundation of his relationships. George and Walter, boy-
hood companions, shared the agony of the vaudeville struggle, were in
the same arena for almost a half-century—and were never friends.
For years they had a casual, teasing relationship. Winchell twitted
Jessel by recalling that when they had appeared together on a vaudeville stage in Harlem, the billing in front of the theater read, "It's
worth five cents alone to hear little Georgie Jessel sing." Thirty years
later Winchell reprinted the remark adding, "And it still goes!"

In his autobiography, Jessel recalled that once, while in Miami
Beach, he had had a spat with his wife, Lois Andrews. She stayed in
her room while he took a stroll on the beach. There he met Winchell,
who told him, "I'm happy to hear that despite what the wise guys
said, your marriage is going so well. I'm saying so in my column
tomorrow."

Jessel raced back to his wife and exclaimed, "Honey, we can't split
up! I wouldn't cross Winchell for anything."

The deterioration of the Winchell-Jessel relationship began the
day that Jessel had panned him. Winchell was incensed. Broadway
friendships were frequently made and broken on hearsay evidence.
When Winchell learned of Jessel's alleged heckling, he banished him
from his column. This was tantamount to Siberian exile. Jessel, who

adored seeing his name in print, was furious. (I once saw Jessel
about to enter the Stork Club. When he was told there were no columnists in attendance, Jessel about-faced and went elsewhere.) Well-
known for his funeral eulogies, he raged, "I can't wait to speak at
Winchell's funeral."

Sometime later, the Friars' Club of California tendered a dinner for
Winchell at the Beverly-Wilshire Hotel. The Committee of the
Friars urged Jessel to serve as toastmaster. George was reluctant until
one of his friends reminded him, "If he doesn't like you now, it certainly won't help much to refuse to speak at his dinner."

Jessel's speech, perhaps excessively, even within the tradition of the
Friars' Club "roasts," bristled with sarcasm, and Winchell never forgave
him. "He slugged me with a feather," the columnist said.

George orated:

> And now, gentlemen, it becomes my function to present to
> you the guest of honor, whose valiant efforts in the fight against
> cancer have deserved our salutations and the lifting of our
> glasses. I have known Walter for forty-five years. We have not
> been close friends all this time, but I have known him for
> forty-five years. We disagree on many things. For example,
> despite the fact that you have heard humorous talks tonight by
> Benny and Burns and O'Brien and others, don't be surprised if
> in Walter's next column, you read of this dinner that Milton
> Berle came in with his front teeth blackened out and was the
> hit of the evening—despite the fact that Mr. Berle is more than
> three thousand miles away. Walter and I are not in accord
> politically. He favors the administration that is in office now,
> while I favor the one that is momentarily out. He favors the
> opinions of the Secretary of State, who has made statements
> to the effect that in the Middle East, Egypt is our friend. The
> Secretary definitely emphasized that when he visited the Premier
> of Egypt (now in the can) he brought him a silver revolver as
> a token of the esteem of the American people. (I don't recall
> the Amercian people chipping in to buy this pistol!) I, of
> course, don't in any way go along with the Secretary's policy
> in the Middle East, and I have been given to understand that
> Walter does. I cannot believe that these pagan countries, that
> have held back civilization for thousands of years, that have
> spent an eternity in the marketplaces smoking strange weeds
> and eating goat doodle, are the friends of modern democracy.
> There are some things that Winchell and myself do agree

upon—that Zanuck is quite a guy and that certain ladies are easy on the eye. But even if we didn't agree on anything, knowing a man forty-five years forges a bond of such great strength that a political or theatrical opinion cannot break it in two. No, gentlemen, everything old becomes a thing religious, and, by a strange irony, ivy often climbs on the wall of a deserted brothel long before it does on a young church. So be it. I now present to you the most listened-to newspaperman of our time, Walter Winchell.

Winchell did not reply to Jessel before the assembled Friars, but exploded later. He was particularly infuriated at Jessel's implication that he, Winchell, was anti-Israel. It simply wasn't true.

Winchell of the *Graphic* was more interested in having his column win friends and influence people. His devotion was directed toward his work, a consuming passion that endured nearly to the end of his days.

If Winchell the columnist was careless about friendship, he derived emotional compensation during the early years of his marriage from the warmth of his family. Mrs. Winchell, happily confined to housewifely duties, took pride in her husband's success and encouraged him. The Winchells had adopted an infant and named her Gloria. Walter was secretive about this aspect of his life, but I believe that Gloria had been born out of wedlock and had been the infant in June Magee's room when June and Walter had first met. The columnist was always sentimental about children. While Gloria and the two Winchell youngsters born subsequently were growing up, he delighted in quoting their baby talk. Many of his listeners winced, but that didn't stop him. "I know it bores some people," he snapped, "but it never bores me." In any case, Winchell would rather bore than be bored.

=5=
Wine, Roses, and Thorns

By the mid-1920s New York's bathtub-gin era was in full swing. Its symbol was Mayor Jimmy Walker, the "master of ceremonies," and he performed his role in a high, hedonistic style. For playboy Jimmy it was truly a time of wine and roses. He wisecracked, patronized speakeasies, womanized, and, in general, had one helluva good time. Walker and Winchell, two denizens of the Broadway night world, went to the same clubs, met at the same parties, and had many mutual friends. Besides, as Winchell once said, "Jimmy liked to see his name in print, and he was good copy, always handy with a quip or news item."

The Winchell column reflected the demimonde of the lurid Prohibition era. The gaudy group included Broadway and Hollywood stars, producers and playwrights, social registerites, influential Wall Street types, wits, writers, clowns, and assorted models, showgirls, and prostitutes—plus other playboys and playgirls of the Western world. However, the true "royal" figures of the period were unquestionably the mobster-tycoons spawned by Prohibition. They bankrolled most of the speakeasies—the essential retail outlets for illegal liquor.

By and large, Broadway reporters and gangsters had casual relationships. As owners of nightclubs and backers of shows, the mobsters naturally gravitated to those who could provide the publicity they needed. In addition, many of the gangsters relished seeing their names in print. In turn, newsmen used them as news sources.

A blurring of moral distinctions made it a status symbol to establish good relations with mob bosses. At the time, the boss of bosses was Owen "Owney" Madden. Madden, Ed Sullivan later recalled, was the "most powerful man in town. He was another Mayor," who condescended to allow politicians and others to dwell in obedience to his brutally strong leadership.

Madden, like Al "Scarface" Capone of Chicago, was surrounded by an atmosphere of fearful respect. He amassed millions and controlled hundreds of legitimate businesses ranging from laundries to taxi fleets. His topsy-turvy success story began when Madden migrated from Liverpool as a youth and settled in New York's Hell's Kitchen. There he served his savage apprenticeship, notching more than forty arrests, including one on a homicide charge that sent him to Sing Sing penitentiary. Paroled in 1923, he quickly engineered a series of coups that made him Mister Big in the criminal community.

Short in stature, with a hawklike face dominated by burning eyes, Madden looked tough, acted tough, and was tough. Strangely, though, he had a shy streak, and his hobby was breeding pigeons.

Winchell wasn't the only newsman in town with a grudging admiration for Madden. Stanley Walker, one of the leading journalists of the time, wrote, "Madden, whose long-ago record caused him to be referred to occasionally as a sneak-thief and worse, actually had a great many admirable qualities. It would have been impossible for even the most strict moralist to have passed an afternoon listening to Owney without feeling that, according to his own lights, he was an honest man."

His own lights? With corkscrew logic, Madden contended, "What's the matter with rackets? They're a real benefit to the small tradesman. Take the laundry racket, for instance. I'll bet you all the tea in China that half the little guys in the business would be starving to death if it wasn't for the racket. They get protection, don't they? If some mug opens a laundry where he ain't wanted, the boys tell him to scram the hell out of the neighborhood, don't they? The racket's a genuine benefit in cases like that."

Madden's munificence was on a par with his sense of social justice. He guaranteed lifetime pensions for widows of his underlings killed in the line of duty.

Unlike Chicago's flamboyant Al Capone, Madden avoided the limelight and carried on his administrative functions quietly and efficiently as he cartelized the city. He employed violence only as a last resort, preferring to operate as an elder statesman in settling underworld disputes.

One day, when Winchell was sitting in a barbershop, Owney Madden came over and cordially greeted him with "I like your stuff, kid. You have the knack. You're good at your racket." The key word was "racket." Mobsters considered every field of endeavor a racket, and they were impressed by success. Winchell and Madden subsequently became "pals"—a relationship that lasted several years. They went everywhere together—to clubs, parties, and Madison Square Garden. Madden was a fight fan and owned several pugilists, including Primo Carnera, the Italian King Kong who became heavyweight champion after flooring a series of setups. At the zenith of Madden's power, practically nothing of importance happened in New York without his knowledge, assistance, or control. Several decades later Winchell insisted that he had secretly despised most gangsters. "Even Owney," he said, "with all his power, was a frightened man. He was always afraid of being betrayed or framed or killed. Besides, the mobsters were wild. They could be as polite as headwaiters one minute and kill you the next."

Nevertheless, while Madden ruled, Winchell maintained an uneasy alliance with him. The columnist once visited the offices of the *Herald Tribune* to chide the paper's editor for referring to Madden as an ex-killer. Winchell contended that this was unfair and downright discourteous. On another occasion the columnist suddenly blurted out to Madden, "Owney, if there's anything I can do for you, just let me know." Recalling the incident, Winchell shuddered. "I'll never forget the contemptuous stare he gave me when he answered, 'What can you do for me?'" Winchell never again neglected diplomatic niceties in Madden's presence.

His most delicate exercise in diplomacy came when Madden decided to present him with a Stutz car. Apprehensive about being "in anybody's pocket," Winchell managed to coax Madden into accepting payment for the car.

Madden's reign ended in 1932 when he was returned to Sing Sing for a parole violation. He came out of jail some years later and faded into the shadows. For the last three decades of his life he lived in peaceful and prosperous obscurity in Hot Springs, Arkansas, where he died at seventy-three.

By the end of 1927, Winchell's success extended beyond the dark glamour of knowing the best goons in town. The *Graphic* raised his salary to $300 a week and relieved him of his duties as an advertising salesman, though he retained his position as the paper's drama critic. The Winchells moved into a fancier apartment at the Majestic, on Seventy-second Street and Central Park West. Broadway was fast becoming his private estate. Both those who feared him and those who liked him welcomed him. Headwaiters gave him the royal treatment. After his serfdom in vaudeville and his novitiate years at the *Vaudeville News*, he had reached a position of considerable financial eminence.

At thirty, Winchell was almost completely gray, and his hair was starting to thin. The silvery frame for his still-boyish, bright-eyed, ripe-apple face gave him an arresting appearance. "In those days," he said, "I was starting to develop my superior look." The Winchell "superior look" was cold, hard, and piercing. It was a way of looking over or through people, staring at them as if they didn't exist. Once he fumed that columnist Leonard Lyons was "one of my gee-dee imitators." I pointed out that Lyons was one Broadway columnist who had made a deliberate effort to avoid the Winchell style. Winchell mused for a moment and then said with finality, "But I gave him my superior look!"

Winchell's expanding popularity deepened the bitterness between him and Emile Gauvreau. For weeks they didn't speak, communicating when necessary through intermediaries. When Edward L. Bernays, Bernarr Macfadden's public-relations counselor, suggested that the Winchell column be moved from the back of the paper to the front, Gauvreau curtly rejected the idea.

There was another problem that came with the initial stages of success. It began as a minor annoyance and eventually became a major nightmare, replete with ghosts. From the beginning, the Winchell column was serviced by numerous contributors, mainly press agents. Winchell's attitude toward his column was like that of Moses toward the Ten Commandments: Once his byline was on the column, he saw the entire creation as his. To believe otherwise would have been extremely painful to him. In his *Graphic* days, when bragging press agents inspired the rumor that Winchell did not write his own column, he responded with the following verse:

> Some toil at night to make the grade—
> To fill the space for which they're paid—
> Or try to pen a grin or laugh
> In every other paragraph:

> Or string some words to make a verse
> Which helps to fill a lanky purse,
> When some chump yap churps in rebuff
> "Say! Do you really write this stuff?"

Winchell never was able to tolerate any suggestion that others helped him to compose his pieces. He once pulled out a column published in *Billboard* in 1920 and proudly showed it to me. "I wrote that," he emphasized, "and don't let anyone tell you different." The column included the following notes:

> According to another trade paper, Mr. and Mrs. Davey Jamison were blessed with a boy on January 23, at Portland, Me. On another page, Mr. and Mrs. J. were blessed with a boy January 25, at Portland, Ore. Some leap. And whose airplane did the proud parents use? Mother and child are doing fine. Congratulations!
>
> Most actors are married and live scrappily ever after.
>
> Did you ever notice the little brass tablet on the door in the room of your hotel which reads: "Stop! Have you left anything?" Apropos of the high cost of living, it should read: "Stop! Have you anything left?"
>
> In New York recently the snow tied up traffic severely. A gang hired to remove same struck at the crucial moment, carrying banners which read: "You took away our beer, now take away the snow."
>
> A certain actress was left a fortune for being kind to a newspaperman. Moral: Be kind to gossip writers."

Truly, Winchell had created a distinctive style and form. He was undoubtedly the Columbus of the modern gossip column. The trouble was that he wanted the public to believe he was the entire crew as well. Ironically, by refusing to share credit publicly, Winchell often deprived himself of the acclaim he deserved.

The year 1927 was marked by Winchell's first major Broadway contest. The confrontation on the theatrical battlefield was the most talked-about incident in the White Light district. It made history of a sort, and, in comparison, the continuing tension with Gauvreau was a private skirmish, a minor, grubby quarrel that lacked the flamboyance and the public interest of this fight with the mighty.

When Winchell became embroiled with the brothers Shubert, the feud generated instantaneous public excitement. Winchell relished the brawl. His fighting disposition was so ingrained and vital that it sometimes seemed impossible for him to live without resistance. He went into every personal struggle with the certainty of triumph, buttressed by Jimmy Walker's sensible admonition "Never fight with a newspaperman—he goes to press too often."

The tussle with the Shuberts, Jake and Lee, was touched off by Winchell's negative reviews of shows they produced. Critic Winchell wrote, for example, "I had a poor view of this Shubert show. The curtain was up." About another Shubert production he declared, "It gave boredom a bad name." He was singled out for exile after he wrote, "I know why the Shuberts are rich, they get dollars for a penny of talent."

The Shuberts were the lords of the theater, the wealthiest and most powerful producers. They were eccentric sensitive plants who refused to understand or accept a critic's basic obligation to render an honest opinion. Consequently, they barred Winchell from their theaters.

The banishment became the talk of the town. Winchell was quick to perceive the advantages of a fight with the Shuberts. He dramatized the sharp humor of the situation, writing, "The Shuberts have barred me from the openings. I'll wait five days and go to their closings." This type of feuding appealed to Broadway's acid brotherhood. Winchell's quip was repeated and reprinted as the struggle was joined.

The Shubert-Winchell war reminded the columnist—and everyone else on Broadway—of Winchell's growing influence. If he was important enough to annoy the lordly Shuberts, he was clearly a man to be reckoned with. Winchell later said, "The fight with the Shuberts taught me that the way to become famous fast is to throw a brick at someone who is famous." In years to come, this quick-success formula was turned against Winchell when his name became big enough for lesser-known sharpshooters to spark a burst of attention by using him as a target.

The Shubert battle endured for several years. Winchell successfully ran the blockade once when the Marx brothers, his cronies from vaudeville days, prevailed upon him to disguise himself with whiskers and attend one of their premiers.

It was becoming clear to the stars of Shubert shows that they needed the showcase of Winchell's column more than the columnist needed his opening-night tickets. Finally, Al Jolson forced the Shuberts to surrender. The star, who was Walter's friend, informed the producers that he would not appear for the opening performance of *Wunderbar* unless they allowed Winchell to occupy a first-night seat. When he marched down the aisle to attend the Jolson opening it was the act of a conquering hero. Some members of the audience applauded.

Winchell's early success was the usual mixed blessing. He soon discovered that the spotlight magnifies—and burns. In 1928, he was shocked to learn that the government was taking action against him. Federal agents padlocked the Artists' Social Democratic Club on West Forty-sixth Street as the front for a speakeasy. The government alleged that Winchell was a member of the board of directors. Years before, he had signed his name to a register that listed him as a director. But though Winchell did visit the place occasionally, he had nothing to do with its actual operation. After a brief legal hassle, Winchell's name was stricken from the complaint. Never again was he involved in entangling alliances. "I don't want to be anybody's partner," he would often proclaim. He was wary of deals that involved the use of his name, steering clear of situations that might cause him embarrassment. Besides, he had a horror of being "used."

Winchell danced on hot coals for several weeks after his experience with the Artists' Social Democratic Club. "Broadway," he commented, "is not as gay as the bright bulbs would indicate. It's rather a glum place for most of its alleged butterflies. It is vicious, merciless, selfish and treacherous." In this case, he was hounded by the supercilious and malicious folk who generally greeted the knockdown of a Broadway name with a hallelujah chorus. More often than not, Winchell was the leader of the hounds. "On Broadway," he often observed, "they pat you on the back—hoping to find a soft spot to plunge the knife."

Winchell's hate-love for Broadway was expressed in a simple verse he composed:

> Broadway bred me, Broadway fed me,
> Broadway led me—
> > to a goal.
> Broadway boo'd me and pooh-pooh'd me,
> Disapproved me—
> > in the role.

Broadway scared me, Broadway dared me
It prepared me—
                    to be shrewd.
Broadway cursed me, Broadway nursed me,
It rehearsed me—
                    how to brood.
Broadway canned me, Broadway banned me,
Broadway panned me—
                    and my muse,
Broadway slammed me, rammed and damned me,
Broadway taught me
                    how to lose.
Broadway ruled me, Broadway fooled me,
Broadway schooled me,
                    how to cry.
Though it trumped me, bumped me and dumped me,
Broadway's where I want to die.

Although Winchell was occasionally victimized by the raw Broadway philosophy, he was nonetheless a willing practitioner of the bare-knuckle style. While brawling with the Shuberts, he had written, "The Shuberts lousy? Why, they are the best mediocre producers in show business." Lee Shubert sued for libel—and lost. The producer was unforgiving. Years later, when he was introduced to Mrs. Winchell, accompanied by her children, he coldly commented, "Well, I'm glad there are some nice people in the Winchell family."

By 1927 vaudeville was moving into its big sleep. Radio had upstaged it. Paul Whiteman's band received $5,000 for a single performance. Al Jolson revolutionized the movie business by uttering, "You ain't heard nothin' yet" on the sound track of *The Jazz Singer,* The new Ziegfeld Theater was rolling along with *Show Boat,* and the opening of the world's largest movie temple, the baroque Roxy, said that movies were here to stay.

The Winchell column was oblivious to Mussolini's Fascists ranting in Rome, Nazi stormtroopers terrorizing the streets of Munich, and Stalin's abuses of power in Russia. Winchell's interest in foreign affairs was confined to noting that Maurice Chevalier had become the toast of Paris.

His participation in domestic politics was limited to echoing the belief of many New Yorkers that Jimmy Walker was a great little guy. (Winchell himself ran fourth in *Variety*'s poll to elect a mythical "Mayor of Broadway." The winner was Eddie Cantor.)

As Winchell moved through the tabloid world of soiled saints, moral riff-raff, sex addicts, and refugees from boredom spewing gossip and gags, he worked hard, very hard. He would be accused of many things, but rarely of laziness.

His hard work was paying off, and he was squirreling away money —in the bank. Winchell resisted the lure of the big-board lottery— first, because he lacked business sense and, second, because he had no desire to risk his hard-earned money. "I remember," he once said, "Eddie Cantor, my friend since the Gus Edwards days, practically pleading with me to invest in Wall Street. Eddie would tell me about the big money he was making in stocks. He once told us that he made over a hundred thousand dollars in a few hours. Eddie and lots of other people in show business were getting rich in a hurry. Wall Street had no interest for me, although I reported some Wall Street news in the column." Incidentally, in the 1929 stock-market disaster, Cantor lost $2 million.

When his daughter Walda was born in 1927, Winchell announced that he would save at least $50 a week. The birth of this second daughter, coyly named after her father, deepened his sense of financial responsibility. Even more, he became an enthusiastic partner in a truly satisfactory love affair—his passion for money. As his savings mounted, he distributed the money in several banks, burbling with delight over what he deemed financial success. He would throw open his bankbooks during nightclub conversations and crow, "Look at those numbers!" His actions titillated some who relished freak behavior and irritated others. Winchell dismissed hostile comments as mere reflections of bitterness and jealousy. He generally considered such backbiting a measure of his expanding success.

Although Winchell was an also-ran in the race for "Mayor of Broadway," he was solidifying his leadership of Broadway's tinsel aristocracy. Like other court circles, Broadway nobility was nourished by money and power. In many cases, particularly among the underworld monarchs, the royal gratifications matched those accorded mad King Ludwig.

At this point, Winchell was not in an upper economic bracket despite his almost sensual feeling about bankbooks. His royal privilege derived from the whip and wand of his column. He could reward or punish, transform nobodies into somebodies, damage shows or nightclubs by his criticism or indifference. He could hurt or help individuals or commercial endeavors. That was royal power indeed.

Winchell relished recalling the flash point in his career. "I knew I was becoming a big shot," he said, "when those who called me a son of a bitch behind my back would ask me for favors. You'd be surprised what some people would do for a line in a column. Another zany thing was happening. Owney Madden wasn't a publicity hound, but most of the other mobsters liked to see their names in print. A lot of the baddies had girls in the Broadway and nightclub shows and they were pitching for them. All kinds of big names started calling me by my first name. 'I've got an item for you, Walter,' they said. Everybody wanted to be a part of the act."

As the Winchell column became Broadway's prime organ of communication, the columnist's method of gossip-gathering changed. For years he had been an explorer in the dark and whispery underground. He buzzed hither, thither, and occasionally yon, discovering Broadway's shiny bits. He cajoled, wheedled, and pleaded for notes and gags. When he heard someone laugh aloud at another table in a nightclub, he would dash over and inquire, "What made you laugh? Is it a gag I can use?" He would confront celebrities boldly with piercing questions about their love affairs. More often than not, those interrogated would reply with a candor springing from shock, as well as the fear of antagonizing Winchell by refusing to cooperate. When he heard something usable, Winchell whipped out a carefully folded piece of copy paper, scribbled a note with his left hand, and departed, sometimes saying, "That's a goodie! I'll run it in tomorrow's column." He was a master of the ten-second interview.

As the columnist's popularity and power sprouted, he was becoming a Broadway broker of trivia. Sources would come to him with items or submit them in the mail. The eagerness of people to spill dirt helped harden Winchell's streak of cynicism. In his opinion, gossip was news—and news was anything that fascinated him, no matter how insignificant. After all, the tabloids in particular had the capacity to make a tidal wave out of a teardrop.

As a matter of fact, he considered gossip about himself newsworthy. Never noted for marital fidelity, Walter made his promiscuity virtually public early in 1929 with a series of columns modeled after Samuel Pepys's diary. Portions of the columns were fiction, but some of the items were true. Mrs. Winchell's strong objections finally put an end to his confessions.

The following excerpts are typical:

> Nursed the sheets till late, being weary from a strenuous tear the night before, having hoofed at a White Light place with Bobbie Folsom and other charming wenches. So to breakfast with Lovey Kent, who is as sweet as her Christian monicker.

> Up betimes and broke fast with a baby doll from "Artists and Models." To the plant and did my Monday copy hurriedly, then to a dice house where the side wagers dented my b.r. and I pledged to dissipate thereafter with the Casino . . . In the rain to keep a rendezvous with Mary Thomas, who coryphees for a living.

> Up early and prettied myself before taxiing through the park to my mother's, where I broke my fast. Mother distressed because my cheeks were wan and worried over my conduct, hearing tales from kin who should know better. Later to visit Vivien and Pearl at the Commodore. The house detective reluctant to permit me to remain, but fell for my police card.

Winchell's whiff of success was perfume to him. Emile Gauvreau refused to be overcome, however. The editor was quick to deplore and ridicule. Whether Gauvreau was moved to envy or honestly offended by the gossip column, the fact is that he overlooked no opportunity to needle Winchell. Gauvreau heaped scorn on the columnist when the latter referred to Emile Zola as a female writer. After Winchell reported that "a party of Broadwayites had stepped off from an ocean liner at the port of Paris, France," Gauvreau presented the columnist with a map of Europe. "I tore up the damn map," Winchell remembered, "and tossed the pieces into his stupid face." The columnist and the editor also clashed over Winchell's penchant for peppering his column with cleaned-up dirty flippancies. "What's wrong with changing effin' to kissing and running the the gag so long as it's funny?" Winchell wanted to know. After Gauvreau deleted such quips, there would be several days of screaming contests, two enraged chickens making the feathers fly.

Late in 1928 according to Winchell, Jimmy Walker told him that the Hearst people were interested in acquiring his column. At first, Walker said that the *Journal*, the Hearst evening paper in com-

petition with the *Graphic,* had a spot for a columnist. But Winchell
wasn't contacted officially and soon dismissed it as a rumor. Several
months later, Jimmy repeated the story to him. The Walker con-
nection is a minor part of this incident. In his autobiography, Walter
conveniently forgot how he extracted the Hearst job: With the assistance of his friend Mark Hellinger, who said *New York World*
editor Herbert Bayard Swope owed him a favor, they convinced Swope
to fake a letter stating he was anxious to hire Winchell. Walter
promptly displayed the letter to Hearst executive Bill Curley, who was
impressed enough to hire him. Years later, Jim Bishop told the story
in his book *The Mark Hellinger Story.* Winchell denied it. Actually,
Walter told it to me before the book was written. He relished the
recollection and concluded: "My success story could not have been
possible without fucking Hearst." The *Graphic* was hurting in the
circulation battle with the *Journal* and was losing about $10,000 a
week. Winchell heard that Hearst wanted to buy the *Graphic* for $4
million but Macfadden refused to sell. There were some preliminary
negotiations before the deal fell through.

Newspaper people didn't give the *Mirror* much of a chance to survive. Hearst himself wasn't too proud of the paper. He didn't have
his name on the masthead. His pet was the *American.* But the *Mirror*
surprised everybody by moving ahead in circulation figures, although
it was a losing proposition as far as advertising was concerned. Two
years after the *Mirror* hit the streets, its circulation exceeded two hundred thousand. But the *News* topped a million.

"When the Hearst people made the offer to me," said Walter, "I
didn't care where I would land, in the *Journal* or the *Mirror.* The deal
was for five hundred dollars a week and a five hundred-dollar bonus
when I signed. That was big money to me in those days. My contract
with the *Graphic* had a few more years to run. But I was anxious to
get out—fast. The money was the big lure, of course. But leaving
Gauvreau was an attraction for me. I told Kobler I would come over
to the Hearst side as soon as possible. But the switch wasn't easy. Macfadden didn't want me to go." When Macfadden refused permission
to leave the *Graphic,* Winchell took it as a presumptuous effort to
block his progress. *Graphic* veterans remember the spectacle of Winchell's shrill demands for freedom from Macfadden's bondage.

His resistance was furious as well as devilishly ingenious. In this
instance, Macfadden was the victim of harassment. Winchell would
phone the publisher at three or four in the morning and bellow, "This

is Winchell! When are you going to let me go?" After a while, he just awakened the publisher and then hung up.

The deadly serious phone-calling farce went on for several weeks. Macfadden refused to budge. Winchell was equal to the challenge. Conflicts involving his career took on the tone of a holy war to him. Everyone on Broadway was aware of Winchell's outrage. He reiterated the ebb and flow of the melancholy clash. "There were times," Winchell said, "when I felt hopeless about my situation. Here was a big break, an immense opportunity, and the bastards were standing in my way. You can imagine the frustration."

His feelings of despair were transient, however. He was not a man given to pondering a difficult situation. When he felt wrapped in a web of circumstances, he hacked his way out, sometimes with a rusty axe, without regard to consequences.

When the phone-call-in-the-middle-of-the-night gambit fizzled, Winchell launched a frontal attack. Macfadden had mounted his reputation on being a health faddist. He was the uncrowned king of the vegetarians. Well aware of this, Winchell rolled up the heavy artillery. He bluntly informed Macfadden that he—and presumably other eyewitnesses—had seen Macfadden eating meat. He was ready to make this stunning revelation public. For Macfadden to be caught *in flagrante* with a lamb chop was unthinkable. The entire Macfadden empire might topple. Winchell's zany blackmail threw the Macfadden forces into panic. Whether or not the charge was true was secondary. The mere airing of the story might damage the Macfadden image beyond repair. Finally, Macfadden capitulated.

On May 31, 1929, shortly after Winchell arrived at the *Graphic* office, Gauvreau informed him that he was fired. Winchell was beside himself with joy. He cleaned out his desk immediately and ran, leaped, floated, and flew out of the *Graphic* office—with visions of gold dancing in his head. Three years later the *Graphic* folded.

Privately, William Randolph Hearst declared, "Winchell appeals to the whims of the younger degeneration." But he publicly extended a cordial welcome to his new columnist. Hearst wrote to congratulate Winchell on joining the fold, urged him to maintain his "readable style," and reminded him that he was among the world's highest-paid newspapermen. The publisher, a compulsive collector of expensive knickknacks, had another one in Winchell.

Walter's first *Mirror* column appeared on June 10, 1929. Several days earlier Walter Howey, the *Mirror*'s editor, had conferred with

him. Howey was the legendary Chicago newspaperman who had inspired the character of the hard-boiled, unscrupulous editor in the
Hecht and MacArthur *The Front Page,* the slambang drama that gave
Broadway and Hollywood their journalistic stereotype. He was one of
the few editors to elicit a friendly response from Winchell.

Winchell said, "Howey wanted to give me a big sendoff in the
Mirror by running the column on the front page. He told me it would
be the only news in the paper. Sure I was flattered. But I thought the
column would lose its form and flavor as a page-one feature. Howey
thought I would jump at the suggestion. I think he was surprised when
I turned it down. He finally agreed to run the column on an inside
page."

Howey's estimate of Winchell's value to the *Mirror* was quickly confirmed. Within a month he was the paper's top mail-puller and his
column its leading feature, a position that was maintained until the
Mirror's demise in 1963.

During Winchell's first month with the Hearst organization, one of
the publisher's friends called to complain about the columnist. "Mr.
Hearst, please do something about that new man of yours, that Walter
something or other. Stop him from writing about my husband that
way, please."

"What way?" Hearst inquired.

"He keeps putting things in your papers about my husband."

Hearst responded, "I'll make a deal with you. You stop your husband
from making news and I'll stop Winchell from breaking it.

Until Winchell's byline appeared, the *Mirror*'s dubious claim to
fame had been its role in the Hall-Mills murder case. Back in 1922 a
coroner's inquest had declared Mrs. Edward Hall innocent of any con-
nection with the deaths of her husband, the Reverend Hall, and his
mistress, Eleanor Mills. The story created a journalistic furor, but it
was soon relegated to the files. In 1926 the *Mirror* splashed page one
with "new" evidence that tended to incriminate the philandering cler-
gyman's widow. She was put on trial for her life.

A headline epidemic followed to which even the more conservative
journals succumbed. Of course the trial was the stuff of a newspaperman's dream: an angel fallen in the quagmire of crime and sex. Moreover, the courtroom goings-on were perfect for a tabloid, brimming
with surprise witnesses, lurid testimony—the cruel and disgusting sadness with which world-weary eccentrics were afflicted. The hypnotic
appeal to the public's sexual fantasies was obvious.

The *Mirror* played the story for all it was worth. It was worth about one hundred thousand in extra circulation. The case ended on an anti-climactic note when Mrs. Hall was declared innocent. The *Mirror* had been guilty of a horrid circulation stunt. But who cared?

In years to come, the *Mirror* could always be depended on for crime stuff. If a crime story failed to exist, the paper manufactured one. On dull news days, a *Mirror* man would squat at a typewriter and tap out something beginning like this: "The Purple Gang is organizing a gang war, the *Mirror* learned exclusively today. Police have been alerted to the underworld struggle that threatens to endanger the streets of our city."

Two months after Winchell joined the *Mirror,* he was stunned to learn that his old foe Emile Gauvreau had resigned his position at the *Graphic* and had been appointed the *Mirror*'s managing editor. "I thought I had escaped that man," he stormed, "and he was following me." Infuriated, Winchell sought to stop the second coming of Gauvreau in his life, but to no avail. "Gauvreau," *Mirror* staffers opined, "was hired to be Winchell's keeper." They were probably right.

The Winchell-Gauvreau relationship remained taut and tingly. The columnist and the editor never spoke to each other. The ice between them could have covered the Antarctic. Their opinions of each other were known to anyone who cared to listen.

In 1929 Winchell was generally acknowledged to be the single most influential personage on Broadway. As he scaled the electric mountain, the age that nurtured him stumbled and tumbled. Hot jazz was being replaced by the blues.

The 1920s had been a parody of American life. More burlesque than satire, they had been dominated by the atavistic urge for acquisition and pleasure, a rampage of sex and silliness. Money was something to be won, not earned. People were convinced that the carnival would never end, though some warned of the rumble of thunder in the gay music. But the indefatigable pleasure-seekers were unlikely to take seriously those who were posting speed warnings on the gilded highways.

On October 29, 1929, it happened. *Variety* summed it up in its classic headline "WALL STREET LAYS AN EGG."

The lighthearted fantasy of American life ended with a crash. Everything toppled in Wall Street except the buildings.

The big moneyquake numbed the populace. The party was over,

and the confetti had turned to rubbish. Mayor Walker had said that the 1920s were a "time when we all got drunk." Now the hangover was national. On November 19, 1929, Will Rogers summed up the national mood: "America already holds the record for freak movements. Now we have a new one. It's called 'restoring confidence.' Rich men who never had a mission in life outside of watching a stock ticker are working day and night 'restoring confidence.'

"Now I am not unpatriotic, and I do want to do my bit, so I hereby offer my services to my President, my country, and my friends around old Trinity Church, New York, to do anything (outside of serving on a commission) that I can, in this great movement.

"But you will have to give me some idea where 'confidence' is, and just what you want it restored to."

"I was stunned by the change in a few months," Winchell said. "People who thought I was a chump for not buying stocks were now envying me. They thought I had been smart to keep my money in the bank. I thought so, too."

Late in 1929 Winchell was dining at a glossy speakeasy that was rapidly becoming his favorite haunt—the Stork Club. Several years before, Texas Guinan had told Winchell, "There's a nice feller named Sherman Billingsley, a country jake from Oklahoma, who has a new restaurant. He has been taking $10,000 a month for nine months out of the sock to keep it alive. Give it a look like a good little boy." He looked and raved in print: "The New Yorkiest place in New York is the Stork Club!" Billingsley later claimed that after the Winchell plug "I started banking $10,000 a week."

While Winchell was spooning his dessert at the Stork as midnight approached he received a phone call. A voice commanded, "Stay where you are. You will be called again in twenty minutes!" Precisely twenty minutes later the phone rang. Winchell recognized the voice of an Owney Madden aide: "The Big Boss wants to see you in Miami Beach." Aware that the only big boss in Miami Beach was Al Capone, Winchell inquired, "What does he want to see me about?"

"He wants to talk to you for the papers."

"Okay!"

Winchell was about to produce his first underworld spectacular. His feelings were mixed during the rail journey to Miami. Excitement was tinged with a touch of apprehension. After all, Capone had never before granted an exclusive interview. There was the possibility that

the published interview might displease him. Gang leaders were sensitive plants. Winchell knew that entertainers in Chicago walked on
eggs. Those who had riled gangsters for one reason or another were
often cut up, kidnapped, or beaten.

Winchell was in Miami Beach for three days before he was contacted by Capone's lieutenants. One morning, two globs of lard called
at his hotel and escorted him to the back seat of a chauffeured car.
Wedged between beefy backsides and knees, he sought to lighten the
ominous atmosphere by quipping, "I feel like a tube of toothpaste."
Nobody laughed. The hush continued as the car moved to Capone's
retreat.

The ganglord's mansion was strategically located on an island. Big
and white, it was decorated with cupolas and spires and scrolled bal-
conies. The postcard beauty of the scene was smudged as soon as
Winchell spotted the entrance guarded by a pair of husky armed men.
The columnist later remarked on the overpowering quiet in the high-
ceilinged house as he was ushered into Capone's office, the flanking
guards performing the rigid ceremony with brisk efficiency. The underworld elite delighted in a certain pomp and flummery.

As he entered the room, the door was shut and locked behind him.
The guards sprawled in corner chairs. Capone rose from behind his
desk. His eyes were black coals in a dough face. Capone was taller
than he appeared in photographs, a six-footer with bronzed oaken
arms. The gang leader spoke in a soft, furry voice: "I'm glad you
could make it, Mr. Winchell."

"Glad to be here."

That ended the social niceties. Capone immediately explained the
purpose of the meeting. As he spoke, Winchell noticed a gun on his
desk and small framed pictures on the wall behind him: One was of
George Washington; the other, of Abraham Lincoln.

Capone made it clear that he was distressed by a splurge of unsolic-
ited publicity. He grumbled, "I don't like those phony inside-stuff
writers who claim to know me. If you ever meet them, give them a
punch in the nose with my compliments. It's a big laugh to read the
things I'm supposed to have done and said. A bigger laugh is those
movies about me. Where do they get their ideas? I also hate the damn
newsreels that sneak pictures of me. How do those things look to my
family?" Ironically, the love of respectability was a primary drive
among underworld chiefs, who considered themselves statesmen. In
fact they were, in a corrupt sense.

Capone went on to say that he received several thousand fan letters every week, many of them requesting money. He yanked a batch of them from a desk drawer and showed them to Winchell. After an hour in which the columnist played the unaccustomed role of listener, Capone ended the interview by lifting the gun from his desk. He banged the butt down with the finality of a judge's gavel.

The first exclusive interview with Capone received considerable headline hoopla. It seemed as newsworthy as a summit conference would be today. The interview added to Winchell's glamorous aura of being Mister Inside. As the national darkness deepened, Winchell's personal star ascended.

King Features began distributing his column nationally. His deal with the syndicate typified Winchell's shortsighted transactions. His contract stipulated that he was to receive 100 percent of the proceeds, although columnists and their syndicates generally split the take, 50-50. In this case, the syndicate accepted Winchell's all-or-nothing proposal simply because it used the column as a "leader" in packaging other syndicated products. Years later, when he was in dire need of syndicate aid and promotion, King Features refused to cooperate because it derived no money from Winchell. Even then, he refused to make any concession to snare more income. When he reached the $1,000-a-week level, $100 a week was earmarked for Mrs. Winchell's account. The sum was later raised to $200 weekly when his earnings increased. The arrangement continued for the rest of Winchell's working days and helped make his wife a rich woman in her own right. "My wife," he often remarked, "is richer than I am, and she deserves more."

Winchell's recollection of the gasping months of the 1920s blended regret and elation: "All around me things were falling. You can't imagine the doomsday feeling that swept the country. Big-name performers were so frightened by the turn of events they were ready to work for a fraction of their loot. Everybody was scared stiff by the nightmare. But things were sunny for me. I was doing much better than good. My family was spending its vacation in Miami Beach instead of the usual Long Beach holiday. The money was coming in. Hearst doubled my salary. I was the highest-paid columnist around. Hell, my only career problem was the unpeaceful coexistence with Gauvreau."

=6=
Broadway Lightning and Berlin Thunder

Winchell's reputation as an all-knowing columnist was taking on mythic proportions. His clout was recognized by his competition. A sign on the bulletin board in the *New York World* office warned staffers not to tell Winchell anything, and in 1931 *Time* magazine wrote:

> Walter Winchell is no ordinary scandal-snooper. Famed is he in theater lobbies, speakeasies, nightclubs. From one gossip center to another he travels to get column material. Alert, the Winchell ear hears all. Amiable, the Winchell disposition makes friendly easily, elicits scandal scraps. Then, at three or four in the morning, he goes back to his typewriter and two-fingers what he has learned, adding here and there the result of an imaginative mind.

Devotees of Winchell's column acknowledged that he was omniscient, because it made them feel privy to secrets that few people shared. Always the showman, Winchell was well aware of the box-office pull of this myth, and he magnified it whenever possible by accentuating the positive. If his prophecies and gossipy guesswork proved to be true, he loudly proclaimed it. If inaccurate, he remained silent or corrected them with a brief so-sorry. He developed the knack of printing retractions without making the reader aware that Winchell was correcting one of his "wrongos," as he called them.

Walter never learned to accept charges of inaccuracy with grace. After all, the image of omnipotence was essential to the Winchell mystique. When Winchell reported that a movie star was a cancer victim, her press agent observed, "I hope it's true; otherwise she's in real trouble."

He hated making retractions, and they were so deviously worded that Manhattan's District Attorney Frank Hogan vowed never to ask Winchell for another retraction. "The retraction was worse than the original," he said.

Early in Walter's career, he reported that a performer named Josephine Sexton had "passed away." She wrote to tell him that she was alive and well. The Winchell retraction: "Josephine Sexton is alive, she says."

As the nation was struggling to survive the first shock of the Depression, Winchell's career was moving serenely upward. The Publix Film Company paid him $17,500 to star in a dozen one-reel films to be shown between double features. The first, with Madge Evans, was *The Bard of Broadway.* "In 1930," Winchell later observed, "I collected more loot in a week than I had once earned a year in vaudeville."

In 1931, *Scribner's* magazine listed several "Winchell words": "Dotter: Daughter . . . Moom Picture: Moving Picture . . . Hahhlim: Harlem . . . Gel: Girl . . . Sealed: Married . . . Joosh: Jewish . . . Tome: Book . . . Hush Parlor: Speakeasy." And Charles W. Wilcox rhapsodized in the same periodical, "Winchell knows his stuff is good, and damn it, it is good. Everybody likes gossip. There is in all of us that ingrained hypocrisy which makes us affect to despise the quidnunc, while we break our necks to hear what he has to say, and run our legs off to repeat it—and with what gusto! Scandalmongers, aren't we all?"

H. L. Mencken publicly declared that Winchell was Elizabethan in his creation and vitalization of the language. Mencken gave his ex cathedra blessing to Winchell's telescoping of words, his staccato phonetics, his intimate bursts, and especially his minting of words and phrases. Among thousands of examples, "blessed event," "Girl Friday," "makin' whoopee," "phffft," and "bundle from Heaven" are probably best known.

More and more Winchell began to believe that he was the darling of the gods, an infallible genius who sifted and funneled all the secrets of Broadway and Hollywood and brought forth daily a bright and flawless column. The column became his single greatest preoccupation. Acquaintances who met him in the street—sometimes even strangers—would be compelled to listen to the problems and triumphs of his work. He took it for granted that every line in the column was read and remembered. Sometimes, if one of his monologues elicited a puzzled expression, he would launch a cross-examination to ascertain whether his listener had indeed done his homework or was just being polite. If the person indicated that he had neglected to read the column or remember what he had read, Winchell would walk away shaking his head, as if his interlocutor were guilty of an utterly unforgivable offense.

Late in 1931 an incident occurred that made him temporarily consider giving up his column. The Palace Theatre booked a number of journalistic notables—Heywood Broun, Floyd Gibbons, Harry Hershfield, and Mark Hellinger—to appear. Winchell was offered $3,500 for a week's engagement. Despite his column's success, he was a vaudevillian at heart. Only a vaudevillian knew what playing the Palace meant. It was hallowed ground. The theater's tradition was rich and wonderful. Sarah Bernhardt had played there and insisted on being paid in gold coins after every performance. All the superstars except Al Jolson played there Ethel Barrymore, Gertrude Lawrence, Will Rogers, and many others. Moreover, the theater itself was something to behold, with its giant crystal chandeliers, gold damasked walls, red carpeting, and rococo ceiling panels.

Decades later, Walter could still recapture the incident. He told me, "All the years of playing the hick towns, getting the rebuffs and the humiliations and hoping that some day you'll play the Palace. It's difficult for people who weren't a part of the old vaudeville days to understand. But for me, playing the Palace was better than being elected to the White House. The cold and rainy days I spent in front of the Palace when I was jobless, hoping for an invitation to share a sandwich, made it all more poignant for me. Not many people see a dream come true. I did. Just seeing my name above the marquee was something unforgettable. I stood and watched my name for hours and took pictures of it. You know, the week before I was due to open, I couldn't sleep. It was my first professional stage appearance in years. I had left vaudeville without a nickel, a flop. And now, here I was getting back at the top. The Palace—boy!"

He danced a little, sang a little, told a few jokes, and titillated the audience with Broadway gossip.

Winchell wrote his own review for *Variety*:

> Another freak attraction on the current Palace bill is Walter
> Winchell. . . . This sort of headliner is too anemic for the best-
> known music hall. His appearance was oke—he has a natty
> tone about him. He can be heard in the last rows, too. But
> he is hardly bigtime material. He simply won't do. . . . Winch-
> ell should have known better and stuck to columning.

Despite the *Variety* notice, Winchell was gratified, even over-
whelmed, by the audience response. He thought his vaudeville stint
would be something more than a one-time pleasure through which he
would collect big money, and he considered the idea of devoting himself to it once again. In recalling the incident, Winchell said that this
was not mere idle chatter. It was complicated by a problem that arose
as a consequence of the Palace engagement.

Mirror publisher John Kobler contended that the paper should
share in the columnist's vaudeville earnings because it was the column
that had made him a valuable vaudeville property. Winchell was outraged by what he judged a mercenary assault. Kobler, who spoke with
a heavy accent, was mimicked by Winchell. "Vinchell, the Meerorrr
must share in you muneee. Vinchell, don't be an eengrate." At one
time, they called each other "Jew bastard." That didn't help matters.

The columnist refused to deliver a penny of his vaudeville salary to
the *Mirror,* of course. Kobler retaliated by removing Winchell's secretary, Ruth Cambridge, from the *Mirror* payroll and ordering
Winchell to pay for his own secretary and telephone and telegraph
tolls. From that time on, Winchell did pay for his own secretarial
assistance, but the *Mirror* eventually restored his phone, wire, and
stationery privileges.

But Winchell's campaign of civil disobedience in *Daily Mirror*
country paled as the shadow of Vincent "Mad Dog" Coll loomed on
his personal horizon. At the time, Owney Madden's hegemony in the
New York underworld encompassed various spheres of influence and
gave it a degree of stability. While Madden's power was concentrated
in the downtown area, the less lucrative uptown territory was ruled by
Arthur Flegenheimer, alias Dutch Schultz. Among Schultz's young
lieutenants was an ambitious radical, the aforementioned Vincent Coll,
who went into business for himself and stole from his former boss.

Coll's uncommon audacity demanded swift reprisal, and Schultz ordered his gunmen to kill the rebel. Unfortunately, the professional assassins were not very professional. They mistakenly killed Vincent's brother Peter.

Coll retaliated with a brace of kidnappings. He first seized Sherman Billingsley, the Stork Club host, and held him captive in a Bronx garage for three days, beating him daily. Billingsley was released by being tossed from Coll's speeding car after friends paid $25,000 in ransom. The Billingsley kidnap story remained a secret until Winchell mentioned it about three decades later.

Coll then undertook a second snatch, "Big Frenchy" Demange, Madden's close friend and partner. Madden paid $35,000 for his release.

Schultz was Coll's next target. One sunny July afternoon, Schultz visited an East Harlem political clubhouse. Coll and his henchmen drove up, machine-gunned the area and roared away. Schultz was still breathing after the attack, but the spray of bullets had killed a five-year-old child playing in the street and seriously wounded four other youngsters.

The atrocity caused a community uproar. Coll went into hiding, and for good reason: he was being sought by the police as well as by gun-bearers of Madden and Schultz.

On February 6, 1932, Winchell made his nightly news-gathering visit to the club run by Texas Guinan. It was hardly a secret along Broadway that Texas was on intimate terms with the gangsters who financed her club. On the evening in question, she stopped at Winchell's table and whispered to him. "My eyeballs almost dropped out when I heard Texas's words," he later said.

The following night, the column carried an electrifying item. It was reprinted in a late edition of the *New York Times,* where Winchell's tangy style was as strange as a tap dance done to Beethoven's Fifth.

Walter wrote, "Five planes brought dozens of machine gats from Chicago Friday to combat the Town's Capone. . . . Local banditti have made one hotel a virtual arsenal and several hot-spots are ditto because Master Coll is giving them a headache."

About six hours after the seven o'clock edition of the *Mirror* hit the streets with the item, three gunmen entered a shop on West Twenty-third Street and riddled Vincent Coll in a phone booth.

Winchell was attending a movie at the time. As soon as he learned the news, he rushed to the scene, then returned to his *Mirror* office brimming with exhilaration. A front-page scoop was the high point of journalism, and this was the true romance of Winchell's life.

Winchell's delight was of brief duration. It ended with the ringing of a phone. The tone of the caller was fiercely insistent: "Walter, you told too much in the column. You may be in trouble with the boys." Walter, properly frightened, instantly called Madden, who spoke to Coll's assassins and then called the jittery columnist. Winchell was informed that it had been difficult to persuade the killers, but they had eventually agreed to spare him. Freed from the specter of an underworld death sentence, Winchell expressed his gratitude to Madden. Several minutes later, Madden called again. "I'm sending a few boys over to escort you for the next few days," he said.

"Thanks," Winchell sighed, "I was afraid to leave the office."

Several days later the columnist requested police protection, and his column was filled with grim portents, including his own epitaph: "Here is Walter Winchell—with his ear to the ground—as usual."

The district attorney summoned Winchell to appear before a grand jury. He testified that the Coll tip had come anonymously, via the mail. The real source—whose friendship with Winchell was well known—was ordered exiled by mob czars for "talking too much."

Winchell was exiled too. Shocked and frightened by the Coll incident, Kobler intensified his feud with the columnist by barring Winchell and his secretary from any part of the *Mirror* building except Winchell's own office.

Time magazine reported:

> Every move by Kobler and the *Mirror* is carefully considered lest it give Winchell the supreme satisfaction of breaking his contract. The instant that should occur Winchell would skip three blocks downtown to Joseph Medill Patterson's big little *Daily News.* . . . The *News* offered Winchell $1,000 a week for a Sunday column alone.

Patterson told Winchell, "Anytime you want to come here you're welcome. Ed Sullivan owes his job to you. If you gave up your column, I would get rid of Sullivan." Patterson had hired Sullivan to write a Broadway column for the *News* when he saw that Winchell's product was gaining readers for the *Mirror*.

At the time, survival rather than advancement was uppermost in Winchell's mind. The *News* offer was forgotten in the troubled tension of his bodyguarded existence. Eventually he cracked. In his words,

"I decided to chuck the whole thing." It was announced that he had had a nervous breakdown, his column was temporarily discontinued, and he headed for California with his family to recuperate.

Six weeks of California sunshine seemed to dissipate the terror of the Coll affair. Winchell returned to New York to resume his column. But only a week after the family's return, his lovely nine-year-old daughter, Gloria, was stricken with pneumonia. She died three weeks later. Mr. and Mrs. Winchell had witnessed and shared the youngster's agony. They were at her bedside when she died.

Winchell never fully recovered from the tragedy. Years later he would discuss it. After the child's death a reader sent him a cheap ring as a token of remembrance. Except for a wristwatch, it was the only piece of jewelry he ever wore. He kept her shoe on his desk at home. Winchell would touch it before he began working.

Winchell's life was always a blend of dark tragedy and explosive flashiness. Beneath the dynamic, vibrant personality and the self-congratulation was a recurring sadness. The sadness was frequently a consequence of physical illness and emotional stress in his family. Mrs. Winchell, an asthmatic, was ill during the greater part of her married life. In later years, their other children brought him disappointment and tragedy. He never could expiate his guilt for his infidelities by showering his wife with material possessions.

Winchell's friendships were primarily business-based. Insecurity haunted him. Frequently he wondered aloud, "What if I lose my column? What if I lose my voice and cannot broadcast?" He never had profound or lasting trust in anybody or anything, not even banks.

Nevertheless, despite the undercurrent of melancholy, Winchell was generally a happy man during his heyday. He gloried in his work and relished the fruits of success. "I want all the money in the world and all the stories in the world," he told me. Then he added, "And I want a few laughs."

I'll never forget Winchell's laughing jag when he read the latest malapropism uttered by producer Sam Goldwyn. In a toast to Britain's Field Marshal Montgomery, Goldwyn said: "A long life to Marshall Field Montgomery Ward."

A few days after his return from California, Winchell received a call that opened new media horizons. The call came from William Paley, head of CBS. "I would like you to meet Mr. Gimbel," Paley said, "who is in the department-store business. I think you can slant your style of reporting for the radio, and Mr. Gimbel is willing to be the sponsor."

Winchell had rejected radio offers before. He lacked radio experience and was skeptical about public acceptance of a Broadway column wired for sound. But Paley's insistence overcame Walter's misgivings and he signed up for a local newscast. Within months Paley's prescience was confirmed by the popularity of the Winchell newscast. It was the ideal mating: flashy words and a slam-bang voice. As his audience increased, he attracted additional sponsors.

Winchell's newscast was confined to the New York City area, where George Washington Hill, president of the American Tobacco Company, heard it. Hill immediately called Tom McAvity, of Lord and Thomas, who supervised the production of American Tobbaco's program "Lucky Strike Magic Carpet." Hill, an eccentric genius, told McAvity, "I want Winchell on my next show." Within twenty-four hours Winchell was signed for $1,000 a week.

Hill ordered a heavy promotional campaign. Billboards, posters, radio spots, newspaper ads all proclaimed the coming of Walter Winchell to the "Lucky Strike Magic Carpet." The program was hosted by several emcees who introduced famous bands scattered around the country. In the early radio era, listeners were awed by the hop, skip, and jump from city to city. It seemed an electronic marvel. Hence the "Magic Carpet" title.

Winchell introduced the bands in his commanding, exciting manner with a phrase that soon became a popular tag line: "Ohhhkkkayyy, Aaaammmmerrricca!" Soon Winchell added entertainment news to the program and his memorable greeting: "Good Evening, Mr. and Mrs. America and all the ships at sea!" He had become a national voice.

While Walter was riding the magic carpet, the nation's economy continued to plummet. Late in February 1933, financiers put unofficial observers at the doors of the Federal Reserve Bank to watch the outflow of gold. There was widespread agreement with Bernard Baruch's dictum before a Senate committee that the nation was confronted with a condition "worse than war."

President-elect Franklin Delano Roosevelt drove in an open car to Miami's Bay Front Park, where he was welcomed by twenty thousand cheering Floridians. Roosevelt waved to Chicago's Mayor Cermak, who was sitting on the bandstand. He then pulled himself onto the car's down-folded top, was handed a microphone, and began to speak. Several minutes later, five shots rang out in rapid succession. One bullet hit Mayor Cermak and four other bystanders. Standing on a wobbly bench among the spectators, not thirty-five feet from FDR, was the gunman, Joe Zangara, a blurry-minded transient.

At this time, Winchell was spending his annual winter "workation," as he called it, in Miami. He had just filed his column in the Western Union office when a messenger dashed in with news from the park. Winchell sprinted straight to the jail, where he talked his way up to the cell block and eavesdropped on the sheriff's examination of Zangara. He wired the *Mirror* that night that Zangara "gave every indication of being crazy." The story was Winchell's first international exclusive. "At last I'm a newspaperman," he later crowed.

Sidney Skolsky, a *Daily News* columnist and a good friend of Winchell's, arrived at Miami police headquarters at the same time as Walter. When the police allowed Winchell in and barred Skolsky, Skolsky shouted, "Hey! I'm a newspaperman too. Ask Winchell." Winchell looked back and muttered, "Never saw him before in my life." Skolsky didn't get in.

Incidentally, Winchell's editor-enemy Emile Gauvreau refused to pay the $11 long-distance toll, even though the *Mirror* published the scoop. When William Randolph Hearst subsequently visited the *Mirror*, he handed him $11. "This," he smiled, "is long overdue."

While the front pages headlined the attempted assassination of FDR, the inside pages reported on German Chancellor Adolf Hitler's election-speech promise that, no matter how Germans voted on March 4, his government would retain power. "If the German people should desert us, that will not restrain us! Whatever happens we will take the course that is necessary to save Germany from ruin!"

The Berlin Bureau of the London *Times* cabled that Hitler's henchmen "are in a position to brush aside any suggestion that their ambitions can be thwarted from any quarter." Nazism's long night had begun and, among other things, it would help transform a hard-driving Broadway hustler into an international crusader.

The transition was a slow process. Winchell brought a raffish Broadway quality to the international scene. He began his campaign against Hitler in a frivolous tone, by publicly scorning Hitler's alleged homosexuality after foreign correspondent Quentin Reynolds had told Winchell, "Hitler is a fag."

On March 28, 1933, Winchell gagged, "Cable. March 26, Berlin—to Walter Winchell, care of Paramount Theatre, Brooklyn—What are you doing over the weekend? Would you like to spend it with me?

I think you are cute—Adolf Hitler." A later column asked readers, "Didn't you scream laughing at the pansy way Adolf lifted his eyes in that photo in yesterday's *Mirror?*"

In June, 1933, he cracked, "Hitler turned down the chance of entering a beauty contest because he found out that the first prize was a free trip to the Bronx." He added, "Henceforth this column will call him Adele Hitler." Later he quoted Marlene Dietrich: "If Hitler can wear pants, then I can."

In Hitler, Winchell had someone to despise. Concurrently, the New Deal gave him—and millions of others—someone to revere. Shortly after Roosevelt's inauguration, Winchell gushed in his column, "They should give the Nobel Peace Prize to FDR's smile." Another typical Winchell valentine: "They're making the postage stamps bigger so that when the time comes to put President Roosevelt on it there'll be room enough for his heart."

For the next fourteen years, his contempt for one leader and his adoration of the other were the twin passions of his professional life.

Granted that Winchell's initial thrusts against Nazism were pinpricks, the fact remains that he was a pioneer in the struggle. Not many Americans—or their leaders—were quick to fathom the monstrous possibilities of the Nazi philosophy. For example, in 1933, Secretary of State Cordell Hull casually dismissed the Nazis' anti-Semitic campaigns as "mild." Winchell publicly protested, "The Hull you say!"

Today it is shocking, even preposterous, to imagine that in the early 1930s it was difficult for a columnist or news commentator to express opposition to Hitlerism. Nevertheless, it is true that Winchell endangered his career by challenging the German horrors. NBC feared that German authorities would retaliate against its correspondent in Berlin, and William Randolph Hearst deplored his columnist's anti-Nazism, because he owned a news service that did a big business in Germany. Besides, Hearst was anti-British.

Winchell continued the offensive. On September 27, 1933, he wrote, "I wondered for a long spell if my barbs were being seen by the Nazis—and if they were irked by them, even a little. It is so nice to know that my efforts haven't altogether been snubbed." This remark was occasioned by a front-page story in Hitler's paper, the *Voelkischer-Beobachter.* It carried the columnist's photo with the caption "A New Enemy of the New Germany."

Winchell began carrying a gun after receiving threats from Nazi groups. And he advertised his gun-toting as a psychological deterrent.

"If they know I carry a gun," he said to me, "the Nazi creeps will be scared shitless." To my knowledge, he never fired a shot in anger.

His mother was frightened by his gun-toting. She called several times and pleaded with him to surrender the weapon. "I haven't been able to sleep," she said, "since I read you are carrying a gun." To placate his mother, Winchell promised to disarm himself. But he never did.

Although he was funnybone-deep in international affairs, Winchell continued to peddle such staple items as "Helen Henderson, ex-Follies femme, who divorced Bob Rice of George Olsen's crew to wed rich Aaron Benisch only to phffft with Aaron and be resealed to Rice, was melted from him last month." Always a shrewd showman, Walter never surrendered his patented crowd-pleasers. After all, crusaders without an audience were merely voices in the wilderness.

In time, the simplicity of his exhortations against Nazism helped alert the average American to the menace. Winchell's huge audience was aware of the danger long before most statesmen and editorial writers reached the same conclusion.

Late in 1933 the Winchell column reported, "Fritz Kuhn, who poses as a chemist for a motor magnate, is Hitler's secret agent in the United States." With the discovery of Nazis in America's own backyard, Winchell launched a prolonged battle against Hitler's supporters here. Several days later, Winchell revealed that Kuhn was the leader of the German-American Bund, a Nazi-financed propaganda arm of the Third Reich.

Within weeks the Winchell column had disclosed that the Bund had seventy-one units scattered around the country, twenty-three of them in or near New York City. For the next four years, while the press in general ignored the Bund, Walter maintained a steady barrage. One editor dismissed it as "just another Winchell sideshow." Winchell's quarry screamed "dirty Jew!" and vainly used intermediaries to plant items with the columnist in an effort to trap him in a libel suit. Kuhn's repeated countertactics were crude, farcical, or both. He once showed up at the Stork Club and sat about twenty feet from Winchell downing drink after drink. Finally he staggered out of the club. The next day, Winchell ran an item: "Fritz Kuhn and a columnist swapping stares at the Stork Club." When Kuhn charged that Winchell's "real name was Lipshitz," the columnist cracked, "*Ja,* me *und* President Rosenfeldt!"

Incidentally, soon after Kuhn came into the Stork Club, the columnist went to the men's room and stripped the bullets from his gun. Apparently, he feared a loaded gun in Kuhn's presence might be a temptation hazardous for all concerned.

As time passed, Winchell began digging out additional "Ratzis." In addition to the Bundists, numerous other Nazi groups came out of the wall.

The columnist's peers remained indifferent. It wasn't until 1936, three years after Winchell had begun to hoist warning signals, that several newspapers, notably the *Washington Post,* joined him in exposing domestic Nazis. Some years later he griped, "The Nazi nightmare here was becoming clearer and I was surrounded by journalistic Rip Van Winkles, including some of my editors along the syndicate."

Perhaps they were diverted from one nightmare by the pervasive effects of another one—the Depression. Still, the year 1933 had one bright note: Prohibition was repealed. Some of Winchell's old Prohibition sidekicks were hardly jubilant. Owney Madden, who had saved Winchell's life little more than a year before, languished in Sing Sing for parole violation, and mobster Larry Fay, who owned Texas Guinan's club, died broke.

Winchell flourished, however. He kept the Lucky Strike show when he was tapped for his first network news show, and it put him among the nation's top money-makers. At $1,500 per program plus the $1,000 per week from the *Mirror* plus his syndicate income, his earnings totaled more than $200,000 per annum. Winchell was well on his way to his first million.

In later years, he often boasted about "going down to the bank to dust off my money." I remember walking into his bedroom at the St. Moritz Hotel and seeing the bed neatly covered with stacks of hundred-dollar bills. "What a bedspread!" I thought.

Winchell beamed. "Know how much money that is?" I shook my head. "A million dollars!" I was truly impressed.

On March 1, 1932, the child of the world's most famous celebrity was kidnapped. The victim was Charles Lindbergh's infant son. Kidnappings are generally high-yield journalistic material. In this case, the public concern was incredible. For more than a year various tragic and bizarre ramifications of the case dominated the headlines. The discovery of the bruised corpse of the baby led to the greatest manhunt in history.

Winchell covered the Lindbergh story and covered himself with

distinction after a series of exclusive revelations about the FBI's progress toward solving the case. Eventually, the FBI took into custody
a man it believed to be the kidnapper. He was Bruno Richard Hauptmann, a German carpenter. Winchell learned about it less than an
hour after Hauptmann had been nabbed.

FBI chief J. Edgar Hoover asked Winchell to withhold the news
for twenty-four hours. The columnist complied, thus sacrificing the
biggest scoop of his career, though he reported that the case might soon
be solved eight days before the official announcement.

Shortly thereafter, Hoover reciprocated in kind: Winchell was allowed to inform his readers and listeners that one rail of the ladder
used to climb into the Lindbergh nursery matched the wood flooring
of Hauptmann's attic. This piece of evidence was considered decisive
in Hauptmann's subsequent conviction.

The Hauptmann trial in 1934 was a journalistic three-ring circus,
and one ring was occupied by supersleuth Walter Winchell. Courtroom visitors were almost as interested in seeing Winchell in the flesh
as in observing the suffering Lindberghs. In his reports the columnist
dubbed himself the "thirteenth juror."

About a year after Hauptmann was found guilty, Hoover wrote
to Winchell:

> Yesterday I had the occasion of speaking before the newspaper
> editors of America, who are in convention here in Washington,
> at which time I pointed out some of the things that newspapers
> help us in and some of the things in which they hurt. I pointed
> out, without, of course, mentioning the name specifically, how
> a well-known columnist had refrained from printing a truly
> national and international scoop in the Lindbergh case for
> twenty-four hours in order not to harm the investigation which
> was being conducted in that case. Of course you know who
> that person is. The entire speech is "off the record," but I thought
> the editors should know that there was at least one columnist
> who put patriotism and safety of society above any mercenary
> attitude in his profession.
>
> With best regards, I am
>
> > Sincerely,
> > JOHN.

After Hauptmann's conviction, Winchell accelerated his campaign
against Nazis at home and abroad. Because Hauptmann was a German

alien, Hitler's propagandists countercharged that Winchell was using the Lindbergh case to whip up hatred against the Fatherland.

J. Edgar Hoover, who adored publicity, courted reporters in general and Winchell in particular, because Walter had the largest audience. Although their relationship had been casual before the Lindbergh case, mutual admiration evolved afterward. Naturally, it was believed that Hoover was the source for the columnist's exposes of American Nazis. On the contrary, Winchell's revelations had roused the FBI and other government agencies to examine the domestic Nazi legions. After Winchell demanded "that the authorities ascertain the source of Fritz Kuhn's finances," New York's district attorney investigated and discovered illegal manipulations. Kuhn was indicted for grand larceny and forgery. Furthermore, he and other native Nazi leaders were called before various congressional investigating committees. Subsequently, Kuhn was tried, convicted, and imprisoned.

Shortly thereafter, Winchell was accosted near Central Park by two men with heavy German accents. After voicing several anti-Semitic remarks, they mugged him. He suffered a split lip and a broken tooth. The culprits were soon apprehended. One of the Broadway detectives who had collared them asked Winchell, "Do you want us to take care of them?" Winchell nodded. Presumably, harsh justice was dispensed in the backroom of a police station.

=7=
The Bronx Kid, King Walter, and the President

A variety of circumstances, fanciful and realistic, led me to Winchell's office one humid evening in August 1936.

As a youngster, I had haunted the darkened movie temples, where celluloid fantasies nurtured my dreams of becoming an actor, then a tap dancer, and finally a playwright. In February 1936, then aged sixteen, I was stricken with pneumonia and, after a period of hospitalization, recuperated at home for almost two months. I twiddled away the hours listening to the leading radio clowns: Eddie Cantor, Ed Wynn, Jack Pearl, Fred Allen, Jack Benny, and others. Possessed by another dreamy notion, I decided to become a humorist. At any rate, to kill time, I began writing gags in a notebook. After compiling about a hundred jokes, I impulsively sent a batch to Milton Berle, then appearing at Loew's Paradise in the Bronx. Berle responded with an encouraging note, a heady experience for a sixteen-year-old.

After receiving Berle's note, again acting impulsively, I mailed a page of quips to New York Post columnist Leonard Lyons. Three days later I had the dizzying delight of seeing my words and my name in print. I was hooked. Imagine a kid in a third-floor walkup in the Bronx finding his name in a glamorous Broadway column. For several months I continued submitting material to Lyons, who found more than one usable quip in my contributions, which he would credit to such humorists as George S. Kaufman and Robert Benchley—and sometimes Mrs. Lyons.

In July 1936, then working as a $12-a-week errand boy in the garment district to pay for my evening courses at City College, I received a note from Leonard Lyons inviting me to come to see him to discuss my "making some extra dough in press agenting." We met in Lyons's cubbyhole office at the *Post.* Slat-thin and hawk-faced, the columnist greeted me cordially: "I think you can make some money as a press agent."

"What is a press agent? What do they do?" I wanted to know.

Lyons patiently explained, "They swap gags and gossip for plugs in columns. If Al Jolson is your client and you send me a usable gag, I'll pin it on Jolson. That's how the publicity business works on Broadway. A lot of the boys make big money in this field."

Lyons arranged an interview for me with a press agent in the resplendent RKO edifice, which adjoins the Radio City Music Hall. As soon as I entered the sumptuous lobby I decided to ask for $15 a week or maybe even $20. After waiting half an hour, I was ushered into the presence of the press agent. He offered me $10 a week and I eagerly accepted.

My mother, the business head of the family, and my father were appalled by my decision to leave the garment industry—and take a $2 cut. The field of press agentry was alien to them. As it turned out, for the first month, their forebodings were warranted. When I launched my career as a press agent, Winchell was on vacation. Except for Lyons, the columnists were unimpressed with my work. After the first week, therefore, my salary was cut to $6. The third week I collected $4.

When Winchell returned in August, I sent him the material the other columnists had rejected. This was contrary to the customary procedure. Winchell always came first, and his rejects were then submitted to his competitors, whom he dismissed contemptuously as "my wastebasket."

Winchell liked my gags. One morning his secretary called and said that he would like to see me that evening at seven. As soon as word of the call got around the office, my salary zoomed from $4 to $15 a week.

Promptly at seven I walked into Winchell's office on the third floor of the *Mirror* building. It didn't look at all the way I had imagined. Dingy, narrow, and cluttered, it was sparsely furnished with several hard chairs, a row of files, a long table, and two desks. Winchell, nearly bald except for graying hair at the temples, was seated at a desk typing furiously with two fingers. He seemed older than he appeared in his photos. As I approached, he pushed himself away from the typewriter and said, "You have a way with words, kid." I glowed, simply awed to be in his presence.

He resumed his typing and only looked up briefly when a beefy man, who turned out to be his bodyguard, lumbered in and stationed himself in a far corner of the office.

Winchell signaled the completion of his chores with a loud sigh. After he put on his jacket, he whipped out a pencil, wrote a few words, and passed the paper to me. It read, "Ed Sullivonce and Ed Dullivan." Then he bragged that Hollywood producer Darryl Zanuck was tempting him with "a big-money contract" to star in a film. I was impressed, of course.

He turned toward me. "Do you want to be a writer?"

"I'm taking an accountancy course at City College three nights a week."

"Accountant? Accountants don't have fun. I have two accountants. They get mad when I call them bookkeepers."

"Well," I quickly added, trying to agree with him, "I would like to be a writer."

"To be a writer you must have some talent and you must write something every day. Never give up."

I nodded.

He went on: "I like your stuff. Some of my contributors have become gag writers for the top clowns on radio."

"Wonderful," I said.

Then he asked how I had joined the press agents' ranks. After I told my story and mentioned Leonard Lyons's contribution, Winchell commented, "Len is a good kid. I named his column 'The Lyons Den.' He used to be one of my contributors. His real name isn't Lyons. But, like all my imitators, he'll probably end up hating me."

He glanced at his watch and rose.

As we were about to leave, he displayed a photo of his son, Walter, Jr., who had just celebrated his first birthday, and his daughter, Walda, then nine.

While waiting for the elevator, he donned a gray snap-brim fedora. The transformation was stunning. With his baldness masked, he suddenly looked like a younger man.

As we walked down Forty-fifth Street, he complained that his bosses were "giving me migraines complaining about the anti-Nazi stuff." Then, for the first time, he offered a comment he was frequently to repeat over the years: "Don't get too friendly with your boss." With that parting advice, he wished me luck and hailed a cab. He and his burly companion climbed into the taxi and moved into the night.

At the time, Walter's militant anti-Nazism and fervent support for FDR displeased the Hearst brass. For Winchell it was simply a case of the good guys versus the bad guys. He despised Hitler without reservation and revered Roosevelt without qualification.

When Nazism slithered onto the stage of history, even well-educated Americans could not conceive of its potential monstrosity. Certainly there was some contempt for Hitler in some American minds. But few could imagine that he could possibly be as vile as he seemed.

As a Jew, Winchell was quick to recognize the monstrous threat of Nazism. As a reporter who was familiar with the underworld, he was equally vigilant to the peril of a gangster.

To say the least, Hearst did not share Winchell's attitude. He had visited Germany in 1934 and had had an interview with Hitler. On his return to the United States, the *New York Times* reported, "While condemning dictatorships, Mr. Hearst added his belief that Chancellor Hitler seemed to be popular with the German masses largely because of 'his advocacy of a united Germany capable of resisting encroachment of injustice from foreign powers.' He predicted that some Nazi policies would be modified, 'particularly with regard to the Jews." He did not believe Hitler a war threat, but insisted that France and Italy were arming to the teeth.

Furthermore, the German press had quoted Hearst: "If Hitler succeeds in pointing the way of peace and order . . . he will have accomplished a measure of good not only for his own people but for all of humanity."

Hearst later declared that he had been misquoted.

Aware that his militant anti-Nazi position infuriated Hearst, Winchell wrote a letter to the publisher in May 1937. He discussed his political stance and reminisced about his career with the Hearst paper since 1929. Among other things, he observed that he had always disliked the slogan of Hearst's King Features Syndicate: "All the Stars—While They're Stars!" Winchell commented, "When they are no longer stars—they are fired, huh?"

Hearst responded:

> Stars are stars as long as they desire to be and deserve to be. What extinguishes stars is liquor, indolence, egotism, indiffer-

ence, temperament and such noxious developments. The quality
which makes success does not die out. It is often choked—killed
by the toxins which a swelled head breeds. We WANT stars
and we want to KEEP them, and we DO keep them as long as
they will let us. . . . We take care of the stars all right, but we
expect them also to take care of themselves. The stars are independent. We cannot compel them to behave properly. We
do not OWN stars. We do not BUY stars. We buy their product.
We try to help them MAKE it good and KEEP it good. Sometimes it is a hard job.

Winchell published a portion of the letter. He was aware that
Hearst's use of the words "egotism" and "temperament" were pointed
directly at him.

Although Winchell's anti-Nazi zeal was the main source of Hearst's
displeasure, the publisher was also irked by the columnist's fervent
support of President Roosevelt. An early FDR admirer, Hearst was
soon disenchanted by Roosevelt's social programs.

But Winchell's sympathy for the underdog was forged in the cru-
cible of Harlem and vaudeville. He grew up in an atmosphere of unre
lieved poverty, was humiliated by his dismal experiences in school and
frustrated by his obscurity as an itinerant entertainer. A quarter of a
century of struggle had left Winchell with a persistent sense of insecurity and a feeling of compassion for the underprivileged that were
apparently latent until he fell in love with Franklin Delano Roosevelt.

As his consciousness was raised, his conscience was broadened. Walter's visceral sympathy was transformed into understanding by his personal affection for FDR and his vigorous, even ferocious, support of
New Deal measures on behalf of the ill-fed, ill-housed, and dis-
possessed.

Through an assistant U.S. attorney who knew Winchell, FDR extended an invitation to the columnist to visit the White House in May
1937. When he was escorted into the Oval Office, Winchell said,
"How do you do, Mr. President."

FDR broke the ice by grinning and saying, "Walter, I've got an
item for you."

They spoke for more than an hour. Winchell regaled the President
with Broadway and Hollywood tidbits and off-color jokes, and Roosevelt touched lightly on several domestic and international issues. The
President delighted him with a quip: "Senator Taft is a horse's aft."

Winchell roared when he heard it and couldn't wait to see it in print. But the *Mirror* editors had other ideas. Time after time Winchell sought to publish it, and time after time it was deleted. The arguments were long and furious. "I got it from FDR! How can it be in bad taste?" he screamed. He threatened to quit the paper over what he termed "censorship," but to no avail. Months later, he managed to sneak it into the column disguised beyond recognition: "Sennnntffffttttizahuzzzsfffttt!" It made no sense, except to those aware of the behind-the-scenes ruckus. But the gibberish inspired questions from readers, and Winchell happily translated it for them.

Thereafter, the columnist and the President communicated regularly. Whether it was a face-to-face meeting, a phone call, or a letter, every contact with FDR left its exuberant mark on Winchell. After their initial meeting, the columnist enthused, "Franklin Roosevelt means more to me than any other man." Until the end, his devotion was constant, and he measured succeeding chief executives by his giant image of Roosevelt.

Meanwhile, friendly editors sought to divert Winchell's attention from his major issues. The *Mirror*'s editor, Glenn Neville, circled an item in an old column and noted, "Why don't you do more stuff like this?" The item read, "The most interesting person I've seen in ages is a young lady from Ohio, whose specialty is making a muscle in her shapely chest wiggle. She came to join a girlesk show and her aunt— a former member of the Beef Trust, who did it for years—taught it to her."

Winchell's one-word reply: "Nuts!"

As the weeks passed, his column of personals become more and more a column of principles. As Winchell matured, so did his contributors. My initial Winchell material was a series of one-liners. Within a year I was contributing anti-Nazi editorials. Early in 1938, I sent him a feature called "The Headliners," in which I quoted people in the news, particularly Nazi leaders, and added my own editorial comments.

Winchell called the following morning. He liked the feature and offered to double my salary if I would work exclusively for him. I accepted on the spot, abandoning my career as a press agent.

As a paid Winchell writer, I was at first anonymous. I picked up my paycheck at the Winchell office and signed it there, and it was cashed while I waited. Walter apparently feared that I might show his check around, thereby confirming rumors that his column was ghost-written.

The check-secrecy routine soon ended, but my work for Winchell remained a trade secret for years.

Shortly after I joined the Winchell ranks, his feud with Hearst escalated. Hearst had been objecting for some time to Winchell's anti-Nazi paragraphs. He usually "recommended" or "suggested" policy. In Winchell's case, his recommendations and suggestions had had little effect. Finally, on March 28, 1938, the Press Lord transmitted a teletype from his San Simeon domain:

> To editors of all Hearst newspapers using Winchell—please edit Winchell very carefully and leave out any dangerous or disagreeable paragraphs . . . Indeed, leave out the whole column without hesitation, as I think he has gotten so careless that he is no longer of any particular value.
>
> W. R. HEARST

This was an unmistakable command. Its immediate effect was the deletion from Winchell's column of virtually all comments on events beyond Broadway's borders.

Winchell reacted by resigning five times between April 1 and April 15. As a matter of fact, he resigned four times in three days. The flurry of resignations was ignored for two reasons: Circulation experts knew that the Winchell column attracted about one-third of the *Mirror*'s readers, and Hearst was well aware that the rival *Daily News* would welcome his star.

Winchell effectively countered the Hearst censorship in his newscast, in which he aired many items deleted from the column. Hearst countered with a radio speech in which he ignored Hitler's Germany but vilified France and Britain.

After a phone conference between the columnist and the publisher was arranged by Hearst executives, an uneasy truce developed. Parenthetically, despite his long association with the Hearst organization, Winchell probably spoke to the publisher no more than a dozen times. Winchell never called him "Mr. Hearst." Impishly, he addressed him as "Daddy."

It would be misleading to imply that in the late 1930s, or at any other time, Winchell completely abandoned gags and gossip to cover the doings of dictators. While the Nazi menace and his support for FDR were central in his thinking, he continued to attract the multitudes with his trade-marked sass and Broadway spangles. Manhattan, not Washington, was his home base. Further, he was still the *Mirror's* drama critic.

In the fading months of 1938 he was the only daily critic to rave about a show called *Hellzapoppin.* It was a slapdash, slapstick thing in which every time a guy shook hands water squirted out of his ear and a banana tree grew four inches when someone sneezed. The inanities convulsed Winchell, though the show was panned by every other critic. He decided to billboard the stage riot, which became an immediate hit. For the first time in Broadway history a show triumphed over almost unanimously negative reviews. Winchell's raves made *Hellzapoppin's* producers more than $5 million richer.

Late in 1938, when he was tangling with Hearst, Winchell wrote a self-pitying note: "What if I lose my column? Then I'm no different than the loudmouth in a bar. The man who sells papers on the corner may have a more secure future."

But such dire musings are not exaggerations to Winchell. He was never sure of himself. The public Winchell was full of fiery self-confidence, but the private man was constantly plagued by an inner instability. Part of the problem was an abnormal family relationship. As a father and husband he was generous but delinquent. He purchased a large estate in Westchester, not far from New York, where he installed his wife and children. His visits to the family were intermittent. Among other things, he said, the "cooing pigeons in the country" prevented him from sleeping late. Besides, it was more fun for Walter to sleep with shapely city "doves" in New York.

His favorite environments were Miami Beach's Roney-Plaza and Manhattan's Stork Club, particularly the latter.

Winchell was Broadway, and he carried his own electricity. When he was in Miami Beach in winter, it was Broadway. Wherever he moved in Manhattan, it was Broadway. That he vibrated with nervous energy is something of an understatement. He *was* nervous energy. From the second he opened his eyes in the late afternoon until he closed them at dawn, he was bubbling and churning. His own little world in which he was the dominant player fascinated him.

Walter once described a typical Winchell day:

"I usually open my baby blues at about one in the afternoon. I call my office to check for late news, mail, and column changes. I breakfast at Lindy's: orange slices, baloney and eggs, coffee. Delish. I've eaten so much baloney I think I'm growing a baloney cock. Then to the barber for the usual. People are always coming to me with newsy tidbits and gags—in restaurants, in the barbershop, on the street. After barbering I go back to the apartment to check the late mail and read the papers, then to the Stork for dinner. After that, maybe a show or a movie, then back to the Stork for more gabbing. When things get dull, I hop in the car and chase police calls. Or I go chasing girls—and finding them too. I love the city about five or six in the morning. That's when I dash home and try to sleep."

=8=
Reporter, Statesman, Showman

Several weeks before Neville Chamberlain's historic trip to Munich, Walter met British Ambassador Lord Lothian at the Stork Club. When Winchell asked him about the British response to Nazi expansionist policies, Lothian replied, "We must try to fatten the tiger without strengthening him." The next day the Winchell column capsuled the story in a single line: "Britain will marry Hitler in the fall and the marriage will blow up via World War." Later, when the Munich Pact was signed, appeasers hailed the illusory peace, but Walter saw the tragic reality.

The isolationist-interventionist debate was enacted in the press. The case of those who believed America could remain aloof from the oncoming European war was argued by the Patterson family papers in New York, Washington, and Chicago and the Hearst chain. On the other side was a committee formed by William Allen White, famed editor of the *Emporia* (Kansas) *Gazette*. Widely respected by his fellow newspaper editors, White urged all aid to the Allies short of war. White's group gained the support of Walter Winchell as well as Drew Pearson, the *Washington Post* editors, and other journalists.

At first, the debate was a struggle of ideas actuated by honest convictions. But as time passed, it became savage, personal, and unreasoning.

The debate was highlighted by an interview in the early part of 1939. Winchell was at his winter headquarters—the Roney-Plaza in Miami Beach. One sunny afternoon, Joseph P. Kennedy, then U.S.

Ambassador to Great Britain, was visiting friends there when he spotted Winchell and went over to say hello.

Walter greeted him with a pointed question: "What about Munich, Joe?"

Kennedy was happy to discuss it. "It's great," he said, "and I think I had a part in it."

"How?" inquired Winchell.

"Lindbergh dropped in at the embassy. He had just inspected the Luftwaffe. What he told me was so important that I had him sit down at a typewriter and write it out himself. It was so important I myself brought it over to Chamberlain."

"What did Lindbergh say?"

"He said the Luftwaffe was by far the most powerful air force in the world, absolutely tops."

"Do you think the Lindbergh memorandum had anything to do with Chamberlain's decision at Munich?" asked Winchell.

"I think it was the decisive factor in his mind."

"Do you mean," said the columnist, "Chambelain reached the Munich agreement with Hitler because he thought Germany was Britain's military superior?"

"Yes. Absolutely."

"What about the British fleet?"

Kennedy replied, "The British fleet is capable of defending one of three strategic areas, and only one: home waters, the Mediterranean, or the Far East."

"Has any decision been made on which area would be defended in case of war?"

"Certainly."

"Which area?"

"Home waters, of course."

"What about Australia?"

"Australia," asked Kennedy, "is vulnerable to any two capital ships of the Japanese Navy."

The interview was cabled around the globe within hours and caused diplomatic and editorial eruptions on both sides of the Atlantic, as well as in Australia.

Kennedy met Winchell again several weeks later. "How did you like the story?" Walter asked. Kennedy responded by shaking his head in wonder: "I liked it. They didn't like it elsewhere. I wonder why."

The Kennedy interview not only propelled Lindbergh into the isolationist-interventionist brawl; it also expanded and embittered the controversy. Years later Joseph P. Kennedy's part in this historic incident would be recalled to discredit his son's Presidential campaign.

Of course, the Kennedy story was a major exclusive for Winchell. But late in 1939, in terrain more familiar to him than the international landscape, he achieved the most sensational news beat of his career.

From the time Texas Guinan took him by the hand and introduced him to the underworld, its rulers courted him, appointed themselves his bodyguards, believed it was a mark of distinction to be in his company, and hoped he would mention them—or their girls—in the column. Of all Winchell's acquaintances and friends in the underworld, the one he most admired was Frank Costello. He was impressed with powerful men on every level. The chemistry between Costello and Winchell was good; besides, he was a prime news source.

For about a dozen years both Winchell and Costello resided in the Majestic, at 115 Central Park West. As neighbors, they occasionally met in the lobby. Their relationship could be described as cautious but cordial. They usually engaged in animated, lighthearted discussion. Walter called his Francisco. Oddly, they resembled each other— both were dapper, cocky men who sported conservative suits, the same gray hats tilted at a rakish angle, and the same direct gaze—in brief, two major powers.

Walter introduced me to Costello by saying: "Meet Mr. Costello, the gambler." Costello wisely corrected him: "The people who come to my places are gamblers, Walter. I'm a business man."

J. Edgar Hoover tolerated Costello. He once told Frank, "Just stay out of my bailiwick." Because gambling was the only illicit operation that could be pinned on Costello—and gambling was not a federal offense—he was outside Hoover's territory, and the détente was maintained. Hoover, a rabid horseplayer, received tips from Winchell. The information originated with Frank Erickson, the nation's leading bookie, who relayed it to Frank Costello, his financial backer, who passed it on to Walter.

The scoop began with a call to Winchell's friend Irving Hoffman, a Broadway and Hollywood publicist. The caller, who was apparently known to Hoffman, told him, "Lepke wants to come in. He's heard the New York cops will bump him off and say he was trying to escape. He wants to surrender to Winchell, no strings attached. Just assurance that he won't be killed." Hoffman publicly testified that "the caller was not connected in any way with Frank Costello," but Winchell told me much later that Costello had used Abe "Longie" Zwillman, a New Jersey gang chief, to tip Irving Hoffman.

Incredibly, in his autobiography, Winchell ignores Hoffman's role in the Lepke story, although Hoffman disclosed the facts in "The Hollywood Reporter" shortly after Lepke surrendered. Winchell never denied Hoffman's public statement. Privately Winchell confessed: "It was a helluva scoop. But I knew I was being used. Actually John [Hoover] had warned Costello through an intermediary that if Lepke didn't surrender, the FBI would declare war against the underworld buddies. As a result Costello convinced Lepke to turn himself in."

About three decades later, Walter's statement was confirmed by George Wolf, Costello's attorney.

Lepke Buchalter was the chief of Murder, Inc., the underworld's own ruthlessly efficient police agency. For years, Lepke was a malevolent force looming over New York's garment, fur, and bakery industries. It was rumored that the garment industry alone yielded $18 million annually in "protection" money.

Fugitive Lepke was wanted for murder in New York and had good reason to be frightened. New York's District Attorney Tom Dewey had branded him as "probably the most dangerous criminal in the U.S." and posted a $25,000 reward for his capture dead or alive. At the time Dewey was grooming himself for the Republican presidential nomination by racket-busting. On the other hand, Democratic Attorney General Murphy wanted the credit—and the headlines—for busting Lepke. So did J. Edgar Hoover.

In light of Dewey's dead-or-alive proclamation, Lepke figured he would get a lighter narcotic-selling rap from the feds.

Hoffman relayed the phone message to Winchell, who called his friend Ernest Cuneo, a White House aide. Cuneo in turn contacted Murphy, who agreed that Lepke would be allowed to come in unharmed if he surrendered to Winchell.

In his newscast, Winchell turned in a powerhouse performance. As millions listened, he addressed Lepke personally. He extended his personal guarantee that Lepke could come in unharmed, by offering to walk in with him.

Lepke didn't jump at the offer. For the next two weeks, intermediaries called Winchell with various arrangements for the surrender, then changed their minds.

Finally Winchell lost patience. One day when a Lepke intermediary called, the columnist barked, "If Lepke doesn't surrender by 4
P.M. tomorrow, Hoover and Murphy say no consideration of any
kind will be given to him!"

The next evening Winchell got a call at his Scarsdale estate telling
him to drive to a theater in Yonkers. Mrs. Winchell, concerned for her
husband's safety, spread nails along the driveway, hoping that a
flat tire would prevent the meeting with Lepke. The tires moved
across the nails undamaged. In Yonkers another car pulled up along-
side Winchell's. A man got out, holding a handkerchief to his face.
"Go to the drugstore on the corner of Nineteenth Street and Eighth
Avenue about 9 P.M.," said the stranger, who quickly disappeared.

Winchell was on hand at the appointed hour. Another stranger appeared and instructed him, "Tell Hoover to be at Twenty-eighth
Street on Fifth Avenue between 10:10 and 10:20." Winchell got out
of the car and called Hoover at the Waldorf. The lawman promised
he would be there. When Winchell returned to the car stranger
number two asked him to move over and took the wheel. The man
drove the car around the waterfront, weaving through the deserted
streets, veering under the Brooklyn Bridge in a maze of crossings
and crisscrossings in an obvious effort to shake off anyone who might
be tailing them. Around 10:15 he whizzed uptown at high speed,
stopped at Madison Square, and got out, saying, "Give this to Lep
for me and wait here"; then he slipped into the night. The object he
had handed Winchell was a religious token.

After a short wait, a mustached man, wearing dark glasses, with his
hat pulled over his ears, got into Winchell's car and said, "Hello,
I'm Lepke." Winchell drove a few blocks until he saw the J 42 license
plate of J. Edgar Hoover's black limousine. Inside, also in dark glasses,
sat the FBI chief.

"Mr. Hoover," said Winchell, "this is Lepke."

"Glad to meet you," said Lepke.

Winchell parked his car and entered Hoover's limousine.

Hoover ordered his driver to proceed to the Federal Building. En
route Winchell got out and ran to a phone booth.

He was bursting with the biggest exclusive story of his career. His
finger whizzed around the dial. The *Mirror*'s city desk answered.
Winchell spilled the news. He had the Big Scoop at last. He had just
delivered Lepke Buchalter, Public Enemy Number One, to J. Edgar
Hoover.

"Walter," said the editor, "we can't give it a page-one headline."

"Can't give it the headline?" Walter shouted in amazement.

"No," said the editor. "Hitler just invading Danzig. The war is on."

Hitler had scooped Winchell.

After Lepke had been tried and given a fourteen-year-rap, the gangster requested a meeting with Winchell in prison. Lepke wondered whether Walter knew about a "deal" that would reduce his sentence to six years. When Winchell professed ignorance, Lepke raged that he had been double-crossed.

Later, on FDR's direct order, Lepke was turned over to the New York County authorities, tried for murder, and sentenced to the electric chair. Hoping for commutation of his sentence, Lepke vowed to turn state's evidence. Dewey, who was then governor, delayed his execution for seventy-two hours so that Dewey's close friend, New York's DA Frank Hogan, could hear Lepke's confession. Later, Winchell prodded Dewey and Hogan for details of the Lepke revelations. Both remained mum.

The day the story of Lepke's surrender was published, Walter called Mrs. Winchell for her reaction. He respected her judgment. As a matter of fact, he called after every newscast and listened solemnly to her opinions. Apparently she was in no mood to hear about his conquests. Young Walter had fallen and injured himself painfully, but not seriously. She reprimanded her husband for "not being around when she needed him" and hung up.

Mrs. Winchell wanted him to come home. But her husband's home was his work.

By 1940, the world was not only Winchell's oyster but his beat as well. Hitler's ascendancy had caused a fundamental change in Walter's journalistic aims. The alteration was not the result of profound self-examination or historical analysis. It was purely an emotional response.

As a Jew he was sensitive to every threatening flicker. Nazism outraged his sensibilities and menaced his very existence. Inevitably Winchell discovered America. His columns and broadcasts not only pledged allegiance but also expressed his satisfaction with his nation's power and security and pilloried America's foes at home and abroad.

Being anti-Nazi automatically made Winchell a liberal. And his enormous audience made him a "leading liberal."

Of course, his adoration of FDR opened his mind, as well as Washington news sources. Until the mid-1930s, Winchell had probably visited Washington about a dozen times, usually as a touring vaudevillian. After that, he had become a steady visitor, welcomed at the White House and fawned over by politicians. A Winchell visit to Washington usually was covered by the news services and news magazines.

In time, the political arenas, domestic and foreign, emerged as prime news sources for Winchell. Government officials, correspondents, civil-rights leaders, and industrial lords gravitated toward Walter at the Stork Club, the Roney-Plaza, and his other haunts. But he didn't exile himself from Broadway and Hollywood. He understood the box-office value of stars. He had, however, become a world force.

The day after World War II broke out, Winchell cabled British Prime Minister Neville Chamberlain and U.S. Ambassador Joseph P. Kennedy, urging them to have Allied propagandists emphasize that "we are fighting the Nazis, not the Germans." Both men immediately cabled Winchell that it was a "good idea" and thanked him for the suggestion.

About 90 percent of his newscasts and 50 percent of his columns during this period were devoted to political events and trends at home and overseas, taking the form of political exposés and comments both grave and humorous. His "Man About Town" column, which had been show biz–oriented for years, now offered Washington and foreign coverage in addition to investigative reports of pro-Nazi activities.

Thus, Winchell at the pinnacle of his career radically altered his interests and attitudes. Oddly enough, his newspaper and magazine biographers at the time—and later—ignored the change, continuing to dismiss him as nothing more than a "Broadway gossip." That this description was manifestly false never deterred detractors or careless writers.

President Roosevelt and his advisers were aware of Winchell's power. They had made shrewd use of it, with Winchell's active cooperation and knowledge. Although Walter did not have a monopoly on White House news, he got some beautiful exclusives, and among them was the most exclusive of all, that the President would run for a third term in 1940.

The third-term propaganda campaign was launched in a speech by Michigan's Governor Frank Murphy. Winchell began enthusiastically announcing that FDR would run again early in 1939. The public responded quickly. Winchell forwarded thousands of letters and wires to the White House. This enormous outpouring of public comments gave White House strategists an idea. They prevailed upon Walter to alternately insist that FDR run again and suggest indirectly that he might not. The public reaction pro and con was evaluated by the White House. Winchell was single-handedly conducting a poll by issuing contradictory items, as follows:

"You can safely wager that FDR positively will not run in 1940."

"If Roosevelt decides not to run for a 3rd Term Justice Sam Rosenman will resign and open a law office which FDR will join after 1940."

"Insiders say that if the President doesn't run again he will connect with a New York eve'g paper as editor."

"FDR will run for a Third Term!"

"FDR up to now is ignoring his personal doc's advice against a third term."

Years later, *The New Yorker* and the *New York Post* used these items as evidence of Winchell's inaccuracy.

In fact, Winchell was used not only to check wind direction but also to blaze a trail, to help overcome opposition to the unprecedented third term. In 1971, Ernest Cuneo, who played a backstage role in the third-term campaign, recalled the historic episode: "Actually, the reason the President waited to declare his candidacy was based on Winchell's tremendous circulation; no effective opposition could be formed against him within the party because Winchell so consistently declared he would run and no significant alliance would take on the President in the face of Winchell's statements. The President, astute in these matters, became so convinced of Winchell's power to deal with adversaries that in the last few months he actually encouraged party opposition."

After FDR was nominated, Winchell told a White House aide, "I was afraid he wasn't going to campaign."

"Don't you know, Walter," was the response, "that you were his campaign—and you elected him?"

The White House aide who credited Winchell with electing FDR was, obviously, prone to hyperbole. Walter undoubtedly played a major role in the third-term campaign, but to contend that he was the whole show is ridiculous. His columns and broadcasts favored FDR and were critical of Wendell Willkie, the GOP standard-bearer. Incidentally, when editors censored his sniping at Willkie, Winchell countered by writing a daily anti-Willkie column for *PM,* a now defunct New York newspaper. It was bylined "Paul Revere II." After the elections, Willkie and Winchell became friends. As a matter of fact, Willkie proved to be a source for many Winchell exclusives.

On August 18, 1940, Walter's father, Jacob Winchel, died at the age of seventy. Although his father had deserted his family, Walter had retained some slight affection for him. It was an affection tinged with pity for a man who was an abject failure on every level of human existence. Winchell sent his father expensive suits, which the elder man promptly sold. I met Jacob Winchel in the studio during one of his son's newscasts. He was a gray-haired, wispy man who kept repeating, "My son is a good boy." He had come to ask for money, and Winchell gave it to him.

While there was a slender line of communication between Winchell and his father, communication was practically nonexistent between Walter and his younger brother, Al, who lived in middle-class comfort in Forest Hills, New York. Al sometimes called the Winchell office for tickets to a Broadway show. In all the years I was associated with the columnist, I never once heard him mention his brother. They were alien people who just happened to be blood brothers.

FDR regarded his third-term election as a mandate for all-out aid to Britain. Subsequently, the isolationist-interventionist debate was transformed from a noisy controversy into a fierce, bitter struggle.

Early in 1941, the Hearst-Patterson-McCormick bevy of isolationist publishers were joined by a powerful, well-financed group called the America First Committee, headed by Robert Wood, chairman of the board of Sears, Roebuck. Wood firmly believed that England should seek a negotiated peace with Germany that would allow Britain to retain its fleet and colonies and cede to Germany economic control of the Continent. The United States, Wood believed, could hold its own in world trade.

For Wood and many other isolationists, the issue was strictly business. To side with Britain would be as one of them put it, "just like a well-organized, money-making business deciding to take a bankrupt firm as a partner." In general, they ignored the moral imperatives, as well as the military peril, raised by a triumphant Nazi Germany.

In April 1941, Charles Lindbergh joined the isolationist crusade and immediately became its white knight. He wrote his own speeches and refused to discuss them with isolationist leaders before he delivered them.

Winchell immediately dubbed the man known as the "Lone Eagle" as the "Lone Ostrich." He focused his criticism on Lindbergh and to a lesser degree on the congressmen and native Nazis who climbed on the bandwagon.

In May 1941, Winchell warned:

> The European nations that failed to get down to brass tacks are now in iron chains. These captive nations agreed that Hitler was their common enemy and that they all faced general attack. But they could not agree on a common defense. Hitler capitalized on it. He pitted their private opinion against their common welfare—and he won.
>
> The same general plan is actively under way in America. Joe Goebbels boasts that if Von Ribbentrop could separate 15 nations, he can divide 48 States. . . . Goebbels' job this summer is to produce rioting on American street corners.
>
> They have made a fine start. They have already divorced the President from the national hero and they've got nearly all of us taking sides. After arguments in the corner drugstore comes the fist-fight. After that, weapons. Then the foreign rulers send supplies and men to the side they want to win. Remember Spain? The foreign master who comes to help remains to conquer. The bed you have made for your nation turns out to be your grave. Everything is ashes and tastes like it.
>
> And what happens to you and you and you? Well, this is what may happen. A few of you who are American traitors will be in temporary power. Some of you—such as me—will be shot. Many of you will be put in concentration camps. And the rest of you will be slaves.

In the months that followed he lashed at the isolationists as dunderheads, utter babes in the woods who had been duped into fronting for Hitler. For their part, the isolationists damned Winchell as an irresponsible journalist, a warmonger, a hysterical fool who would destroy the nation if his audience believed him.

Senator Burton K. Wheeler of Montana, among others, ranted, "I do not know, but it is possible that Walter Winchell is in the pay of the British government."

In his next Sunday-evening broadcast, Winchell replied, "No, Mr. Senator, I am not in the pay of the British Government; I am eternally in their debt."

FDR received a jolting reminder of the isolationists' power in the summer of 1941 when the House of Representatives extended the Selective Service Act by the wafer-thin margin of a single vote. In retrospect, one congressional vote might have tipped the balance between victory and defeat for Nazism.

When his aid-to-the-Allies policy was staggered by isolationist blows, FDR retaliated by wiretapping the opposition, relaying wires critical of his defense program to the FBI, and ordering the Attorney General to convene a grand jury to investigate America First's finances.

Winchell was aware of all this, especially the FBI's activities. He also realized what the headline value of breaking the story would be. But he quickly decided to bury the news because disclosure might have endangered the national welfare. In private he explained, "You don't shoot the soldiers who are fighting on your side."

In September 1941, at an America First meeting in Des Moines, Iowa, Lindbergh charged that the Jews, the British, and FDR's administration were pushing the nation toward war. A week later, *Time* noted:

> The most articulate group in the United States last week faced a crisis. The America First Committee had touched the pitch of anti-Semitism and its fingers were tarred. It had failed in its specific purpose of halting U.S. progress toward a shooting war. It could show its adherents nothing but a record of a campaign fought bitterly, spectacularly and with plenty of money, but without success.

Lindbergh's venomous thrust demanded a swift and drastic response from America First Committee leaders. Instead, they vacillated more than two weeks and then issued a bland statement: "Colonel Lindbergh and his fellow members of the America First Committee are not anti-Semitic. We deplore the injection of the race issue into the discussion of war or peace. It is the interventionists who have done this."

Winchell concluded that Lindbergh's "halo has become his noose" and intensified his campaign against the sinister fringe of pro-Nazis who had been encouraged by the Des Moines outburst.

Winchell went after them with a nagging persistence. He exposed and exposed again. All were targets of his shoot-from-the-hip style—Bundists, Silver Shirters, Gray Shirters, Black Shirters, Christian Fronters, and the white-sheeted Ku Kluxers. He named the hate peddlers—Joe McWilliams, Gerald Winrod, Gerald L. K. Smith, George Van Horn Moseley, Edward James Smythe—and did not neglect some of their supporters on Capitol Hill—Clare E. Hoffman of Michigan, Jacob Thorkelson of Montana, Robert R. Reynolds of North Carolina, Ernest Lundeen of Minnesota, John Rankin of Mississippi, Burton K. Wheeler of Montana, and Gerald Nye of North Dakota. Some of the names he blasted for months; others came and disappeared.

He aimed broadsides at isolationist publishers and editors, including his own, and appointed himself chief guardian of FDR's reputation.

=9=
The Winchell News Machine

At this time Winchell's news-gathering frequently involved nothing more arduous than lifting a phone or cocking an ear. It was usually confined to the "city rooms" at the Stork Club and his barbershop. During these sessions, the velocity of his mouth was jetlike. He exulted in his work, and his unencumbered zest was downright awesome. At such times, Walter was playful, witty, the quintessential Winchell.

A daily whirl, for example, took place at 6 P.M. every evening while he was in the barber's chair. He was shaved, clipped, manicured, shoeshined, and sunlamped, but he never permitted these activities to interfere for an instant with his marathon talking jag and news-gathering activities. Phones were brought to his ear, and he would give directions while being lathered; he would even argue through a hot towel while it covered his face. Once I accompanied him to a dentist's office and, so help me, he hardly stopped talking while being probed, poked, and drilled.

Here are my notes from a typical session:

> Cary Grant is Jewish gave the UJA $10,000 this year wonders why they don't approach him more often wonder why non-Jew Sinatra is solicited year after year but he is ignored I checked and discovered UJA didn't know Grant was Jewish how do like that bitch the Duchess of Windsor, a few years ago Taylor Caldwell invited her for a luncheon with fifteen others the Duchess's secretary phones Mrs. Caldwell to ask what transportation she was using and Mrs. C. replied her

husband would drive over to pick her up the secretary said, "I'm sorry Mrs. Caldwell your husband is Jewish and the Duchess is Protestant and does not mix socially with Jews." Mrs. Caldwell then exploded, "tell the Duchess I am Dutch Protestant and I don't mix socially with prostitutes." Bob Hope told me a funny about the fag who became ecstatic when he discovered his gums were bleeding how do you like cheap-ass Justice Frankfurter at the Stork Club he received a bottle of champagne as a gift and told the waiter don't open it wrap it and I'll take it with me one for the oy-gevalt department that Arthur Godfrey is a pain in the ass he knows damn well the Hotel Kenilworth restricts Jews but pretends it isn't so and he plugs the damn place on radio does Paley know about it? Irving Mansfield tried to set him straight but Arthur blew his top and told Irving to mind his own business said he would stay where he damned please and didn't give a hoot in hell how anybody felt about it Godfrey can be a fuck Carl Sandburg walked into the Stork and Billingsley asked what does he do the schmuck never heard of him Paul Scheffer, a newspaperman tells everyone he writes Dotty Thompson's stuff maybe it's bullshit but she's getting more and more pro Arab George Jean Nathan and H. L. Mencken are always telling me not to get so damn mad about things I tell them its part of my act hell I don't get ulcers I give them Sinatra is in bad shape since the breakup with Ava wants me to help him get a job Meyer Berger gave me some items that drove the New York Times nuts I'm not worried about anything except tomorrow's column I never ask J. Edgar Hoover about his sex life I showed my son an FDR letter where the Prez asked about him my son Howard Hughes never phones or mails news to me he has one of his people fly across the country and hand it to me in person he flew Steve Flagg from Hollywood to give me an item I couldn't use try not to talk to your bosses I've spoken to Hearst less than a dozen times usually on the phone the problem with having a mistress is not the screwing part it's having to eat dinner twice in one night.

His monologue was accompanied by myriad facial expressions, body movements, hands never in repose, fingers darting, and eyes effectively punctuating every sentence spoken in his resonant voice. His chattering ebullience enlivened the most mundane aspects of his existence. His alleged insomnia, eating habits, likes and hates—he took for granted that everything concerning Winchell interested everybody, especially his more constant listeners.

Sometimes he handed out assignments on the fly. Once he spotted me crossing the street at Fifty-seventh and Park. He told the driver of his cab to pull over and yelled, "Herm, I need you." In the next few moments he gave me an oral diary of his last twenty-four hours. Then he thrust a paper into my hand, with the admonition to "write a column about this," and he ordered the cabby to drive off.

The slip of paper was a note from Groucho Marx. It was attached to a clipping from the *Nation* that reported on a plague of anti-Semitic propagandists. The note was dated April 14, 1943.

> Dear Walter:
> The enclosed is from *The Nation.* You probably are familiar with this situation and I image that J. Edgar Hoover also knows about them but there are so many places to be covered and so many evil forces to fight that perhaps this one has been overlooked. At any rate, I send it to you for what it's worth. Regards.

As a part of his working philosophy Walter assumed that practically everyone read and listened to Winchell. I remember walking with him on Fifth Avenue after a broadcast. He met a *Journal-American* editor.

Walter greeted him: "What did you think of the broadcast?"

The editor responded, "I'm sorry, Walter. I didn't hear the broadcast. My mother died this morning."

Thereupon Winchell snapped, "That's no excuse" and walked on.

When mulling over such gaucheries he would express regrets, but he rarely apologized. Actually, he made a crude art of cutting people dead. When he met people he disliked, he reacted by giving them the back of his head, ignoring them or refusing to extend his hand. At times, such behavior was essential. His life was frequently invaded by cranks, bores, and ordinary pests.

Nevertheless, he occasionally dripped with sentimentality. One day he spotted a pretty child in the street with her parents. "What's her name?" Walter inquired. "Christine Fisher," one of the proud parents replied. "She's two years old today." The columnist beamed and said, "Listen to Winchell at nine o'clock tonight. I'll mention her on the air."

That evening at nine Winchell said to the world, "Birthday congratulations to Christine Fisher who is two years old today. She is a sure bet for pictures."

He found things to tell Mr. and Mrs. America in the street, in the barbershop (of course), and in the Stork Club's Cub Room, where the "Winchell news service" operated continuously. Specifically, the center of communication was the table in the left-hand corner as you entered the Cub Room. This was table 50, Winchell's office and throne.

For years Walter held court there. A throng that can only be described as motley passed by and stopped from time to time to give him news or exchange flippancies. They were, by and large, the leading newsmakers of the era.

Grace Kelly told Winchell about her engagement to Prince Rainier in the Cub Room. Lana Turner and Artie Shaw announced their divorce there. Clark Gable was there with two of his wives, and Elizabeth Taylor with four of her husbands.

Ernest Hemingway told Winchell that after a two-hour dinner discussion with Spencer Tracy, one quotable line emerged. It was Tracy's: "Sometimes I think life is a terminal illness."

John Steinbeck approached Walter and told him, "We all think you are doing a fine job for your country. Don't stop. Your enemies are the enemies of your country."

Joseph P. Kennedy first became a fruitful source of news after Walter ran a blind item: "A top New Dealer's mistress is a mobster's widow." The New Dealer was JPK, then the SEC commissioner. Thereafter, he continued tendering news to Winchell—his way of feeding the lion.

During his reign at table 50, almost everybody treated Winchell with deference, including those who feared and hated him. Besides, when you were in his presence you felt something important was happening. He was gifted with a magic stage presence whether he sat at table 50 or in a barber's chair.

His wide acquaintanceship and his supersensitive antennae enabled him to accumulate an enormous store of secrets about the famous and infamous and to make some startlingly accurate guesses. He could keep you mesmerized by recounting sex stories about the great and near great. He appeared to have a salacious anecdote about every prominent personality in contemporary America. Some stories eventually appeared in his column as "blind" items. For example, "If that politico doesn't stop fooling with Miss Monroe, Joe D. says he will hit him for a three-bagger," or "Mister FBI knows the White House staffers who are talking too much. Stew stuff."

Drama critic George Jean Nathan, a Cub Room regular, was occasionally joined by his friend and fellow iconoclast H. L. Mencken. Although Nathan and Mencken were thunderers in their fields, the Winchell personality overpowered them. When Walter sat with them, they became enraptured mutes. After one half-hour talkfest at his table, I asked Nathan what Winchell had said. "He said," Nathan smiled, "in several thousand words how wonderful it was to be Winchell."

By 1940 Winchell had become a dominant force in the two major communications media. His column was carried by approximately a thousand papers, and his newscast was rated among the top ten. Often it zoomed to the number-one spot. His combined radio and newspaper audience exceeded 50 million according to various pollsters. Before the end of the decade, he emerged as the highest-salaried American, his annual income exceeding $800,000.

Never before (or since) had an individual journalist commanded so overpowering a position. Under present-day conditions, it is hard to imagine any newspaperman emulating his accomplishment.

The wonder encompassed gold and glory, but it included his delight in news-gathering. Each day was full of discoveries for Winchell. He had more pipelines than Standard Oil. Tips and quips flowed in from every direction.

Information poured into his office daily by wire, phone, and mail. The sources included presidential aides, diplomats, intelligence agents, bank presidents, generals, admirals, other newsmen, police chiefs, judges, office boys, congressmen, stage and screen stars, and gangsters. Truman Capote, Clifford Odets, Clare Boothe Luce, and Woody Allen were among his contributors. George Bernard Shaw wrote a column for him. J. Edgar Hoover submitted tips in plain white envelopes and stationery without official insignia. Battalions of press agents scurried around gathering news, gags, bright ideas, and assorted paragraphs, and eagerly presented Winchell with heaps of tidbits. The columnist's unpaid legmen outnumbered those on the payroll of an average newspaper. About 10 percent of the press agents' material was column fodder. The payoff, as previously noted, was a plug for a client. Sometimes he received a plaintive note from a press agent:

Dear Walter:
Would you please use the indicated note? I need a plug. Could use some cheer these bleak days. Wife and kid hospitalized.

He usually succumbed to such pleading notes from steady contributors. In the foregoing case, he also provided some financial aid for the press agent with the ailing wife and child. Unfortunately, his generosity was as rare as it was impulsive.

Once I read proof copy of a new book exposing pro-Nazis. I liked it, Winchell plugged it twice on the air, and John Roy Carlson's *Undercover* became one of the all-time best-sellers. About a million copies were sold, and it made the author more than $800,000 richer.

Government leaders, Broadway and Hollywood stars, obscure entertainers, famous and unknown writers and composers—all came to Winchell for assistance. Sometimes he was called upon to iron out a problem between a chorine and a nightclub-owner or a dispute between White House aides. Quite often, in fact, he was a successful mediator. Once, a Mafia chief sought to take over Billy Rose's Diamond Horseshoe club. Billy came to Winchell for help, as did Sammy Davis, Jr., when underworld characters threatened him after he had rolled up a mountainous gambling debt in Vegas. And Walter helped them. He once rescued Frank Sinatra from agents who were grabbing 70 percent of his earnings.

Winchell power animated his army of contributors and gained their diligence and loyalty. This vast group, however, was dominated by the "big three"—his editorial Palace Guard, consisting of Ernest Cuneo, Arnold Forster, and myself.

Forster, the guiding force behind the Anti-Defamation League, first met Winchell early in 1940, when Arnold approached him with Henry Ford's apology to the Jewish community for permitting his paper, the *Dearborn Independent*, to traffic in anti-Semitism. Forster asked Winchell to break the news on his broadcast. After Walter made the Ford apology public, he told Arnold, "I could use information like this as often as you have it."

Forster began submitting material, and they gradually became friends. Arnold not only was a rich source of news about pro-Nazis; he also checked and evaluated other stories. Now and then Winchell called on him for unpaid legal counsel in special situations. As much as Walter trusted anyone, he trusted Forster.

Public exposure was the Anti-Defamation League's primary weapon against bigotry, and Winchell was the single most effective means of reaching the largest number of Americans. Thus a powerful alliance was forged. "Winchell," Forster once told me, "did more to light up the dark corners of bigotry in the United States than any other individual. He was read, heard, and admired by millions. His readers and listeners believed him. If he said bigotry was wrong, then it was automatically wrong. He was Mister America."

Forster was right. Winchell's credibility was a potent force.

Cuneo, an FDR confidant and adviser who later became liaison man between the OSS, the FBI, and the White House, was first introduced to Winchell by columnist Leonard Lyons. Soon Cuneo, with the approval and assistance of Tommy Corcoran, FDR's chief domestic adviser, began funneling White House exclusives to Walter. After several years as an unpaid contributor, Cuneo went on Winchell's payroll. Eventually, he earned as much as $100,000 per year. But the remuneration was variable. "If Walter was displeased with one of Ernie's contributions," Arnold Forster recalled, "he threatened to cut him to $500 a week or stop paying him. But when Winchell detected tears in Cuneo's eyes, he would relent and rehire him at the old salary."

The Cuneo and Klurfeld functions were clearly defined. The newscast was generally Cuneo's turf, though he contributed an occasional column too. Sharp editorials were his forte, as well as the Washington and foreign news. When Cuneo failed to deliver, I was enlisted to fill the void. One night Winchell expressed his displeasure with Cuneo's efforts by leaping atop a desk in the ABC newsroom and screaming obscenities. Such tantrums rarely had lasting effects. Winchell never stayed mad at people he needed.

And he needed his Palace Guard. For the fact is that the Winchell column was a Winchell–Klurfeld–press agent column. And the Winchell broadcast was a Winchell-Cuneo-Klurfeld-Forster broadcast. I wrote three or four columns a week in addition to one page of the five-page newscast, the page containing exposés of pro-Nazis and others. I originally entitled the feature "The Fifth Column vs. the Winchell Column." Later it was called "A Reporter's Report to the People."

The spine of the newscast, in Winchell's opinion, was what he called the "eddy" (the editorial, of course) and the "lasty" (the sign-off line). Over the years, my most arduous chore was writing the "lasty." Winchell said, "The last thing you say is what people remember; that's why the lasty is important to me." Besides, in the vaudeville tradition, he believed in a wow finish.

I began the "lasty" ordeal Thursday evening and often failed to produce one he liked until five minutes before the broadcast on Sunday night. I wrote hundreds of lines every week. And it was an enervating chore. After one exasperating marathon "lasty"-writing session, I wrote to him, "Now I know why people go to church on Sunday to thank God. It's because they don't have to write the damn lasty."

He replied, "I know, kid. But doesn't it feel good when we get one we like?"

I wrote his most-quoted line about six months after going to work for him. "She's been on more laps than a napkin."

The "lasty" touched on any of numerous themes. It could be a safety slogan: "Watch the car behind the one in front of you," or a philosophic tidbit: "Greater than the great are the good," an expression of sentiment: "FDR's mother, a great lady, went to Heaven, and left a great son who is trying to make a Heaven on Earth," or a quip: "Here's wishing you a happy Father's Day with a toast to every mother's first child—her husband," or a pious admonition: "God belongs to every religion."

In twenty-seven years I turned out more than four thousand columns, each consisting of about 1,500 words. Sometimes it was sheer drudgery, of course. More often, it was exciting fun. Seeing your stuff in print within twenty-four hours was a thrill every time. I particularly relished writing controversial editorial comments, poetic valentines to New York, and weekly reviews of Broadway shows, films, radio or TV programs, magazines, or books. Oddly, the columns that attracted the most favorable reader response were not show-business or political pieces. One was "America Through a Train Window," verbal snapshots of the U.S. landscape, and another was a year-end essay: "Time: 1951."

Although Winchell received enormous help from writers, his editorial contributions were as indispensable as they were extraordinary. Editor Winchell explored surgically as he prepared his column or newscast. During each session, he would attack a paragraph or a line with a pencil. It would dart onto the paper and move swiftly across the page, crossing out a line here, changing a word there, condensing, distilling, highlighting, and sharpening. He was quick to ascertain what pleased him and what would please Mr. and Mrs. America.

His word-burnishing and personality synthesized the broadcast. He would fuse two long sentences into one short one, dramatize an item that was ponderous, cut the fat away from a wire-service paragraph, and gloriously encapsulate everything. He also would underline phrases he wanted to emphasize and phonetically spell words that might cause him to stumble as he raced along at breakneck speed. He was the consummate actor who made the playwright's words his own. As a result, any lowering of standards in his newscast or column actually made him physically ill with digestive upsets.

If one of my columns failed to meet the Winchell criteria, he relayed a message via his secretary: "Tell Herman he's not trying." A believer in positive thinking, he once told me, "If you want to do something, you can lift trolley cars." I must confess that the weekly grind of columns, broadcast, and an occasional magazine piece sometimes made my burden feel heavier than a trolley car.

Before the broadcast he concentrated on last-minute news. The way he reported often had more impact than the news itself. Once, Attorney General Frank Murphy mentioned casually to Ernest Cuneo that he was moving Al Capone from Alcatraz to Atlanta because Capone was dying af paresis and the Atlanta Hospital had better facilities. Cuneo thought it was an interesting little item and asked Murphy's permission to mention it to Winchell, who might find use for it in that night's broadcast. Murphy agreed, and Cuneo called Winchell and told it to him, just that and nothing more.

When Winchell went on the air, in a voice trembling with excitement he shouted, "Needles, California: Moving across the desert tonight at high speed in a darkened Pullman car is a man under heavy guard. He is Al Capone, chief gangster of them all. He is being moved to a certain prison on the Eastern Seaboard."

From the breathless manner in which he delivered it, the train might have been under bombardment. Winchell told the exact truth, but he made the truth sound unique, exciting. The streamliners always move at high speed across the desert, picking up time lost in the mountain passes. Thus, there was scarcely any news in this. And of course the train was dark. They turn the lights out in every Pullman at night. And of course Capone was under heavy guard. It would have been absurd to hand him a railroad ticket and tell him to show up in Atlanta. But why "a certain prison on the Eastern Seaboard" instead of naming the city? Because every other news service would have covered the story. Winchell wanted a sensational exclusive.

Dashing Walter—star snooper of the *Daily Graphic*. (United Press International)

Walter and Mayor Jimmy Walker in the days of wine and roses. (United Press International)

Cissie Patterson, the powerful Washington publisher. She despised Winchell, and he returned the compliment. (United Press International)

Good evening, Mr. and Mrs. America and all the ships at sea. Let's go to press!
(United Press International)

Walter and son in 1940 in sunny Miami Beach. The clouds came later. (United Press International)

The good old days: The Walter Winchells and daughter Walda. The photo was taken in California when he was recovering from his Vincent Coll scoop. (United Press International)

Lieutenant Commander Winchell and his Hollywood crew: The stars include Charles Boyer, James Cagney, Ronald Colman, Claudette Colbert, Jack Benny, Spencer Tracy, and Cary Grant. (United Press International)

King Walter on his Stork Club throne at Table 50, welcoming the Elliott Roosevelts. (United Press International)

The hoofer and his adopted China Doll, at the Stork Club, of course. (United Press International)

Walter and Walda in 1954—the pride before the fall. (United Press International)

The Big Two meeting in Miami Beach: Winchell and Frank Costello. (United Press International)

WW and Bob Hope in Las Vegas. Bob said his rapid-fire gag delivery was inspired by Winchell's newscasting style. (United Press International)

The old hoofer's last fling in Las Vegas. (United Press International)

Walter and Ed Sullivan: Old age transforms old enemies into old "friends."

That's exactly what he got. The switchboard at the Department of Justice was frantic before Winchell had been off the air five minutes. J. Edgar Hoover, Winchell's bosom pal, was bitterly accused of having given another "great exclusive" to Winchell, but he knew nothing about it. In any event, the movement of Al Capone was a routine item, but Winchell made it a front-page story. He was well aware of this talent and power. A young schoolgirl, after witnessing one of his broadcasts, asked, "Mr. Winchell, why do you talk so rapidly?" "Young lady," said Winchell, affecting his wistful pose, "if I spoke slowly, people might realize I didn't have much to say."

That wasn't true. Winchell had a great deal to say, but it does illustrate his awareness that Winchell himself was as much news as what he reported.

With rolled-up shirtsleeves he worked feverishly on his five-page double-spaced script until the last two minutes before air time. He packaged his show by rearranging, revising, and inserting short and vivid action words. He edited the foreign news "so that Mr. and Mrs. America could understand it." He marked the script so that pauses came at the right spot, thus achieving a dramatic rhythm. He demanded an explosive beginning. "Get me a good murder," he said, "or a train wreck, so that I can get off to a good start. Get your audience, keep them interested, sell them an idea in the middle, finish with a great line, and get off for bows." His newscasting style was dominated by vaudeville's fast pace.

One Sunday night, as Winchell was completing his newscast, the announcer handed him a news item hot off the teletype. Datelined Moscow, it read, "The Berlin radio reports that Adolph Hitler has been killed while inspecting Eastern Front defenses."

Winchell's eyes bugged; his mouth fell open; his hand shook. The flash of flashes had arrived a split second too late. He was off the air. "Damn those bastards!" he shrieked. "That fucking Hitler! He couldn't die and give me an opening item! It's a damn conspiracy! I'm being framed!" Before apoplexy hit, the announcer disclosed that it was a practical joke. The newsroom pranksters had concocted the phony item to celebrate his ten years on the air for the same sponsor. It was at least ten minutes before the turbulence subsided and Winchell could appreciate the gag.

For a typical broadcast, he walked into the studio with his script at two minutes before 9 P.M. and sat down at a table flanked by his sound effects, Morse code, and telegraph instruments. His announcer sat at another table. ABC vice-president Tommy Velotta sat beside him to feed him the copy. Winchell put on his hat. "I always broadcast with my hat on. Habit," he often explained. Actually, it was more superstition than habit. He opened his collar and loosened his tie and belt, zipping down his fly about an inch. He was where he wanted to be. My wife once sat behind him during a broadcast. During the commercial, he turned to her and whispered, "Jeanette, I want to die doing this."

After the opening commercial the announcer introduced him, and he began with a rocket's velocity: "Good Evening, Mr. and Mrs. America and all the ships at sea. Let's go to press!"

Winchell zoomed along at 237 words per minute, covered a hundred news items in twelve and a half minutes of news time, and in one year broke seven out of the ten stories voted by editors the outstanding stories of the year. At his peak, Winchell drew $16,500 for twelve and a half minutes' work. Remember, that was in the 1940s, when taxes were relatively low and the dollar was worth something.

In the wake of his opening flash, he whizzed along with Broadway and Hollywood news, coupled with stories of national and local interest. Page two opened with international datelines. His sources for foreign news were international diplomats as well as British and American intelligence agents. He then swung into a half-page of news and comments on the domestic scene.

Page three was his "eddy"—a 200- or 300-word editorial crackling and bristling with well-honed comments. Being a superb actor, he would underline his comments with snorts or derision, a long "hmmmmmmmmm" or a harsh "huh?" or a groaning "wwhhyyyy???" His delivery provided an editorial innuendo not present in the words themselves: "I do that," he once explained, "because they won't let me say certain things." The truth is he generally did it because it was dramatically effective.

Throughout the broadcast, he introduced as much physical motion as possible into what was virtually a sedentary routine. He wriggled, waved his arms to emphasize a point, thumped the desk, rocked around in his chair, and scuffed his feet as though beating out a bunt to first base.

A commercial intervened. Then Winchell went on to the page-four bombing of the native Nazis and other assorted nuts. Page five went back to Hollywood, Broadway, Wall Street, Main Street, and Pennsylvania Avenue. As he neared the last thirty seconds, the announcer signaled him to go into his "lasty." "If you have Fascism or Communism on your mind—you cannot have Americanism in your heart."

Winchell would collapse for a moment or two, then he would be bouncing around again. He accepted several phone calls from listeners, but the only one that really mattered was the one from Mrs. Winchell. If she liked the program, he was elated. If she was enthusiastic, he was jubilant. If she didn't like it, he was desolate.

He had a standard reply for listeners who called and said, "You don't know me, but . . ." Winchell would interrupt with "Oh yes, I know who you are. You are Mrs. [or Mr.] America."

He could be amazingly patient with phone complaints. He usually told the caller, "You didn't understand me. You listen too fast." As for crank calls, he spotted them before the completion of the first sentence and hung up.

Then he listened intently to a replay of Walter Winchell speaking to Mr. and Mrs. America. If his pace was erratic or he stumbled over a word, his face showed his anguish. "I know how a Winchell program should sound," he once told me, "and I get sick when it doesn't sound right."

After the broadcast, everyone's burdens were lightened. Unless he was disappointed by his Sunday-night effort, Winchell was in a light-hearted mood as he headed for the Stork Club. He walked upstairs to the Stork's barbershop, where he was expected. Later he descended to the Cub Room for dinner. There the emperor was properly welcomed. Waiters, other columnists, the Stork Club host, editors, reporters, diplomats, show-business names—all expressed approval of his broadcast or discussed a particularly controversial item.

For millions of Americans, Sunday night at nine meant Walter Winchell. He had become a national institution, the most read, most listened to newspaperman in history. No journalist, before or since, has ever reached such heights of popularity and influence.

=10=

World War II and the Winchell Wars

Hell descended on Pearl Harbor on December 7, 1941. A member of the naval reserve since 1934, Winchell had been commissioned a full lieutenant. After passing the required examinations, he had been elevated to lieutenant commander. A day after Pearl Harbor he applied for active duty.

On December 8, 1941, Rear Admiral A. J. Hepburn, then the Navy's public relations director, wrote to him, "While we all appreciate your desire to get into active harness, we all feel that you are doing better work for the Navy in your present broadcasting and newspaper activities than you would do in some active station of minor importance." But Winchell was insistent. A week later he reported for active duty and was assigned to the press section of New York's Third Naval District.

I was at his apartment the first time he wore his uniform. He cut a handsome, dashing figure. Still in uniform, he sat at his bedroom desk and typed out his will. I signed it as a witness. Apparently, he was ready for any eventuality, including a sneak attack on the Stork Club.

He worked four days a week without pay for the navy and continued his regular newspaper activities. Proud of being overworked, he asked a *Time*-magazine interviewer, "Did you ever hear of anybody doing a bit more than he has to?"

The outbreak of the war made the isolationist-interventionist controversy academic for everyone except certain diehard isolationists, notably Cissie Patterson, publisher of the Washington *Times-Herald*. Cissy had been a Winchell admirer. She frequently invited him to the soirees at her Dupont Circle mansion. The columnist and the lady publisher shared a fang-and-claw style of personal journalism. But their mutual admiration was a casualty of the ideological collision.

Cissie Patterson launched broadsides against Winchell and her former son-in-law, columnist Drew Pearson. She assigned writers to prepare diatribes against both men and arranged to have them read into the *Congressional Record*. Her vituperation continued even after World War II had ended.

Because of the *Times-Herald*'s editorial position, the newspaper was quoted with approval by pro-Nazi propagandists here. At first Cissie probably despised the lunatic-fringers who echoed her opinions, but she refused to repudiate them publicly. As the war progressed, Cissie's malice alienated some members of her staff. One day the *Times-Herald* carried a photo of American casualties with a caption indicating that FDR was responsible for their deaths. The paper's managing editor, George DeWitt, had pleaded with Mrs. Patterson to delete the remark. Because she had refused, he resigned from the paper Over the years, about a dozen editors left the paper because they couldn't stomach the publisher's capricious methods and blind prejudice.

In February 1942, Winchell took an ad in the *Washington News*: "Attention, Mr. and Mrs. Washington, D.C. A certain Washington newspaper whose initials are the Washington T-H omits considerable material from the column I write for King Features Syndicate. The omissions are usually about certain so-called Americans, pro-Nazis and pro-Japs." The Winchell ad put it mildly. Actually, Cissie had killed nineteen of the twenty-eight Winchell columns submitted during February.

Early in March Winchell went to Washington to get FDR's autograph on a copy of *Into Battle,* which its author, Winston Churchill, had inscribed and given to him for auction at a Navy Relief benefit. Winchell told Washington reporters that his opinion of Cissie Patterson was unprintable. Mrs. Patterson returned the compliment that evening when she said to guests at her home, "There isn't a night goes by that I don't get down on my knees and pray they take that bastard Lieutenant Commander Winchell off shore duty and put him on a destroyer that will sink."

At about the same time, Winchell announced that he would ask

Hearst to remove his column from the *Times-Herald* and sell it to the rival *Washington Post*. At first Hearst refused, but when the columnist threatened to leave the syndicate as soon as his contract expired, Hearst caved in.

Patterson and her congressional robots then demanded Winchell's resignation from the navy. The navy publicly declared itself well pleased with the services performed by Lieutenant Commander Winchell. He had, in fact, done yeoman work for Navy Relief. He had produced a star-studded show at the old Madison Square Garden that had raised more than $1 million. But Cissie and her cohorts never diminished their firepower, and eventually the navy decided that Lieutenant Commander Winchell's position was untenable. He was ordered to report to the Navy Department by the Chief of Naval Operations himself, Admiral King. The columnist learned that King would be joined by Admiral Jacobs, chief of the Bureau of Personnel, King's hatchet man. Aware of the dire possibilities, Winchell went to see the President before his meeting with the navy brass.

Admiral King compelled the lieutenant commander to wait for about half an hour before seeing him. After Winchell entered the Admiral's office, King and Jacobs made themselves busy with other things. They exchanged some remarks between themselves indicating that lieutenant commander was not a very high rank. Finally, King spoke to him: "Commander, you might be forced to disenroll yourself from the navy."

Before King could complete his sentence, Winchell interrupted: "Admiral, I guess you haven't received your orders."

King was shocked. "My orders? Who gives orders to me?"

Winchell retaliated with the crusher: "The commander in chief. His orders are that I am to remain in the navy and from now on report to him and no one else."

It may have been the only time in naval history when a lieutenant commander told an admiral to go to hell—and got away with it.

In the succeeding weeks, Winchell cajoled and badgered Roosevelt to assign him to active duty in a war zone. On November 20, 1942, he was ordered to report to the commander of the South Atlantic Fleet in Brazil.

At a stopover in Miami, Winchell told a reporter, "I'm running an errand for Uncle." Within hours the story hit the news wires that Winchell was being "sent overseas on a secret mission." The fact is that "secret" was a routine classification for all wartime overseas orders. Winchell had no specified assignment.

Vice-Admiral Jonas H. Ingram, his commanding officer in Brazil, liked him at once. And Winchell also charmed the lower-ranking officers. "Walter," said Ingram, "I'm going to send you down to Rio as a special ambassador. Give them our viewpoint and get theirs."

Winchell tore into his assignment like a terrier. He worked tirelessly, meeting leaders of government, industry, and the media, as well as ordinary citizens. He diligently memorized appropriate Portuguese phrases to work into his conversation. His greatest success occurred at a press banquet in Rio, when he raised his cup of coffee in a toast: Never above you. Never beneath you. Always beside you." The Brazilian press adopted the toast as a slogan.

At the inauguration of South America's first 50,000-watt short-wave radio station, Winchell told Mr. and Mrs. Brazil, "For 20 years the Nazi press has been telling our respective countries that we are separated by a language. Your warm welcome to my countrymen tells the Nazi press again, I hope, that our countries are united in ideals. . . . Hitler failed to wreck London and Moscow from without and he failed to wreck your country and mine from within. . . . Brazil and my country—the twin Gibraltars of freedom—will stand guard in the Western Hemisphere . . . more than good neighbors . . . good brothers!"

After about three months in Brazil, Winchell was ordered stateside. Admiral Ingram told a reporter, "We hated to lose him." The Admiral also revealed that during his tour of duty, Winchell had manned a machine gun on a navy bomber and used it against several Nazi submarines cruising in South Atlantic waters.

Winchell returned to Miami Beach brimming with his usual fascinating trivia: "Half the rich Brazilians are married to former U.S. models and chorus girls. . . . I went to nightclubs only twice in three months. . . . What I missed most in Brazil was a hamburger. . . . I spent Christmas in bed. What a bellyache!"

After Winchell's tour of duty, his Capitol Hill detractors were again demanding that he be stripped of his uniform. One managed to bull through the House a resolution directing the Secretary of the Navy to answer some leading questions about Lieutenant Commander Winchell.

Admiral King sent for him once again and sternly informed him, "You no longer are to reply to any kind of attacks, published or otherwise. That is part of your game. Some men have to go to Guadalcanal; others, to Africa. Your duties will not be revealed until the war is over. At this time your job is to fight the war over here—with both hands tied behind your back."

Winchell again appealed to FDR, who wisely counseled that his unblemished navy record effectively answered his critics.

The day after Winchell appealed to the President, Navy Secretary Knox gave a point-by-point reply to Winchell's congressional critics, completely exonerating his naval record. Twenty-four hours later, Winchell's active service with the navy was terminated, because he had officially completed his tour of duty.

Congressman Clare Hoffman of Michigan charged that "Winchell had been stripped of his uniform because his conduct became so offensive to so many Americans." That was a lie, of course. Congressman Warren G. Magnuson of Washington read the naval record of Walter Winchell into the *Congressional Record* to forever refute the idea that he had been thrown out of the navy for misbehavior of any sort. Then-Congressman Henry "Scoop" Jackson of Washington also hailed Winchell's accomplishments.

Winchell remained fiercely defensive about his naval record. "I want my children to be proud of me when they read it," he once said. In the late 1940s, he publicly supported a man who was rumored to be the next Navy Secretary. When Arnold Forster pointed out, "This man lacks any qualification for the position," the columnist explained, "But if he is appointed, he will be grateful to me. Some anti-Semitic bastards have sent letters to the Navy Department attacking me. Every letter sent there is put in my file. If he becomes Navy Secretary, believe me, those letters will be burned."

Winchell returned to the airwaves with a two-fisted attack. He informed his Sunday-night audience, "Those who have tried to force me off the airwaves have failed. I am now free to carry on, no longer strangled by gold braid. The navy is to fight the underseas threat, and I'm to continue fighting the undercover menace. . . . You bet I'm prejudiced against those in high office who guessed so wrong before Pearl Harbor. They are still guessing wrong. . . . What worries me most are all those damned fools who re-elected them."

Another furor burst in the press. "My fangs have been removed," Winchell bellowed after the network deleted similar controversial items the following week. When Mark Woods, the network president, called him to discuss the problem, Walter screamed, "I think your network should be taken over by the people!" Woods remained calm until his star newscaster simmered down and conceded he was wrong to question the intelligence of voters. Woods told him to go ahead as before, but to use better judgment.

Several weeks later, Winchell told a network executive that President Roosevelt "is saying the very thing you would not let me say." The executive replied, "Yes, but the President doesn't have a sponsor."

Winchell resented any threat to his broadcast, no matter how indirect. One day, Mayor Fiorello La Guardia of New York announced that there would be a blackout on Sunday at 9 P.M., the time of Winchell's broadcast. Winchell swiftly notified the mayor, "If you proceed with your plan to have a blackout Sunday at 9, I will announce that the only lights on in New York City are those at City Hall, where a poker game is in progress." La Guardia moved the blackout time to 10 P.M.

When Winchell tangled with network censors during the war, he hinted at powerful backstage figures who sought to muzzle him. These sinister goings-on were denied by network executives and generally ignored by the press. Nevertheless, the military, goaded by Winchell's congressional foes, attempted to intimidate the network. Somehow J. Edgar Hoover learned of the censorship attempts and informed Winchell and the President. More than once FDR cut off the "bad guy" censors at the pass.

Years later, Drew Pearson disclosed in his memoirs:

> Shortly after Pearl Harbor, two of Army Chief of Staff George C. Marshall's generals, who could not very well have acted without his O.K., called NBC officials to Washington and demanded that both Winchell and I be put off the air when the first opportunity arose. NBC acted within two weeks to remove Winchell, merely because he had inserted two words without prior approval in writing.
>
> I have always wondered also just how J. Edgar Hoover found out about the meeting of the two generals with NBC. He called me on the telephone and read to me the brief transcript of what happened at the meeting.

The source of the censorship thrusts was probably Cissie Patterson. She never stopped pouring out vitriol or using her powerful Washington allies. One day Winchell suggested, "I think we have been too kind to Cissie. No more jabs. Let's try to retaliate with a knockout blow." One of my subsequent contributions provoked Mrs. Patterson to hit Winchell with a $200,000 libel suit. Winchell reveled in the libel action. It meant that he had drawn blood. Besides, he was protected by insurance against libel. For months afterward, though, he introduced me to strangers as "the one who got me into my biggest libel suit."

Eventually the suit was abandoned. Winchell's lawyer was John Sirica, who later would make history as the presiding judge in the Watergate trials.

Cissie's fury reached another shrill peak in November 1945. Her abuse was spread across eight columns, under the heading "CRAZY—CRAZY LIKE FOXES!"

She had once visited an insane asylum, she wrote, and "for a while we had fun cataloguing the better-known 'liberals' according to the various types" she had seen there. Her examples included Henry Wallace, Marshall Field, Drew Pearson, and Winchell, of course. *Time* magazine described the attack as "some of the most vicious personal slander since the days when all journalism was yellow."

About Winchell she wrote, "Hard to tell just what's biting this middle-aged ex-chorus boy. False shame of his race . . . may be the root of it all. Anyhow . . . he suffers from a chronic state of wild excitement and venom."

Soon after the attack was published, Winchell told his radio audience, "Very special bulletin! The craziest woman in Washington, D.C., is not yet confined at Saint Elizabeth's Hospital for the insane. She is, however, expected any edition."

Winchell eventually grew bored by the vendetta, but Cissie was indefatigable. Winchell sent me a copy of one of her blasts with his penciled comment: "Haw! The same stale shit!"

While in Washington for a meeting with his attorney about the Patterson libel suit, Winchell went to see FDR. He had heard that the President was depressed because the Roosevelt-haters had mounted a vicious campaign charging that FDR's sons were enjoying safe and cushy military assignments. One of the boys wrote to his father, "I hope one of us is killed in action so that your political opponents will be satisfied."

FDR was always happy to see Winchell. He relaxed the President and gave him a chuckle. At this meeting, however, there was no laughter. In fact, Winchell was stunned to see tears rolling down Roosevelt's cheeks. Embarrassed, Winchell was about to leave. "Before I go," he said, "I would appreciate getting your permission to print a certain letter written by one of your sons, Mr. President." But FDR refused.

The diehard isolationist press continued its barrage of lies. Winchell decided to break his promise to the President and published the gist of the letter, followed by a full-column historical flashback disclosing that President Lincoln had suffered similar attacks during the Civil War.

The Winchell column also reported that the son of Representative William P. Lambertson of Kansas, who led the band of slanderers, had attempted to register with his draft board as a conscientious objector. After publication of the story, the legislator suddenly became sphinxlike.

Several days later, FDR thanked Winchell.

In April 1942, my draft number came up. When I informed Winchell that I might soon be inducted, he complained, "That's a damn shame. I need you more than the army." I submitted my last civilian column with a brief note of farewell. He replied, "Good luck, kid! I'll miss you, Hoym! Walter."

The night before my scheduled induction, Walter and I had dinner together. As I rose to leave, he wished me luck again, then called me back.

"Herman," he said, "while you're in the army, are you going to write to your mother?"

I was startled by the question. "Of course."

"In that case," Winchell said, "you will have time to write columns for me."

The next morning the army deferred my induction. Winchell was overjoyed—and immediately put me to work preparing material for the next column.

His disregard for anything except his work was unswerving. It was difficult for him to accept any interruption of this process, for his writers or himself.

Once, Ernest Cuneo was critically ill with pneumonia and unable to fulfill his word quota for his boss. Winchell, who suspected him of malingering, called the hospital and spoke to Cuneo's nurse, who advised him that her patient was too ill to speak. But Winchell was insistent. The nurse slid the receiver under the oxygen tent. Cuneo wheezed, "Walter, I have trouble breathing. I'm very weak. I didn't sleep last night."

"Neither did I!" snapped Winchell, and hung up.

When FDR decided to run for a fourth term, Winchell once again used his column in Roosevelt's behalf. Having campaigned successfully for FDR in 1936 and 1940, the columnist was in the forefront of the 1944 torchlight parade.

Apart from his fervent personal allegiance to FDR, Walter believed that the climax of the greatest war in history lay near at hand, that the decisive issue of the 1944 election was the nation's postwar foreign policy, and that continuity of Roosevelt's leadership was essential to the nation's welfare.

Winchell's support for Roosevelt was boundless, although he knew that the President was ailing. For example, in November 1943, the columnist learned that FDR's doctors had considered major surgery for the chief executive but had deemed it too risky in view of his weakened heart. Few, however, believed that the end would come as soon as it did.

Roosevelt took little part in the campaign, making only a few speeches in major cities. In an effort to still rumors about his failing health, spurred in part by a shocking photograph of the President delivering his acceptance speech in San Diego, FDR rode through rainy New York streets in an open car. He toured the city in a large limousine, wrapped in heavy furs, with an electric heater under his seat and another at his feet.

After FDR had collected his fourth-term trophy, Winchell hogged the headlines with yet another brawl. This time his opponent was Congressman Martin Dies, Chairman of the House Committee on Un-American Activities. Dies was motivated by personal vanity, partisan antagonism, and the prospect of headlines. His committee hearings were little more than sideshows. A freakish climax was reached when Dies suggested that Shirley Temple, then a six-year-old, was a Communist agent.

In 1943, Dies sent Winchell a letter hailing his exposés of subversives. Sometime later his committee applied the Red brush to Roosevelt supporters. Walter retaliated in a radio editorial. Within twenty-four hours, Dies told the papers that his committee was considering an investigation of Winchell.

That did it. Winchell demanded:

> How long will America stand for this person from Texas? Look at him! What is he? . . . One of the dime-a-dozen statesmen of no particular stature. . . . He got his first appropriation [by saying] that America was threatened with overthrow by the Communists. Whom did he pin the plot on? Stalin? No. Trotsky? No, no. . . . I'll tell you whom he dragged up as the powerful menace to the American way of life. He named Shirley Temple. . . . She was the excuse Dies offered for the hundred and some thousand dollars he wheedled out of Congress at a time when the Bundists and other genuine enemies of democracy were at their strongest.

Frightened, Dies denied that an investigation of the newscaster was planned. Winchell, unappeased, stepped in with more punishing blows. Dies then asked Drew Pearson to arrange a truce with Winchell. Walter responded, "Tell him to go to hell!" The congressman then requested time on Winchell's program to reply. His request was granted. The network gave Walter the following fifteen minutes for his own rebuttal.

By this time the battle was front-page news. Walter flew from Miami to Washington for the confrontation. He was joined by a friend from New York, who arrived with a migraine headache. Walter graciously offered the ailing friend his own luxurious hotel room for his greater comfort. Recalling the incident, his friend said, "I was so sick, I groggily accepted his unusually generous gesture without question. It wasn't until the following day that I learned Walter had been tipped by the FBI that two gunmen were planning to kill him that night."

Congressman Dies took over Winchell's time slot to denounce him as a "smear bundist." Walter sat outside the studio listening and chuckling. When Dies hit him for characterizing Congress as the "House of Reprehensibles" and its members as the "stumblebums in Congress," Winchell jumped up and yelled, "He's using all my best punch lines!" When Dies finished, Walter remarked that it was a "pretty good speech, considering all my stuff that he used."

Walter had prepared three different replies. I wrote one, Cuneo another, and Forster the third. He chose Cuneo's "A Newspaperman's Declaration of Independence" as his response. In part he said, "Far from retracting a single statement, I reiterate every one of them. Far from apologizing for any action, I reaffirm that my conduct has been the product of my deliberate intention."

A New York newspaper summed up the March 1949 battle: "The two men fought in different rooms at different times. Both of them thought they won. There was no official referee, but newspapermen awarded the thing to Winchell on points and Dies' lack of them."

The following Sunday, Winchell devoted his entire broadcast to pummeling Martin Dies. As always, he was relentless. Congressman Dies never called the columnist to testify. Within eighteen months, he was no longer Chairman of the House Committee on Uñ-American Activities.

The morning after his broadcast from Washington, Winchell was at the White House. I met him shortly after he returned to New York. His distress was evident. "The President looked awful. . . . His hands shook. . . . He sat with his hands on his head as if to hold it up. . . . His voice was so weak, so very weak."

In his January 30, 1945, broadcast, Winchell saluted FDR's sixty-third birthday with a touching last line: "Happy birthday, Mr. President. I wish I could add my remaining ones to yours."

On April 12, 1945, the wire services carried the shortest news flash in the history of journalism: "FDR dead."

The death of his father figure devastated Winchell. For Walter, it was not just the end of a man and beloved leader, but the end of an era, the loss of a symbol, a hope. Besides, Winchell feared and despised death more than most. Whenever I wrote the word "died," he always changed it to "passed away."

When Winchell offered his reaction on the radio, I had difficulty recognizing his voice. It was velvety and quiet, utterly subdued by sorrow.

As time passed, his sadness subsided. But he remained a self-appointed protector of FDR's reputation. Years later, when the investigation of the Pearl Harbor attack smudged Roosevelt's record by charging that the commander in chief had ignored the warnings of several military aides who had alerted him to the possibility of a Japanese surprise attack, Winchell lectured Mr. and Mrs. America:

Without Franklin Delano Roosevelt as the protector of the Bill of Rights, the present Pearl Harbor circus, which is trying again to discredit him, could never have been held. All the congressmen now conducting this probe would have been the captives of foreign conquerers. And the irony of it—some of these congressmen investigating FDR were elected in the 1944 elections, which the *Chicago Tribune* publicly feared would be prevented by Mr. Roosevelt.

This newspaperman believes in public investigations. He also believes in a square deal—even for a man who has passed away. There are some very cheap politicians, however, with their eyes on the next elections, who are attempting to blacken FDR's name—who were not fit to blacken his shoes when he was alive.

The truth is, ladies and gentlemen, that Mr. Roosevelt was not to blame for Pearl Harbor, but he was responsible for the grand over-all strategy which gave us victory. And that will be repeated again and again, so long as the mighty Hudson he loved flows to the sea, and so long as electrical current runs to this microphone.

Less than a month afer FDR died, the Nazis surrendered. About ninety days later, a giant American Superfortress flew over the Japanese city of Hiroshima and dropped a small bomb with the destructive force of 20,000 tons of TNT. Then another, more powerful atomic bomb was dropped over Nagasaki. Soon the Japanese called it quits.

Shortly after the war ended, Winchell received from J. Edgar Hoover a letter that stated, "The men in the government service have been cognizant of the big job you did to bring this war to a successful conclusion." Another note came from Britain's Lord Louis Mountbatten: "We who have been in this war fully appreciate your great efforts in bringing it to a justifiable ending." Assistant Secretary of State Adolf A. Berle also lauded Winchell's contribution to the war effort.

Sir William Stephenson, chief of British Intelligence in the Western Hemisphere during World War II, wrote to me, "There has never been Winchell's equal in the field which he created to begin with. He was enormously constructive where it mattered most."

In the spring of 1945, Winchell scaled radio's equivalent of Mount Everest. When I arrived at his apartment with broadcast material, he handed me a clipping from the *New York Times*. The headline read, "Winchell Program Tops Hooper List." It went on: "Walter Winchell's Sunday night commentary leads the popularity poll conducted by C. E. Hooper, Inc., moving up from fourth position." "Congratulations," I said. "It looks like you're a big shot." Winchell smiled and said, "It shows what can happen with hard work and determination."

Indeed, few men have been more determined. When Walter wanted something, he craved it. What he described as determination can also be viewed as pure selfishness motivated by a chronic sense of insecurity. He never had enough. The impoverished youth was a constant companion of the rich, powerful adult.

One evening about this time, I dined *chez* Winchell, in the kitchen, on pot roast and potatoes, one of his favorite dishes. Walter heated the food and served it. Then he suggested that we have dessert in the dining room. As we were about to leave the kitchen, he walked back to the table. With one hand still grasping the dessert dish, he picked up an uneaten slice of bread and placed it in the breadbox. "You never can tell," he remarked solemnly, "when I'll need that again." I waited for some sign that he was joking. But he remained grave.

I was appalled, unable to reconcile the millionaire broadcaster and columnist with the man who was hoarding a single slice of bread against an uncertain tomorrow. It probably made sense to Winchell, though. His insecurity manufactured its own logic.

He frequently confided, "I need money to pay hundred-dollar call girls, and I save money to be able to pay someone a hundred dollars a day to push my wheelchair."

His unblushing passion for dollars was common knowledge and inspired countless anecdotes. As a financier, he considered liquidity sacred. He used a checking account for business expenses, of course, but the bulk of his fortune was in cash. Once he invited Arnold Forster to join him on a visit to his bank, from which he wished to draw money to buy war bonds. He led Arnold down to the bank's vaults, where he opened a steel box "the size of a miniature coffin, about four feet long and two feet deep." Forster was astonished to see the money-hive. Stacks and stacks of neatly packaged bills almost filled the box. When Forster expressed surprise about his cash hoard, Winchell shrugged and said, "I don't trust banks."

=11=
The Private World

At the time of his great public triumphs, Winchell's private life was anything but triumphant. Mr. and Mrs. Winchell were not your average American couple. In the 1930s he wrote several columns entitled "Mr. and Mrs. Columnist at Home." Here is a sample from the first one:

"How's the baby? I havent' seen her for days. Is she well?"
"Yes, she's fine. She's growing fast—too fast."
"I met some man who said he met Walda—and that she threw him with one of her words. He asked her to go to an ice-cream parlor and she politely told him that she couldn't go with him but that she 'sppresheated' it very much. She's a stylist like her pop."

Walter discontinued the "Mr. and Mrs. Columnist at Home" columns after the following appeared:

"Did you read the column I did about you and . . .?"
"Don't you mention that thing, do you hear!"
"What's the matter? What's wrong with it?"
"I said don't mention it to me! I threw it down three times—although it got me so curious I had to pick it up and finish the darn thing. Don't put me in the paper. Don't make me say things I didn't say. People will think I'm silly or something. Walda, come here. Be careful what you say in front of your Daddy. He'll put it in the paper!"

"Oh, cut that out! Everything I said, you said! Maybe not in the same way—but you said those things. It's a good idea for a column, and I'm gonna do it every now and then—and what do you think about that? It's intimate, personal stuff about us—and several people have written in to say they liked it. Get me some orange juice."

Almost from the start of their marriage Walter and June were parted for frequent and extended periods. June yearned for his homecoming, but he rarely had the time or inclination. They were separated for months every year while Walter played in Miami Beach or Hollywood. While he was in New York, he phoned her daily in Scarsdale but visited infrequently.

Mrs. Winchell made her own life. She raised their children and adopted two Chinese tots, and she enjoyed reading and interior decorating. She frequently refurbished their New York apartment as well as the Scarsdale house. The sixteen-acre estate was surrounded by a high fence with an iron gate. The children's windows were protected by iron bars and a system of electric eyes connected to huge sirens. Walter had a consuming fear of kidnappers.

Walter confided, "She spends more on furniture than what the house costs." Not quite, of course; he had paid $167,000 for the estate —in cash. But, compared to the niggardly Walter, June Winchell was extravagant—probably in a conscious effort to avenge herself.

While Walter referred to his wife with affection and often quoted her, he chose his sexual partners at random. In New York, Hollywood and Miami Beach, he enjoyed call girls, movie stars and starlets, show-girls, waitresses, and the mistress of a prominent gangster. Along Broadway, the whisper was that Walter was a "great cocksman."

He was a sexual athlete, a stud, a man for all female seasons. His friends speculated that his demise would be the result of terminal orgasm. "When I'm around," he once cautioned me, "watch out for your wife." The girls in his life were usually busty, blond, and beautiful. Walter approached a woman sexually by sniffing. "I determine how much I like a girl by the way she smells," he once said. A remarkable number had sex-and-scent appeal.

By age forty (and probably before), Winchell's sexual relationship with his wife had dwindled as a result of their frequent protracted separations and Mrs. Winchell's chronic illness. A lingering respiratory ailment had left her with a weakened heart. Eventually she migrated to Scottsdale, Arizona. Thus logistics and the easy availability of other feminine companionship doomed Walter's fidelity. In fact, from early manhood on, monogamy was alien to him. As a lonely vaudevillian, he found warmth and comfort in having sex at random. This pattern continued the rest of his life.

Winchell bragged freely about his sexual prowess. Handsome, vigorous, and powerful, he attracted flawless young creatures to his bed. Unknowns believed that a tumble with Walter might elevate them to the aristocracy of stardom. Movie queens sought to maintain or improve their careers by being "nice" to Walter. When he was in Hollywood, producers such as Samuel Goldwyn and Harry Cohn provided willing nymphs for him. It was fascinating to hear him grade the bedroom performances of Hollywood royalty. Oddly, he described Marilyn Monroe as "average." He gave detailed descriptions of the anatomies of prominent movie stars. Being an experienced reporter, he noticed everything from the shapes of their nipples and vaginas to their sexual aptitudes and proclivities. His knowledge of this subject was practically encyclopedic. For a time he patronized Polly Adler's elegant "house is not a home," along with other big names, including a Rockefeller. The Winchell column once carried this social note: "Wallace Beery, the movie star, and Polly Adler, walking down Fifth Ave. arm-in-arm, bowing to their respective fans."

Generally, Winchell picked a girl, enjoyed her, and then discarded her. Several, though, lasted for years.

His longest-running affair was with Sarah Jane, which isn't her real name. She was a show girl, but Winchell, being Winchell, got a bargain rate, paying her only $75 a week. The relationship lasted, on and off, for almost a decade. He sent her love notes or bits of poetry and was happy in her presence. She was usually with him at the Stork and joined him in Miami Beach. He liked her, maybe even loved her. I was impressed by her capacity to absorb alcohol. She drank and drank and never got drunk. In time the relationship deteriorated. Sarah Jane eventually married an army officer, moved to a small town in New York, and had several children. The last I heard, she was a happy housewife.

His other eduring affair was in the 1950s, with an actress who later became a TV star. Winchell's daughter once spotted them in a theater and stopped speaking to her father for weeks. When the actress was in a Broadway musical that was scorned by critics, Winchell's plugs kept it alive for months. Walter claimed that Brooks Atkinson, the very proper *New York Times* critic, "panned the show because he didn't have a girl in it."

One of his more daring dalliances was with a Mafia leader's girl. For years, he rented a room at the Waldorf Astoria (he coyly called it his "sin den") under an assumed name. Winchell ended the affair when he decided the pleasure wasn't worth the risk.

Once, a major-league star announced his engagement to a lady, unaware that she had been one of Walter's playmates. Winchell admired the ballplayer and considered him a friend. So, when, before his marriage, the sports hero asked Winchell if he "had anything" on his prospective bride, Walter gallantly gave her a clean bill of health.

His intimates couldn't understand why frugal Walter would use call girls, paying for something he could receive for peanuts or a plug in the column. The answer is that he considered call girls safe, especially after one notable Hollywood experience. As he walked out of a nightclub into a parking lot, a nude girl leaped out of a nearby car and rushed toward him, trailed by a photographer. Fortunately, Winchell spotted them and dashed back into the club for refuge. He privately accused pro-Nazi groups of being responsible for the incident. Thereafter he was always concerned about being compromised. His obsession inspired one of his friends to quip that "from now on Walter will get laid while wearing an overcoat."

Until the onset of his final illness, at age 70, he continued to carry on with young, busty blondes. Only the inroads of illness withered what he once described as "my favorite sport—bending, stretching, and coming." For more than half a century he enjoyed the sport. He conquered. He saw. He came.

Mrs. Winchell was aware of Walter's indiscretions. Nevertheless, publicly and privately she wore the mask of toleration. Walter loved both his wife and his sexual freedom. Besides, he believed that sex and love are two different things. After all, you can usually recover from sex in a few minutes, whereas recovery from love can take years. He never forgot actor John Barrymore's plaint "There is so little time, and so many girls."

But inevitably, June's husband's neglect created a personality pyramid of frustration, loneliness, bitterness, and anger for her. The relationship between Walter and June was evaluated by a family friend: "They loved and hated each other, loved and mistrusted each other. Almost always, she was angry with him for being away from home.

If you offered comments detrimental to Walter in her presence, you would risk her rage; but she freely criticized him on numerous occasions. In her judgment, he was cruel, selfish, and cold. Sure, she was proud of the success he achieved and she enjoyed the material advantages. But she never was impressed with his work. After all, she was a native of Mississippi. His campaigns for civil rights did not sit well with her. She was not politically oriented. But his enemies were automatically her enemies." One evening she was dining in Dinty Moore's restaurant when another columnist approached her and offered a cordial greeting. June remembered that the columnist had offended her husband the previous week. She returned his greeting by bellowing, "Don't say hello to me, you big heel!"

In her presence, Walter underwent a remarkable transformation. A man ordinarily awash in sycophantic gush and mindless public adulation, he was strangely subdued by her forthright manner. She held center stage. Incredible as it may seem, the omnipotent Winchell was downright henpecked.

The stark contrast between Winchell the columnist and commentator and Winchell the husband and father fascinated me. In his professional world, Walter could intimidate powerful men. In public places he was treated like a lord. But at home he was fallible and almost spineless. Walter's surging dynamism evaporated when he was with June. Superb actor though he was, he was never convincing to Mrs. Winchell in his role of "The Great Winchell."

Throughout Winchell's life, in the best of times, private misfortune was devilishly insistent.

At seventeen, his daughter Walda was a lovely girl with reddish-blond hair. One evening, while dining with her father in a midtown restaurant, she told him of her wish to become an actress.

At first, Winchell dismissed Walda's ambition as a youngster's whim, but she had inherited some of her father's determination. An admirer of Anthony Eden, the British statesman, Walda adopted "Toni Eden" as her show-business name. She went to Hollywood, won a starlet contest, and entered the studio's drama school. Subsequently, she was offered a role in Mike Todd's musical *Up in Central Park,* which was then having a pre-Broadway tryout in Philadelphia. After rehearsing for a month, she quit the show, saying, "I wanted to act, not parade around the stage in period costumes." Later she won a role in the Broadway drama *Dark of the Moon.* It was a minor part, but she worked hard and eventually was chosen to understudy the star, Carol Stone.

Consistent with cliché show-business tradition, Carol Stone became ill and Walda replaced her for a week. The Winchell column plugged the name Toni Eden without further identification. Walter asked George Jean Nathan, the toughest critic in town, to evaluate his daughter's talent privately. Nathan gave her high marks. Winchell went to see her several times, sitting in different parts of the theater to get varying views of his daughter. At the end of the week he enthused to friends, "I have an actress in the family."

Walda—or Toni—was showered with bids from Hollywood as well as Broadway producers. She accepted a costarring role in *Devil's Galore*. The critics were unimpressed with the play, which closed after a few days, but singled out Toni Eden for special praise.

Winchell meanwhile played the role of proud papa to the hilt. He carried clippings of Walda's good reviews and displayed them at the slightest provocation. He urged everybody within earshot to buy a ticket to see his daughter, the actress. At the Stork Club the lovely young Walda and her father often gave rhumba exhibitions, moving with graceful ease. Both were superior dancers. Often, others on the dance floor stopped to watch them whirl by.

It was during the run of *Dark of the Moon* that Walda eloped with William F. Lawless, a staff sergeant in the army signal corps. The elopement was news to the columnist, who complained, "I've been scooped by my own daughter."

Three months after Walda eloped, the *New York Daily News* headlined, "Flash! Winchell Sergt. Asks Alimony."

Walda Winchell Lawless was sued for divorce by William Lawless, who sought part of her estate as alimony.

Typically, Walter was not at home when the case hit the headlines. He was in Hollywood, where he quoted his daughter: "We made a mistake. After a heart-to-heart talk we decided to call it off. Lawless is a very nice boy, but we realize that we will not be happy in marriage."

Actually, they had never lived together as man and wife. Less than an hour after the wedding, Walda had changed her mind and walked out on her husband. Ultimately the marriage was annulled and Lawless's suit for alimony was dismissed.

The episode was a tragic crisis in the life of Winchell and his daughter. He had had an unrealistic image of Walda as virtually a saint.

When he discovered that the model was flawed, he was unable to cope with her imperfection. Instead of offering understanding and consolation, he felt and acted as though he had been betrayed. Like many libertines, he was a puritan at heart. After that incident, their relationship was disfigured.

Soon after Walda and her husband split, malicious rumors floated along Broadway, inspired by her marriage and divorce. Winchell was horrified and furious. Ironically, he had always valued his family's privacy.

I'm sure that part of his unhappiness with Walda was the adverse publicity provoked by this incident. Privately, he shook his head and sighed: "I'm sad, disappointed and sick."

Winchell dismissed the rumors as "shitty gossip"—although he himself was the king of gossip. His sole comment in his column was indirect. He quoted an observation attributed to Socrates concerning the youth of Athens in his day:

> The children now love luxury. They have bad manners, contempt for authority, they show disrespect for elders, love chatter in place of exercise. They no longer rise when their elders enter the room. They contradict their parents, chatter before company, gobble up dainties at the table, cross their legs, and tyrannize over their teachers.

=12=
Power and Glory;
Gold and Brass

Private setbacks rarely interrupted Winchell's bold participation in the public arena.

The United States had emerged from World War II with unparalleled power and prestige. Nevertheless, the inevitable postwar economic problems and international tensions plagued the country. They were aggravated by fumblings of a new and untried President.

This stressful period was summarized by Winchell in a radio editorial:

> December is always inventory month. All kinds of businesses and organizations take stock of themselves in December. But they seldom take stock of their own country. . . .
>
> What's wrong with America? Plenty is wrong. So much is wrong that the wonder is not that it threatens to stop running but that it ever runs at all.
>
> We Americans are trying to fit the twentieth century into the nineteenth—instead of preparing for the twenty-first. There is blame enough for all. Labor unions are so busy collective-bargaining they have forgotten that unless there is production there will be nothing to divide.
>
> Investment bankers won't buy stocks unless they have them sold before they buy—and then expect to get paid for taking a risk. Industrialists work together for a general wage reduction —mass suicide for free enterprise because they destroy each other's customers.

124

Our government has a tax system which makes it the greediest partner in history. It takes nearly all the profits, assumes none of the risk, and then boasts that it believes in free enterprise. Unless born to money no American can accumulate enough to even try free enterprise.

It is time—if it isn't too late—for the so-called big boys in business—industry, labor, and government—to grow up. We are living under the same roof, but this time the well-known fight to the finish is wrecking the house.

Truman's incompatibility with the press embittered postwar issues. Hence, Charlie Ross, the President's press secretary, decided to try to win friends for the White House. He sent Winchell a short note.

> En route to the Potsdam Conference.
>
> Dear Mr. Winchell:
>
> We stopped at nine p.m. to listen to your radio program. The President enjoyed your commentary, and wishes me to extend greetings to you.

Several weeks later, Winchell was invited to meet the President. As it turned out, it was more of a collision than a meeting.

Winchell had not expected Truman to behave like Mary Poppins, but he was disturbed by the President's stream of profanity. Even more distressing to Walter was Truman's abrasive attitude toward press critics. Most unforgivable was Truman's slur directed at the publisher of the *New York Post,* Dorothy Schiff. According to Winchell, Truman called her "that damn Jew publisher in New York." Several days later, Drew Pearson told Winchell that Truman had referred to Walter himself as a "kike."

Winchell was stung by the President's bigoted outbursts. Moreover, Walter had revered Roosevelt as a moral leader, a man of supreme dignity and charm. Truman, by contrast, seemed crude, petty, bitter, and vindictive. When Winchell returned to New York after meeting Truman, his constant refrain was "He is not a President! He is not a President!"

Damon Runyon, the first person to hear Winchell's opinion of Truman, observed, "I would rather meet a heavyweight champion than a President anytime." Winchell and Runyon had become close friends, although Runyon never shared Winchell's intense interest in national politics and foreign affairs. One day he deliberately teased Winchell by maligning FDR. As a consequence, Walter didn't speak to his friend for about two weeks.

Despite an occasional spat, however, their friendship flourished, and soon they were inseparable. Although he had once said that "gossip columns are for women only," Runyon respected success and was impressed with Winchell's journalistic power. He immortalized Walter in his Broadway fables as "Waldo Winchester." Both men were sentimental cynics whose formula for success was "get the money!" And they were both denizens of Broadway whose unique journalistic styles had elevated them to Hearstian heavens.

Once, when Winchell was driving Runyon through Harlem after midnight, they noticed two men fighting on the sidewalk. One was trying to strangle the other. Walter stopped the car and dashed out to separate the combatants. When Winchell returned, Runyon reprimanded him for stopping the fight. "I've never seen a man choked to death before," explained Damon.

Cancer robbed Runyon of his voice, and his wife divorced him six months before he died. During that period, Damon and Walter were together nightly at the Stork Club. They were frequently joined by sportswriter Jimmy Cannon, Sherman Billingsley, and other Broadway characters. Runyon would write messages on a small paper pad. And he never wanted to go to sleep. He stayed up until even Winchell became weary.

Ironically, the friendship between the two cynics inspired a remarkable charity and in some respects its story parallels the Runyon yarns involving hard-as-nails guys and dolls who suddenly turn to marshmallow.

On a Sunday night in December 1946, Winchell told his radio audience about his friend Damon Runyon, who had died four days earlier. He wondered whether his listeners would like to send "a buck or so" to help create a Damon Runyon Memorial Fund to fight cancer.

"It seemed like nothing much at the time," Walter said later. "For more than a year I had watched one of my oldest and dearest friends dying. In all that time we had talked of everything but death, because you don't talk of death with a man whose voice has been choked out of him, a man who has to write down on slips of paper every word he wants to say. When Damon was released at last from the pain he never talked about, I had to say something, if only to get it off my chest.

"There I was with the mike in front of me, and the words came hard. But what I did say, they told me afterward, was that maybe other people felt the way I did about the thing that killed Damon, and maybe they'd want to send a buck or so and take a share in building a Damon Runyon Memorial to fight cancer.

"I didn't have the slightest idea how much we could raise, twenty or thirty thousand, maybe even seventy-five thousand tops. But that wasn't the point; it was just one of those things you do first then reason about afterward."

The money came pouring in almost before the broadcast was over. As the avalanche of contributions continued, Winchell called attorney Morris Ernst to charter the fund, and officers were appointed, Broadway columnist Leonard Lyons was vice-president, sports columnist Dan Parker was president, Leo Linderman, of Lindy's Restaurant, was secretary, and Winchell appointed himself treasurer. Later the Runyon Fund's honorary directors included Bob Hope, Milton Berle, Arthur Godfrey, Joe DiMaggio, and many other stellar names. Not one penny was spent for overhead and administative costs. Every cent of the donor's dollar was funneled into cancer research.

Among the early and generous contributors were underworld chiefs: Bugsy Siegel gave $8,000, Frank Costello contributed $25,000, Joseph "Socks" Lanza sent $250 from Sing Sing, where he was serving a term. A few months later, Lanza's friends learned he was suffering from cancer and collected $6,000 for the Runyon Fund. When Winchell expressed some concern about the underworld donations, I told him, "It doesn't matter where the money comes from—it only matters where it's going to." He published the line to exonerate himself. Actually, the underworld's contribution to the total fund was minuscule.

Bernard Baruch sent $5,000, as did Stevens Brothers, the ballpark caterers. There was $58 from the candy butchers at Madison Square Garden, $25 from a cabbie, and 9,000 pennies from a bunch of Bronx kids. The panhandlers on New York's Bowery decided to turn over a day's take. A soldier stationed in the Panama Canal Zone sent ten money orders of $100 each in the hope that they would be of some help in curbing the disease that had killed his wife. Show-business celebrities raised funds—Frank Sinatra, Dinah Shore, Bob Hope, Bing Crosby, Jack Benny, and many others. Milton Berle raised more than a million dollars in the first telethon in history—which also marked Walter's first television appearance. In the first four years of the

Fund's existence, the contributors exceeded a million individuals, including General Eisenhower.

By far the most singular donor was a Hollywood starlet turned hooker. A blond stunner, she roamed the film studios providing afternoon "quickies." One day, an aging executive convinced her to stop free-lancing in Hollywood and give him her exclusive services in New York. Before leaving she called Winchell and disclosed her new deal. She then confided her intention to "moonlight" without her benefactor's knowledge. She assured Winchell, "All the extra money I earn I'll donate to the Runyon Fund."

Officials of other philanthropic organizations were amazed by the Runyon Fund's burgeoning financial success. The surge was powered by Winchell, who raised thousands of dollars by creating a nationwide contest for the best anticancer slogan. The winner: "Arrest cancer! It's wanted for murder!" In column after column and broadcast after broadcast, he reported the progress of the Fund.

Several years after the charity was organized, the West Coast branch of the Friars Club held a dinner in Winchell's honor. Attorney Jerry Giesler spoke for about two or three minutes. The incident was recalled by Maurice Zolotow in a *Saturday Evening Post* article:

> Giesler is one of the greatest criminal lawyers in the world and quite a spellbinder. But he made a simple speech, just citing the amount of money the Damon Runyon Cancer Fund had taken in and the money it has allocated for research and how not a penny is deducted for expenses—it was just facts and figures—but in a way it was a more eloquent tribute to Winchell's humanitarianism work than if Giesler had given a fancy speech with big words and quotations from Shakespeare.

Walter had the ability to synthesize everything. In his judgment, nothing he did or said was contradictory or inconsistent. The paradoxes, shifts, reversals, and sacrifices of truth for expediency all were for the purpose of enlarging his career.

When it suited him, Walter was willing to ignore his personal code and journalistic principles. He often bent our ears with his reasons for avoiding friendships lest they create obligations that would restrict his freedom of expression. But early in 1947 he ignored the movie *Crossfire*, which dealt with anti-Semitism, because his friend Darryl Zanuck was producing *Gentlemen's Agreement*, which had a similar theme.

In response to a rumor that "Zanuck had Winchell in his back pocket," he exploded, "I don't believe in movies that trade on anti-Semitism!" Of course, the struggle against anti-Semitism had been one of his staples for years. Yet he continued giving *Crossfire* the silent treatment and welcomed *Gentleman's Agreement* with raves. Subsequently, conscience-stricken, he tossed several crumbs to *Crossfire*. It was, he wrote, "an RKO hit, still packing them in."

If there was one consistent thread in his crazy-quilt life, it was his Jewishness. Winchell did not observe the High Holy Days or attend a synagogue; yet he clung proudly to his religious heritage. After all, his grandfather had been a rabbi and cantor. He made regular financial contributions to Jewish organizations and had a radar-like sensitivity to any form of anti-Semitism. Winchell had no gift for deep analysis of as complex a subject as anti-Semitism. But he had the assistance of authorities on the subject, especially Arnold Forster. He translated their views into a language people could understand and expressed himself with a passion he imparted to millions of his readers and listeners.

It should be noted here that not many of his friends were aware that he spoke Yiddish fluently. Once, Arnold Forster was anxious to convey confidential news to Winchell. The busy columnist said, "Tell me in the car. I'm on my way to the racetrack." As they entered the car, Arnold noticed that the driver wore a loud suit and had a foot-long cigar sandwiched between his teeth. "He looked like a Mafia-type," recalled Forster, who tried to tell his story to Winchell in halting Yiddish, so that the driver would not understand. As Forster spoke his fractured Yiddish, Winchell and the driver began to converse in rapid-fire Yiddish. The flabbergasted Forster then learned that the driver was producer Mike Todd.

The independence of Israel inspired an eloquent Winchell column. It began:

> Wars are the result of old hates and the cause of new ones. I respect the leaders of the new State of Israel for accepting the issue of force. They had no choice. But though they are defending themselves by force, they have set an example for the civilized world by fighting without hate. They have not called upon the civilized world to exterminate the Arabs: They merely ask all decent people to help them defend their homes. They did not order out all Arabs within their new boundaries. Nor

did they treat them as prisoners. Instead, this new land of refugees called upon all Arab inhabitants to play their part in the development of the State, with full and equal representation in all its bodies, provisional or permanent.

The column concluded:

These people have felt the full weight of years of sorrow and it has cleansed their hearts of all hate. They prove that by their integrity to their ideals of democracy, even as they fight for their lives. At least they die with peace of mind. Do not mistake the call from Israel as a cry for assistance with a local war. It is the cry of peaceful world citizens calling for world forces of law and order—without which YOU are likely to be killed.

He raised his voice against anti-Semitism wherever and whenever he found it.

Nonetheless, when he was attacked, he echoed the frenzied idiocy of ordinary bigots. When *Time* magazine clobbered him, he privately denounced its writers and editors as "smart-ass intellectual Jews." And when he was reprimanded by a Jewish organization for assailing Andrei Y. Vishinksy, the Soviet deputy foreign minister, Winchell sarcastically said to Arnold Forster, "Here it is again. Some Jewish groups are attacking me. Good heavens, you mean it's true what they say, that the Commies and the Jews are the same? Oh, Arnold!"

A month later the same organization wrote asking him for a donation. "Get your money from the *landsmenn* [*sic*] who are giving me only headaches," Winchell shot back. But he stopped pouting the following day and sent a check.

Winchell's headlined clash with Vishinsky in October 1947 followed a steady deterioration of U.S.-Soviet relations. With the end of World War II and the formation of the United Nations, peace-hungry Americans craved international friendship in general and friendship with Russia in particular. But the euphoria faded with the revelation of the spy story of the century. Americans were shocked to learn of a vast Communist espionage network in the Western Hemisphere. Winchell hinted at the story in a column item, and Drew Pearson broke the details the following day, February 18, 1947. Almost immediately, the cold war turned colder. In the months that followed, hopes of favorable U.S.-Soviet relations became a mirage.

As the situation worsened, Winchell erupted. In mid-September 1947, he fumed:

> The Third World War is already being fought. . . . We are losing it. . . . When the Communists are ready there will be fifty Pearl Harbors, atomic explosions erasing our cities. . . . The Communists have germ warfare already. . . . The cholera plague in Egypt is suspected abroad of being a Soviet experiment. . . . The next countries the Russians intend to grab are Italy and France as a base to attack Great Britain. . . . American diplomats inside the curtain are under Russian guard day and night. . . . Trained Communist spies are among us locating targets for the sneak attack. . . . We must start rearming now.

These excerpts, from several broadcasts and columns, typify the Winchell-in-crisis style. He would leap and whirl in fury, freeze in a fighting stance, then wait for his quarry's reaction. I had seen his war dance too often to be surprised. As a matter of fact, I had frequently choreographed it.

Vishinsky promptly leaped on the stage with a few militant steps of his own. He called a press conference at the United Nations and bitterly denounced Winchell and several other Americans as warmongers. He orated:

> Radio commentator Walter Winchell also made his voice heard. The new American Baron Munchausen, famous for his utterly absurd lies, disgorged a lot of rubbish apparently intended to cover up the real motives of his lampoon. According to the logic of this sage, you cannot dominate anything or anyone with a demobilized army, a laid-up navy, and a grounded air force. It is an amazingly stunning argumentation. Winchell finds it irresistible as if an army could not be mobilized, as in the case when a war is launched, and as if a navy could not put out and an air force could not take off. But when there is a lack of logic one seeks salvation in cheap lies. All this baloney is based on the order to refute by any means the fact that those monopolies profited by the war, and this is why Winchell wriggles and lies and lies.

The controversy put Winchell on the front page of the *New York Times* and other newspapers throughout the nation. As usual, Winchell himself was as newsworthy as the story he reported. He offered to go to Russia with other American newsmen and report his findings. More-over, with his instinctive sense of showmanship, he wired Vishinsky, "Walter Winchell has requested the ABC Network to offer you free radio time to reply to his statements about yours." Of course, Vishinsky spurned his offer and Walter never went to Russia.

For the first time in years, Hearst supported Winchell. He sent him an approving letter and instructed editors along the Hearst chain to support the columnist's position.

During the Vishinsky uproar, Winchell became downright manic: He rarely slept, and he was constantly in a state of wild excitement. Once, during this time, I was having dinner in Lindy's with some relatives. Winchell came into the restaurant, spotted me, and yelled at the top of his voice, "Herman! Why aren't you home working for me?" Then he came to our table and showed us letters from Hearst, network executives, readers, and listeners. And he never stopped babbling.

Several days later, a group of reporters interviewed him in the studio after his newscast. With suspenders dangling, collar open, tie askew, and the inevitable hat perched on his head, he talked for almost two hours. During the interview he repeatedly leaped out of his chair, waved his arms, held his head, rubbed his eyes, and stroked the back of his head. He had every symptom of a man on the brink of complete exhaustion.

One of the last questions asked was "Do you think an atomic bomb should be dropped on Russia immediately?"

The weary commentator blurted out, "Yes!" Ben Grauer, the Winchell program's announcer, and Ed Weiner, a publicist, then asked to speak to Winchell privately. When Grauer and Weiner told him he had "stuck his neck out with that comment," the dazed Winchell nodded, returned to the interview, and modified his statement: "When I said an atomic bomb should be dropped on Russia tomorrow, I meant it under certain circumstances, of course. For example, it should be used if our military leaders learned that Russia had launched a sneak attack against us."

After the reporters departed, Grauer said to Winchell, "My God, I felt sorry for you. Exhausted as you were, having to go through the ordeal of a long, tough interview."

He was surprised by Winchell's response: "Don't be silly. I loved it. It is the bullshit on which I thrive."

Every Winchell war inspired an outpouring of mail. This one was no exception. Most writers supported him, though a substantial minority condemned him as irresponsible. A west coast organization vowed to remove him from the airways. He sent its letter on to Robert E. Kintner, ABC's executive vice-president.

Kintner replied, "As you must know, we are proud to present you on the air and I know that our feeling will continue to be the same as in the past—that you are doing the public service which is appreciated by ABC and our listeners."

Winchell thereupon headed for his Miami Beach penthouse at the Roney Plaza. At about this time, he took up his first hobby: golf. He enjoyed putting around the hotel's greens and eventually became quite deft at nudging the ball into a hole.

His hobby surprised me. Only a few years before, after failing in an attempt to contact me because I was golfing at the time, he called again and brusquely asked, "Where were you when I needed you?" I said that I had been playing golf. "They should break every golf club in America!" he growled.

After a rainy spell in Miami, Walter decided to seek the sun in Hollywood. There he made another dismal payment on the private cost of his success.

On November 27, 1947, June Winchell called the West Fifty-fourth Street police station in New York City to report that her daughter, Walda, was missing. Mrs. Winchell had spent several frantic days trying to contact Walda at the Gotham Hotel, where her daughter had been residing. Walter, in Hollywood, told reporters, "Walda is very, very ill, according to several doctors, and needs hospitalization and immediate treatment. Walda is the most wonderful daughter in the world." Then he added, "This is a helluva Thanksgiving."

Walda had been undergoing psychotherapy. "She is full of so many fears," Winchell once told me, shaking his head. "I don't know where she gets those fears. Possibly from my mother who has so many anxieties."

Walda, then aged twenty, was planning to wed a Broadway producer. Both of her parents objected vehemently, but she was adamant. Walda was visiting friends of the producer when her mother reported her missing. The Winchells feared that she had eloped.

Several days later, Walda showed up at the Gotham. The following week was a harrowing one for Mrs. Winchell and her daughter. After a series of highly emotional confrontations and legal hassles, their differences were resolved without fanfare behind closed courtroom doors.

Walda ended her star-crossed romance and reluctantly resumed psychotherapy.

Walter was later damned for having remained three thousand miles
away during the family crisis. Actually, he had been anxious to return
to New York but had been dissuaded by Mrs. Winchell and his lawyers, who feared that his presence would attract headlines. Parents who
have endured the anguish and sense of helplessness of dealing with
"problem" children would understand Winchell's private comment:
"All a parent can do is what is best for his children, or what he thinks
is best. After that, what can be done?"

Since her divorce, his feelings about Walda were ambivalent. He
loved her dearly, but he held her responsible for breaking his heart.
Yet he blamed himself too. "The apple," he said, "doesn't fall far from
the tree."

Like many other people, Winchell accepted his work as an opiate
for his personal misfortune. He led a media attack on General Harry
Vaughan, Truman's military aide and longtime friend, who functioned as one of Washington's chief power brokers.

Vaughan was a little too loud and hearty and was given to making
ill-considered statements when he was angry, which was not infrequently. He also incurred the wrath of the press in general and Washington reporters in particular. For example, when he visited a Central
American country and was assailed for being the guest of a dictator,
he berated the press, bellowing that he was "the guy they had to see
when they wanted favors." Truman resented the attacks against his
friends. However, with Russia inciting coups in Hungary and Yugoslavia and with the Berlin blockade on the horizon, Truman's friends
sought to reconcile Winchell and the President. Besides, it was a Presidential election year. The columnist called at the White House and
urged Truman "to get together with Stalin." The President sizzled:
"I don't kiss anybody's ass!" After some small talk, Walter departed,
still convinced that Truman was not a President.

Meanwhile, the *Chicago Tribune* blasted Winchell because his "attacks on Russia were too recent. When others fought the Communists
Winchell didn't." Walter countered by publishing the record of his
long anti-Communist battle. He added, "The difference between us
is that while they fought the Reds we fought the Red, Brown and
Black Shirts."

In 1948, Winchell was locked in battle with the Russians, the

President, and the *Chicago Tribune.* His travails inspired a cartoon in *Collier's* that depicted a patient confiding to her psychiatrist, "I've been listening to Winchell and, frankly, I'm worried. I haven't been feeling nearly as depressed as I should."

However, a number of editorialists found no humor in his fulminations against the Soviet Union. The *Cincinnati Enquirer,* for instance, accused him of "poisoning the well of public opinion." A reader wrote, "Strange that all and I do mean all the haters who hated FDR are working over Truman, calling him the same names, using the same tactics. What the hell are you doing over there with the Hearsts, Patterson-McCormicks and Gerald L. K. Smiths? Hypocrisy, thy name is Winchell." Walter sent the letter to me with a memo: "This guy makes sense! By golly he is so right!"

Nevertheless, he stubbornly refused to alter his attitude. His opposition was subjective rather than political, and Winchell's opinion was frequently a slavish emotional reflex.

Thus, in the Truman-Dewey presidential campaign, he was not so much pro-Dewey as he was anti-Truman. Privately, he said, "I don't think either of them should win."

At the time, the *New York Post* reported:

> The radio voice that Americans listen to most is not that of President Truman or Dewey, but Walter Winchell's. In the midst of a presidential campaign, Winchell is No. 1 on the Hooper rating list. His 23.1 rating is in dramatic contrast to the meager 2 to 5 points that political talks have been averaging. In fact, the top rating of any recent political talk has been a 12, and that was because it followed a big-rating comedy program.
>
> Winchell's position as the veritable voice of America is even more remarkable in the face of the widespread belief of radio stations that the end of the war had "killed off the commentators."
>
> Winchell's explanation is: "I wouldn't have such a big audience if, after all these years, people didn't believe me."

On election night, when Truman scored his upset victory, there was less public interest in the vote count than in whether Winchell should remove his hat while reporting on the election for the ABC television network. After hundreds of phone complaints came in, he uncovered his head, whereupon a greater number of squawks were phoned in by those displeased by the view of his gleaming scalp. His election coverage was a one-shot TV appearance.

Winchell's career zoomed again in the summer of 1948. He split with his sponsor of sixteen years over a commercial: He objected to plugging a deodorant. CBS promptly offered Winchell $500,000 a year. At the time, his radio income was $390,000. Then ABC president Mark Woods made an unusual move to save his network's highest-rated show. He stepped in and offered Winchell a $520,000-a-year contract, with the promise that he could keep any additional money his next sponsor would pay. Winchell accepted.

The new paycheck plus his newspaper earnings put him among the top U.S. wage earners. Yet he was rueful: "I don't give a damn about the money. I won't get any of it anyhow. The IRS gets most of it. I'd have stayed if they had just shoved that commercial over to Parsons." Hollywood columnist Louella Parsons followed Winchell on the air and had the same sponsor.

The foregoing Winchell statement was strictly for public consumption. He always cared about money, cared profoundly. Even while he was the highest-salaried American—and before and after—he refused to pay my business expenses. Not a cent. Naturally, the IRS was surprised by this phenomenon. Consequently, every year or so, he wrote the IRS to explain that I was "not reimbursed for business expenses of any kind."

For this writer, a cryptic memo on a yellowed sheet of paper recalls a memorable 1948 experience. My scribbled note reads, "WW, Hoover, Yankee Stadium."

One spring afternoon I attended a double-header at Yankee Stadium with J. Edgar Hoover and Winchell. It marked the fourth or fifth time I had been in Hoover's company, always with Walter. The first three times we met I had to be reintroduced on each occasion. Either I had a forgettable, noncriminal face or Hoover's reputation as a master sleuth is grossly exaggerated.

Between games Hoover and Winchell were mobbed by autograph-collectors. (Because I sat between them, I was also asked to sign. I wrote "Harry Truman.") Later, as we were gobbling hot dogs, Walter suddenly blurted out, "I'll bet John and I could take over this country." He said it in a bantering manner. I half listened as I studied the pitchers warming up for the second game. Winchell repeated it. Hoover's reaction was strictly deadpan. In Winchell's presence, Hoover listened impassively to the perpetual monologuist. Hoover's stepped-on face and thick neck exuded pugnacity, but in fact he was shy, stiff, uneasy, dignified and spoke in a subdued voice.

After the game, as we strolled toward the exit, Winchell resumed the chatter about taking over the country and even mentioned several potential aides in the takeover. They were former New Dealers. As we taxied to the Stork, Walter dropped several acid comments about Harry Truman. Hoover neither objected to Winchell's cracks nor agreed with them. He merely chided, "Take it easy, Walter." During dinner Walter asked him, "Who would you like to see in my administration?" Hoover smiled, for the first time and he mentioned the names of two multimillionaire Texans. The subject was soon dropped, and they never determined whether Winchell or Hoover would be President—or King.

While listening to this fragmented conversation, I considered it amusing small talk. Later, it didn't seem so funny. After all, Winchell was the voice of America and Hoover the head of America's powerful national police agency.

Winchell's harsh and frequent criticisms of President Truman, nominally the FBI's boss, never affected his friendship with Hoover. While Walter was assailing the President, he published a letter from Hoover in March 1948:

> Dear Walter:
> Just a note to say hello. Do take good care of yourself and don't overdo because you are far too valuable to the country. You must really get a lot of satisfaction now when so many of your "hysterical" assertions and predictions are becoming all too real. Some individuals must surely be having acute hydrophobia in having to recognize finally how true you have been all along. With best wishes I am,
>
> sincerely,
> JOHN.

Undoubtedly, the two men liked and respected each other. In later years their friendship cooled somewhat, but Winchell remained loyal to the FBI chief.

Of course, Walter was not Truman's only major critic. He was joined by Drew Pearson and many other editorialists. When the "man from Missouri" was inaugurated in January 1949, the news from overseas was ominous: China was in Communist hands, and the Russians were dangling the atom bomb over American heads. At home, the Alger Hiss case created the impression that the government was being overrun by Reds. Simultaneously, the conservative Taft Republicans were blasting the administration for spending too much money and extending economic controls that might bankrupt the nation.

At this time, Winchell was tipped by a member of Truman's Cabinet that Secretary of Defense James Forrestal had severe psychological problems. He brooded about being a failure and often babbled incoherently about plots to destroy him. Further, Winchell was told that Forrestal would soon be replaced. In his next broadcast, Winchell repeated what he had heard.

Because Winchell had forecast the removal, Truman spitefully decided to retain Forrestal. Before the question of Forrestal's mental stability had arisen, Winchell had been critical of his pro-Arab stance and his plans for rebuilding Germany. When Truman refused to budge, Walter urged mutual friends to try to change the President's mind. He was joined by Pearson, the *New York Post* editors, and other journalists. None mentioned Forrestal's illness, but they all demanded his resignation for one reason or another. Finally, two months after Winchell had reported that Forrestal would be dropped, Louis Johnson replaced him. Several weeks later Forrestal entered Bethesda Naval Hospital for treatment of an illness officially described as "occupational fatigue." Soon thereafter, he walked out into the hospital corridor, opened a window, and leaped to his death.

Winchell and Pearson were accused of driving Forrestal to suicide. Protesting mail poured into ABC. Executive Vice-President Robert Kintner forwarded some of the letters to Walter, together with the network response. A typical letter read, "You and your company, ABC, Drew Pearson and Walter Winchell and the advertisers are equally guilty in the assassination of that great American James Forrestal by the continued vilification permitted on your network." Kintner replied:

> I would like to explain the policy of the American Broadcasting Company under which commentators broadcast. We extend freedom of opinion to commentators and others speaking on public matters, so long as laws pertaining to defamation are observed. The opinions expressed by such speakers do not reflect those of the network, for a wide variety of commentators

is employed directly by ABC, or indirectly by their sponsors.

While we do not like to put labels on people's views, these range on ABC from opinions expressed individually by George Sokolsky, Earl Godwin, Jack Beall, Henry J. Taylor and Harrison Wood, to those of Elmer Davis, Martin Agronsky, [H. R.] Baukhage, Drew Pearson and Walter Winchell. In this policy, ABC believes that its listeners have the opportunity to consider many opinions from which they may reach their own decisions.

I am glad that you have expressed yourself to us. Your views will help ABC in the future administration of its policies. Meanwhile, your letter has been forwarded to Drew Pearson and Walter Winchell for their consideration.

Inevitably, several legislators lashed Winchell. Congressman Rankin of Mississippi, for example, called him a "vicious little kike." Fellow Hearstling Westbrook Pegler, a well-known character assassin, joined the mob, charging Winchell—without naming him—with "grossly vulgar and often malicious and untruthful gents'-room journalism." As Pegler continued sniping, I wrote to Walter, "Why the hell don't you write to Hearst Sr. or Jr. and ask them howcum they pay you so much money because they consider you such a valuable property and at the same time permit one of their employees to tear you down?"

I was convinced that he should challenge Pegler publicly. But Winchell's response was "He enjoys jerking off. Let him alone, the poor prick."

Walter's attitude toward Pegler was a blend of admiration, sympathy, contempt, and some slight apprehension. He admired Pegler's undeniable gift for word-slinging. His columns had an aerodynamic style. They curved, swooped, and flowed. But Walter was contemptuous of Pegler's attempt to involve him in a brawl that, in Winchell's opinion, "would help Pegler's syndication." Moreover, they had once been friends.

During the Pegler sniping, Winchell was upset but without his customary Donald Duck indignation. Eventually he decided to retaliate. He countered Pegler's "gents'-room journalism" by dubbing him a "presstitute" and hammered him in a column or two.

Sometime later, a friend of both parties wrote to Winchell, "Westbrook P. was in Chicago recently. He ran into an old friend, a police sgt., who remembered from his old sports reporting days. . . .

The officer remarked: 'My family and I never miss the Winchell broadcast. We like him very much. Why do you pick on him?' Pegler replied: 'You know me, I always pick on champions.' "

Walter commented, "Forget about Pegler. I have more important targets."

One of his targets in 1949 was as unfortunate as it was unnecessary. Walter and Drew Pearson had been allies rather than friends. Nonetheless, they had a certain respect for each other. Their break came in a childish dispute. At the time, "Stop the Music" was a popular quiz show on ABC radio. It included a "mystery tune," for which Winchell gave hints on his program. Soon Pearson was giving similar hints. As a consequence Winchell stopped speaking to Pearson.

In December 1967, while I was enjoying cookies and milk with Pearson and his grandchildren at his Washington home, Pearson told me, "I think Walter had the most scintillating columns and no one ever matched the excitement of his broadcasts. I'm sorry he later went politically wrong. A couple of years ago, Walter tried to make up. I was willing. I couldn't forget, though, that Walter was silent when McCarthy was after my scalp. That hurt."

By the end of the 1940s, the ex-hoofer was not only sitting on top of the world, he was dancing on it. Winchell was number one in the newspapers, on the radio, and at the bank. The cloud on his horizon was Mrs. Winchell's poor health.

Winchell was concerned, too, about his 77-year-old mother. Early in October she checked into New York's Doctors Hospital after a year in California's mellow climate. Doctors assured Walter that her condition was not serious and merely required several weeks of rest. When he visited his mother, he regaled her with talk about the Runyon Fund's accomplishments and other aspects of his thriving career. She was in good spirits and listened to him with interest. Reassured, Winchell departed for Miami Beach.

Several days later, the private nurse stepped out of the room to get her patient's evening meal. She returned to find the bed empty and the window open. Mrs. Winchell had plunged to her death from the tenth floor.

A threnody again interrupted his rousing march. Walter was grief-stricken by his mother's death. Among the many condolences he received was one that read, "Your mother's death breaks your last link with childhood." Winchell quoted it. "How true, how terribly true," he added sadly.

=13=
The Turning Point:
Between Darkness and Light

The passage of time, of course, assuaged the anguish brought by Mrs. Winchell's death. In January 1950 Walter returned to his favorite getaway spot, the Roney-Plaza in Miami Beach.

To Winchell, the hotel, an impressive pink castle, was the Stork Club with sunshine. Walter couldn't swim, but he enjoyed spending time at his cabana on the north side where the famous and infamous came to see him, and occasionally strolled around the pool deck. The long-distance and local calls came in continually. Even when Winchell played, he was working.

The hotel's putting green was Walter's playground. Surrounded by admiring spectators, he engaged in putting contests, accompanying himself with a running commentary. His opponents were generally visiting dignitaries or journalists.

When Louis Sobol of the *Journal-American* visited, Walter gave his fellow columnist a putting lesson. Describing their encounter, Sobol noted:

> Winchell prattled on while we played. He discussed the hydrogen bomb, some short-sighted editors who had taken issue with some of his dire predictions of several years ago, some short-sighted Washington authorities who had asked him not to go out on a limb in foolish prophecies, and how they had all been forced later to concede he was right all the time. He discussed a few contemporary columnists, dismissing one or two with contempt, freely according praise to others. All the

141

time, I was taking from one to three or four putts to get the ball into the cup, while for him not only did the birds sing but the ball eagerly rushed into the hole on a single putt—or two at the most.

At the conclusion, having beaten me soundly, he affectionately extended several invitations to dinner, to join him at Gulf Stream the following afternoon and to come over to the barbershop and listen while he was being shaved.

While Winchell was putting and puttering, an ominous force emerged that eventually exerted a decisive influence on his career. In February 1950, Senator Joseph P. McCarthy appeared before the Ohio County Women's Republican Club in Wheeling, West Virginia. The ladies undoubtedly expected the customary proprietary eulogy to Lincoln. What McCarthy told them jolted him from obscurity to national prominence. "I have here in my hand," he intoned midway in his speech, whipping out a sheet of paper, "a list of two hundred and five, a list of names that were known to the Secretary of State as being members of the Communist Party and who nevertheless are still working and shaping policy in the State Department." The following evening during a radio interview, McCarthy reduced the number to "fifty-seven card-carrying Communists."

McCarthy's diatribe caused little stir in the nation's press. Washington's officialdom, however, was apprehensive. Challenged to document his charges, the junior senator from Wisconsin moved to center stage.

Thus began the era of McCarthyism. McCarthy used his forums in the Senate and the press shrewdly to promote himself and his campaign. As a *New York Times* correspondent pointed out:

> He was always available to reporters. When they didn't seek him out, he would find them, often summoning them out of the press gallery with a meaningful wink. He knew about deadlines and edition times and how to blanket an unfavorable story with one that served his purpose. He would throw a heavy arm about a favorite reporter's shoulder while walking down a Senate corridor or would take him to his office for a drink and give him a tip on the next exposé.

McCarthy developed pipelines into various government agencies. He was fed material from security files and other confidential documents and, in turn, leaked it to favored newsmen. One of them was Winchell. The senator or one of his associates, usually Roy Cohn, telephoned Walter several times a day to provide him with inside news.

On the personal level, Winchell, like many other reporters who detested his tactics, found McCarthy likable. More important in Winchell's judgment, J. Edgar Hoover was an ardent admirer of McCarthy. Further, Walter believed Communist infiltration of the government to be a fact, and he thought McCarthy was right in contending that the Communists should be ferreted out of high places as vigorously as pro-Nazis. Finally, McCarthy was anti-Truman, which won Brownie points with Winchell. Thus he failed to see—or else deliberately ignored—the menace of McCarthyism.

In February 1950, when McCarthyism began its weedlike growth, Winchell was more interested in improving his putting in Miami and in participating in a minor international fracas. He had printed an item to the effect that Britain's Queen Elizabeth was expecting a blessed event. Three days later, a typical Winchell retraction appeared: "The Monocle Set discount the recent rumor (that Queen Liz is enceinte). We stole the rumor from a London correspondent for an American newsmag, which is what comes from stealing from amateurs."

The "newsmag" was *Time,* and the item had been lifted from a confidential cable to its editors. Thus began a skirmish with the magazine that flared on and off for years.

Time's March 1 issue berated Winchell for using the item. Winchell retaliated by publishing additional material from the magazine's confidential correspondence. The *Time* executives, infuriated, assigned a reporter to check into a rumor that Winchell had committed a serious crime that had been hushed up. Walter chortled to friends: "Let the schmucks dig. I have never been arrested anywhere at any time. I must be driving them nutz!"

He continued to drive them bananas with the publication of a critical piece entitled "Man Killing Time" and additional tidbits from his informant inside the magazine, disclosing confidential discussions involving labor-management disputes.

On March 14, Winchell's inside source warned him that *Time*'s legal staff was considering a libel action. Shortly thereafter, Henry Luce invited Winchell to a private meeting, and a truce was arranged. But the armistice was ruptured again and again in the following years. When Whitaker Chambers, who had been a *Time* senior editor, confessed his Communist past and turned in the evidence that convicted

Alger Hiss of espionage, Winchell had a field day at the magazine's expense.

Oddly enough, there was a cordial personal relationship between Walter and Mr. and Mrs. *Time*—Henry and Clare Boothe Luce. Henry once submitted a title for the Winchell columns exposing pro-Nazis: "American Crackpottery." Walter used Luce's contribution, and Luce expressed his pleasure. And Winchell and Clare Booth Luce had been friendly for years, even though she had been anti-Roosevelt. Mrs. Luce frequently communicated with Winchell, wrote guest columns for him, and on several occasions was the subject of Winchell items. For example, Winchell reported that when a fellow member of Congress teased her with the question "Don't you think it's beneath the dignity of this House to have one of its members voted among the six women in America with the most beautiful legs?" Clare promptly zinged back, "Don't you realize, Congressman, that you are just falling for some subtle New Deal propaganda designed to distract attention from the end of me that is really functioning?"

Shortly after a truce with *Time,* Walter revived one of his sure-fire spectaculars. On June 19, 1950, another fugitive killer surrendered to him. But this was far different from the Lepke story, which had been a genuine journalistic landmark.

A year earlier, William Lurye, an organizer for the international Ladies' Garment Workers Union, had been stabbed to death. The police soon learned that one of his indicated killers was Benedict Macri, who had vanished. Meanwhile, the ILGWU offered $25,000 for their arrest.

Winchell began building the story by appealing to Benedict Macri to surrender. After three broadcast appeals, on June 19 he dramatically informed his radio audience that he would turn Macri over to the cops that very night. About an hour later, Macri surrendered to Winchell in downtown Manhattan about a hundred feet from a police station. A *Daily Mirror* photographer popped camera bulbs for posterity while Winchell handed Macri over to the police and claimed the $25,000 reward from the union for the Runyon Fund.

Winchell was on the front pages again. In addition, he received editorial salutes from the *Daily News,* the *Herald Tribune,* and the *New York Times.*

Actually, the plaudits were undeserved. The *Mirror* had had the Macri surrender story written three weeks before it happened. The deal was arranged between the Macri family and several *Mirror* executives. Winchell was used for his publicity value.

A week after Macri surrendered, the Korean War broke out. It hardly affected Winchell's Truman-sniping or his drift to the political right. His movements in Senator McCarthy's direction were cautious. Gradually it became evident where he was headed.

"You know, Herm," Winchell insisted to me, "I've never been in anybody's pocket and I never will be."

I argued, "But many of your old supporters are starting to believe you are on McCarthy's team."

"If they think that," he said pettishly, "then they don't really know me and never really respected me. Such people are not my supporters. So let's forget it."

Arnold Forster also tried to make Winchell see the light. In December 1950, Forster wrote to him:

> I want you to speak on the *principle* involved in the Drew Pearson story. Pearson as a person is unimportant. But his right to freedom of speech on the airwaves is vital to all of us— that's America. When Joe McCarthy demands that people boycott the stores which sponsor the broadcasts, the Senator is denying Pearson's right to earn a living because he disagrees with Pearson. You, too, have been the victim of such vicious un-American attempts to silence you. Luckily, they have not been effective even though some of the boycott attempts against you came from highly respected sources. When one of the two giants in radio is brought to his knees, you should start worrying; the next time it may be you.
>
> McCarthy is lucky that you have found no fault with him publicly. Or is it that *you* are the lucky one? I know you well enough to know that the first time you see McCarthy do wrong you will hit him hard. But if McCarthy gets away with his destruction of Pearson, why should you think that another McCarthy won't feel free to try it against you?
>
> The announcement by Pearson's sponsor that it was only a coincidence that they cancelled the contract simultaneously with McCarthy's demand is sheer nonsense. Here is what actually happened: For many weeks Pearson had been negotiating with his sponsor for a new contract. It was proposed that a television

program be added to the Pearson responsibility. Because there were going to be many changes in contract terms and the nature of services, nothing could be signed quickly. The intent on both sides to renew, however, was clearly understood by both sides. In the middle of negotiations the company routinely sent its November 15th notice to Drew that the contract was to be terminated at the end of 90 days. It was McCarthy's boycott *alone* that changed his sponsor's mind.

Winchell ignored the plea. In the first place, he believed that his old ally was strong enough to defend himself. The second and decisive factor was simply that he was sore at Pearson for stealing one of his radio features, tipping quiz-show answers, so the hell with him. Subjective feelings largely determined his decision.

Within a few years, McCarthyism came close to dominating the nation. In the spring of 1954, for instance, the Gallup Poll reported that fewer than 30 percent of the country's adults disapproved of the Wisconsin Senator's tactics.

Early in 1951 the nation's TV viewers were mesmerized by Senator Estes Kefauver's televised hearings on crime. The highlight was ganglord Frank Costello's appearance. Television cameras were barred from showing his face while he testified, but the dramatic impact was heightened when the cameras focused on his fidgety hands while he reluctantly responded to questions in his raspy voice with its New York twang.

In the midst of his testimony, Costello walked out in a pique and was cited for contempt. The hearings ended soon after his exit. Winchell denounced the Kefauver Committee for badgering Costello and infringing on his civil rights.

Costello was not one who forgot friendly words. On April 1, the phone rang at midnight in the office of the International News Service. Editor Larry Klingman answered and heard a shrill, excited voice: "This is Winchell! I'm going out on a boat with Costello for an exclusive interview!" He was calling from Miami Beach.

Klingman flagged down the vocal express. "Just a minute, Walter," he said. "Let's make sure you don't pitch him soft balls so that he can hit home runs."

"Okay, let's have some questions. Call me back pronto."

Klingman, an old friend, called me, then got back to Walter with some relevant questions that the two of us had devised for Costello. But Winchell posed only one or two of our queries during the interview, and Costello offered evasive responses.

When the Costello interview was sent over the INS wires, Klingman was infuriated to read Winchell's lead: "International News Service assigned me to interview Frank Costello, Public Enigma No. 1."

Of course, the news service had not given Winchell the assignment. Walter had lied to protect himself against the charge that Costello was using him for a whitewash job.

Naturally, Costello presented himself in the best possible light. And Winchell, Frank's good neighbor in New York, handled him rather gently. The closest Costello came to self-criticism was his sardonic comment "You can put down that I haven't sold Bibles all my life."

Incredibly, the core of the interview was Frank Costello's advice on how to curb crime! Even more incredible, the advice was both sensible and pertinent.

Winchell asked, "Do you think organized gambling can be legislated out of existence?"

Costello replied, "Not in a million years. First of all it makes me laugh when they call it organized gambling. Gambling is the most unorganized business of them all. The confetti industry is better organized. In the gambling business, it is every man for himself. But it can't be legislated out because there are too many ways of skinning a cat and too many uncertainties in the world on which people will make a bet. Stopping the wire services and jailing gamblers and setting up crime committees won't do any good. If you stop all racing and then stop all baseball games and the college sports it don't do any good, either. People would bet on the weather. The quickest way to wipe out big shots in the underworld is to make gambling legal. I know a lot about the subject, and that's the only way. What became of the big shots in the gangs when prohibition was repealed? I think that anyone who isn't a hypocrite and knows the picture would have to agree with me. Legalize it and you do three things. Get rid of corruption, raise tax money and knock off the underworld."

Winchell asked, "How should this be handled?"

"On a local option basis," Costello counseled. "Let the states, the counties or the cities decide for themselves if they want it. About one-fourth or one-fifth of the nation is still dry because people who live in those places want to be dry. Do the same thing with gambling. Lots of people want to gamble."

After the interview, Costello's longtime friend and partner Phil Kastel told a columnist, "There isn't a newspaperman around who wouldn't sell his grandmother for a paragraph, except Walter Winchell." Walter confided to friends, "Francisco told me some things I cannot print until he is gone." But Costello outlived him. The "Godfather" died quietly of a coronary at eighty-two, having spent the last decade of his life gardening at his Long Island estate and displaying his flowers in local shows.

Winchell's exclusive story created an uproar. The *Miami Herald* ran the interview but followed it with a barrage of letters from readers who felt that Costello had been handled too sympathetically. The opposition paper, the *News,* published a barbed parody of the interview, which drew a retort from Winchell in his column, to which the *News* responded with a front-page blast. In the ensuing free-for-all, Walter accused the *Miami Herald* of hypocrisy for running letters critical of the interview while accepting ads from gambling houses. Winchell's syndicate deleted his criticism of a client paper, whereupon Walter gave the story to Paul Brunn of the *Florida Sun.*

When the *Sun* hit the street, Winchell, his putter still in his hand, grabbed about thirty copies, rushed to a nearby corner, and promptly sold all the papers by shouting, "Extra! Extra! Winchell Shot Dead!"

He continued the "fun" feud by threatening to quit King Features because it had deleted the item. But the syndicate's editor, Ward Greene, told a reporter who requested his reaction, "I get messages third hand from Winchell. I haven't got this one yet. But then, Walter's been mad at us before."

Two months later, Winchell collected another exclusive interview, this time with General Douglas MacArthur, who had been relieved of his command in the Pacific by President Truman. In the ensuing national controversy, Walter naturally opposed Truman and endorsed the general. When MacArthur returned to New York in June, Walter met him at the Waldorf, accompanied by fifteen-year-old Walter, Jr. The young man was so impressed by the experience that he told his father he planned to make journalism his career. That evening his proud papa assigned me to write a column about cub reporters. I subtitled it, "Memos for a Colyumist's Son."

A Winchell column published in the early 1950s encompassed his extensive and varied battle zones. It levied poetic scorn at those who were willing to forgive and forget the Nazis:

Let's not be unkind to the Nazis
If peace is the prize we should earn.
Why make them feel littler because they backed Hitler—
We've millions of youngsters to burn!
How can you forget the poor Wehrmacht?
They're children, it's guidance they need.
So what if their gases destroyed half the masses,
It's just that much less Europe to feed!
Let's pardon their Krupps and their Tyssens;
Let's toast Axis Flagstad and Sally;
Let's make the peace certain! And then raise the curtain—
The third act, my friends, is FINALE!!!

Winchell credited the verse to "Joe Doax." Actually, it was written by a press agent named Art Franklin.

The same column included a snipe at *Time* magazine, a rap at Truman's military aide, Harry Vaughan, a jab at congressmen who discounted the Red menace, and a typical "lasty": "War-ning! Beware of Russian 'peace' talks. When Communists say it with flowers, it's because they expect a funeral."

Winchell enjoyed playing cops and robbers. Although cautious about his cash, he would recklessly endanger his life by running across a line of fire for the sake of a second-rate felony arrest. Statesmen, generals, newspapermen, and movie stars were among those who accompanied him as he wheeled along the canyons in search of adventure. He supplied an engrossing commentary. Passing Lenox Avenue and 117th Street, he announced, "That's the scene of the first nickelodeon in the city of New York. No statues or plaques to tell people who enjoy movies today that here is where it all started." He always pointed out the spot at 126th Street and Madison Avenue where the kidnapper of the Lindbergh baby was apprehended. Of course, roaming the city in the early morning hours enabled him to pick up vivid human-interest paragraphs, such as the following, which was published in *Time* magazine:

At four o'clock one morning two cheap sedans collided at the corner of Manhattan's 86th Street and Central Park West. Eight people were badly smashed up. The driver of one of the cars was laid out on the sidewalk on a seat cushion, and as an uninjured friend knelt over him waiting for the ambulances to come, he kept repeating: "Oh, I'm hurt bad in the chest. My chest hurts bad."

Suddenly the friend looked up, recognizing a face he had seen in a newspaper. "There's Walter Winchell," he said, "Maybe he'll put something in the papers about you."

The man on the cushion stared up at the black sky and said in the same flat unsurprised voice: "Oh I'm hurt bad in the chest—hello, Walter. Walter, my chest's hurt bad."

One morning, as we drove along, Winchell told me, "It's still a secret, but I'm getting the greatest TV-radio deal in history. You'll read about it in the papers." Winchell had been offered $1 million by ABC for forty-five radio-TV programs—and had spurned it. At that time, doing TV would tie him down to New York. *Journal-American* columnist Jack O'Brian quoted him: "I've got to get one more crack at Florida. One more year of the sun at Miami Beach. I'm investing in health and life down there. . . . I'm 54 years old. I feel 64 up here but 44 in Florida."

At fifty-four, he was a remarkable physical specimen: trim, lithe, energetic. He smoked moderately and drank only occasionally—usually Scotch with a twist of lemon. Always a hypochondriac, he considered himself a victim of insomnia, though he got plenty of sleep. His sole physical problem was what he described as "tookis trouble," meaning hemorrhoids. He frequently voiced concern about becoming a cancer victim but expressed confidence that the Runyon Fund would soon develop a cure.

Several days after he had rejected ABC's fabulous offer, stories appeared in the trade papers and elsewhere that Winchell had received offers from CBS and NBC. In fact, Walter had planted the stories to pressure ABC into taking a decision. Within a week, a *New York Times* headline revealed the success of his propaganda campaign: "Winchell Signed for Life by ABC."

The contract—originally written and signed on the back of a Stork Club menu by Winchell and ABC president Robert Kintner—guaranteed Winchell a minimum of $10,000 a week as long as he was physically and mentally capable of broadcasting. If he became unable to perform, we would have a lifetime guarantee of $1,000 a week. Moreover, Walter had the option of determining when to launch his TV career—a blockbuster deal, never before and never since equaled by any other performer.

Three weeks after Winchell's contractual triumph, the Josephine Baker incident splattered the front pages. Miss Baker was a black American expatriate whose scorching song-and-dance act had made and kept her the toast of Paris since the 1920s. When she returned to the United States in 1951 for a series of stage appearances, Winchell's review was rhapsodic. She had a vital stage presence that electrified audiences. After seeing her in action, I wrote in the column, "Josephine Baker has it all. Class, talent and ding-dong." Winchell's glowing review included the observation that Miss Baker refused to "appear anywhere if members of her race are not admitted."

She and Walter met socially several days after he had trumpeted her performance in the column and on the air. She thanked him for the complimentary notices and expressed her gratitude for his crusade against racial discrimination.

The Winchell-Baker orchid exchange ended suddenly when, shortly after midnight on October 16, 1951, Josephine Baker and several friends swept into the Stork Club. As the party was escorted by the headwaiter through the Cub Room, it passed Winchell, who was engaged in conversation with the *Journal-American's* Jack O'Brian and Mrs. O'Brian. After Josephine Baker and her party were seated, Winchell noticed her and waved. She returned his greeting with a smile.

I was dining at another table with a visiting Chicago newspaperman. I could see several drinks being served to the Baker group soon after it had been seated. As in superchic clubs everywhere, there was a leisurely pace to dining and drinking at the Stork, especially in the Cub Room.

About half an hour later, Miss Baker walked past Winchell's table, without saying a word. After a few minutes Walter also departed, to attend a film preview. Miss Baker then phoned Billy Rowe, a black police official, to complain that she had been victimized by the Stork Club's discriminatory policy.

According to the waiters and the captain who served the Baker party, steaks and a rare French wine had been ordered. The wine steward scanned the racks to no avail, then climbed to the fifth floor, where cases of vintage wines were stored, and eventually found the special brand. Within half an hour the wine and steaks were served. It was during the thirty-minute delay that Miss Baker had concluded she was being discriminated against and called Billy Rowe.

When she returned to the table, a member of her party tossed some money on the table, and the group walked out of the Stork, leaving the food and wine unconsumed.

The next day, Winchell was astonished by a wire from one of Miss Baker's friends: "The Stork Club discriminated against Miss Josephine Baker and you failed to intervene in any way." The alleged-discrimination story also appeared in two New York papers.

At first, Winchell dismissed the incident as a misunderstanding. "I was there," he said. "When Miss Baker passed my table I thought she was going into the other room to dance. If she was discriminated against, why didn't she tell me? She knows I'm one of her fans, and I thought she was one of my friends. Why didn't she tell me if she thought there was something wrong?"

It was a refrain he was to repeat for months. Later that night, Josephine Baker appeared on Barry Gray's radio talk show, blasted the Stork as a den of bigotry, and accused Winchell of approving such discrimination by his silence. Ironically, he had had dinner that night at the Stork with Sugar Ray Robinson, the black middleweight boxing champion.

Miss Baker's attack infuriated Winchell. He considered Josephine Baker on a par, at the very least, with Brutus and Judas in the annals of satanic ingratitude.

Several days later, in a period of relative calm, he confessed to me, "Look, the Stork discriminates against everybody. White, black, and pink. It's a snob joint. The Stork bars all kinds of people for all kinds of reasons. But if your skin is green and you're rich and famous or you're syndicated, you'll be welcomed at the club. Irving Hoffman always brings his Negro friends to the Stork, and it doesn't cause any kind of ruckus. But if I published what I'm telling you, all the damn troublemakers would use it as proof that Sherman and I are bigots or something."

Meanwhile, the Josephine Baker incident was picked up by the wire services, flashed around the world and stressed especially strongly in the French papers. Ernest Cuneo sought to head off the gathering storm. He discussed the problem with Walter White, head of the National Association for the Advancement of Colored People.

Cuneo and White arranged a deal. Winchell would publicly rebuke the Stork Club, and White would write a letter extolling the columnist's battle against bigotry. But Winchell undid their work. On his Sunday night newscast he breathlessly informed Mr. and Mrs. America, "I am appalled at the agony and embarrassment caused Josephine

Baker and her friends at the Stork Club. But I am especially appalled at the efforts to involve me in an incident in which I had no part." He damned those who were magnifying the incident as "no friends of mine." Then he read Walter White's letter hailing his fight against racial and religious hatred.

The columnist further proclaimed that no one, including Cuneo, had a right to commit him to anything. Winchell considered it a cardinal virtue never to make "deals" with anyone. According to Cuneo, Walter was aware of the terms of the deal, had originally approved it, and then had changed his mind. Walter White charged a double cross.

The storm intensified. Mr. and Mrs. America flooded the Winchell office with wires and letters, a surprising number of them critical.

A wire from New York:

> I have always admired you as a fighter for justice among the minority races. Now I almost hate you for the course you took on the Josephine Baker affair. . . . How could you do a thing like that when your own people have been subjected to hatred and things un-American? I am hurt to the bottom of my heart to know that someone I have always believed in would take such a quick turn for something that is ungodly.

A letter from Milwaukee:

> I was appalled . . . when I read of your connection with the Josephine Baker incident in the Stork Club and your association with that cowardly snob Billingsley. . . .
>
> I am sure you must realize what harm this incident has done to our foreign policy and what a great disservice you have rendered to America by your connection, and worst of all after having been caught in this compromising position you attempt to evade and deny, in the regular police court shyster style. Your many admirers must be very proud of you. Why don't you snap out of it; it doesn't become you.

A letter from Los Angeles:

> I have read your column and heard you on the radio for many years. I have not always agreed with you, but I have always admired your courage. But tonight something has changed, you were not the man whose courage I admired!

I am very skeptical that an experienced newspaperman like you, upon seeing the Josephine Baker party enter the Stork Club, did not fail to comprehend that a situation loaded with embarrassment was developing.

Hope I am wrong, but your own words lead me to believe you tried to duck out of this situation. . . . You should not have tried to sidestep! I hold no brief for Miss Baker. In fact I do not approve of her putting you, the Stork Club, or herself in such a situation. If the matter were fully investigated, I feel sure the whole thing was staged to take place while you were there, and the net result has been bad publicity for all concerned.

For the sake of millions of people who believe implicitly in you and the free press which you represent, I repeat I hope I am wrong. If I am not wrong, God help us, the people of these United States.

Winchell replied to this last letter by drawing a circle around the words "to duck out" and writing, "I am sorry you assume these things. But I really thought all was well and I did go to a premiere. Why didn't Miss Baker who went to phone a complaint (when I thought she was going to dance) pause at my table and tell me first?" Walter then added an ominous postscript: "Developments now indicate Communist stagemanaging."

I found the mail reaction disturbing and expressed my uneasiness to Walter: "As far as I know nothing happened. You say nothing happened. But Baker thinks something happened."

Winchell interrupted, "Then why are you worried?"

"Maybe the public is wrong, but the public is beginning to think you would rather defend Billingsley than stand up for principles you have been fighting for."

"It may all be a publicity stunt."

"Maybe it is. But lots of people don't think so."

"Lots of those people are ingrates."

"Yes, but why shield Billingsley?"

"I think they're trying to make both of us look like bastards."

"But that isn't the point."

"Fuck 'em."

"To get back to Sherman. You can settle the issue with a compromise, I'm sure. Why be stubborn?"

"I just don't think I'm guilty of anything, and I don't want to act guilty. Hell, I've been in battles before. Controversies are forgotten in two weeks."

"Maybe you're right. I hope so anyway."

At that point Winchell said something that he would reiterate about two decades later: "Sherman and I know too much about each other." Then he hesitated and added cryptically, "Girls." I could see he was eager to drop the subject, so we went on to other things.

Walter's loyalty to Sherman Billingsley was a complicating factor. After all, the Stork was his second home—and his palace.

The Stork Club phenomenon was a blend of Winchell power, extravagance and luxury, snobbery, and sensuality. The club was a rosy stadium—famous people in superb surroundings, polished glass and gleaming silver giving the atmosphere a constant flush of animation. People came to see and be seen. As Sherman observed, "I found out that a flock of celebrities made a café popular. People will pay more to look at each other than for food, drink, and service," albeit the food and service at the Stork were superb.

By the late 1930s, the Stork Club had become an internationally recognized institution. You could look around the Cub Room and see Randolph Churchill, the Duke and Duchess of Windsor, Franklin Roosevelt, Jr., Joseph P. Kennedy, King Peter of Yugoslavia, Lord Beaverbrook, the Shah of Iran, J. Edgar Hoover, Bernard Baruch, Jim Farley, and Adrei Gromyko, plus a skyful of stars from the show-business and sports galaxies.

Imitation Stork Clubs sprouted in many cities, and Billingsley engaged in continual litigation in an effort to stop others from cashing in on his creation. At one time he juggled thirteen lawsuits simultaneously. As far as Sherman was concerned, the Stork had the singular value of the Hope Diamond. But, interestingly, he raised no objections during World War II when Madame Chiang Kai-shek wrote to him, "We're getting a Stork Club in Chungking."

Paramount Pictures paid $100,000 for the right to use the Stork Club name as the title of a mediocre film. Several years later, the Stork Club was the setting for a regular television show. A replica of the Cub Room was built in an upstairs room, where Sherman interviewed celebrities, sometimes with hilariously disastrous consequences. Faced with the Shah of Iran, Billingsley couldn't think of anything to say beyond "How's Iran?" When a famous British actress was his guest, Sherman suddenly blurted out, "How old are you?" She turned ashen and then replied through her clenched teeth, "Twenty-fivish."

Sherman chuckled. "Twenty-fivish. You'll never see thirty again." She never spoke to him again.

Sherman, who was grandly introduced on the show as the "world's most fabulous host," was thoroughly ignorant about most of the subjects he discussed. Besides, his stage fright before the cameras deprived him of any semblance of aplomb. There were other problems too.

Newspaperman Bill Slocum was assigned to write appropriate questions, which were pasted on the backs of cups and coffee pots, where they wouldn't be picked up by the camera. However, Sherman insisted that the waiters keep his table clean, so waiters were forever bearing away empty cups and pots that bore Sherman's imminent ad libs. The result was some of the aforementioned catastrophes, as well as others.

One night the camera caught Sarah Churchill, Winston's daughter, munching celery. Billingsley brightly asked, "What are you doing?"

"Eating celery."

Inexplicably, he inquired, "And what else do you do for a living?"

Talking to Celeste Holm one night, he asked her when her play *Affairs of State* was expected to open. "It's been running for six weeks," Miss Holm informed him.

Not only did Billingsley have trouble with questions; he rarely listened to his guests' answers.

My flashing memories of the Stork over the years are glad, sad, silly, and some are indelible.

I made my first visit to the Stork Club at age eighteen. Winchell introduced me to the lovely Tallulah Bankhead. Lovely she was, but after more than a few drinks she was at her brassy, bitchy best. After shaking hands with me, she gushed, "Glad to meet, Herman," then paused and added, "Go fuck yourself."

"Pardon her French," Winchell countered.

I remember Irving Berlin phoning Winchell to sing his latest song in his inimitable raspy baritone. "It isn't one of your better ones," Walter concluded. The song was "Easter Parade."

I remember too the melancholy sight of a liquor-soaked Westbrook

Pegler being dragged out of the Stork Club and dumped on the sidewalk while he shrieked anti-Semitic obscenities.

Winchell loved the Stork. It was his office, his second home, and his playground. Next to Walter himself, the Stork was the most advertised product in his column. He plugged it repeatedly, though he never had a financial interest in the club, despite the rumors to the contrary. When Winchell was in New York, he saw and spoke to Billingsley almost daily for about thirty years. While Sherman treated Walter as a demigod, Walter regarded Billingsley as a favorite headwaiter. Nevertheless, they had a certain ironclad loyalty toward each other, and Winchell foolishly regarded an assault on the Stork or Billingsley as a personal threat and acted accordingly.

Walter initially regarded the Baker controversy as the latest in a long string of battles. His record as a gladiator was highly reassuring. Winchell was the undefeated champion of smart-ass brawling. Over the years he had regaled his audience with triumph after triumph. In addition, Walter believed that a fickle public usually forgets old animosities in its fascination with new ones. I must admit I shared Winchell's joy in controversy. After all, I was an assistant general in the Winchell wars. More often than not, my typewriter was "top gun." There is no question that the constant strife had a certain exhilarating quality. Winning is always fun, of course. Besides, arguments make for readable columns. On occasion, when things were dull, I deliberately provoked an imbroglio.

In light of his past record, Winchell at first was supremely confident that he could resolve the issues and emerge triumphant. Within the dual fortress of his column and newscast he not only felt impregnable but also believed that he was morally right.

As Walter reveled in the glorious vision of himself as valiant victim, others joined me in trying to open his eyes to reality. As I well knew, it would be a difficult chore. A fundamental difficulty was Winchell's outsized ego, which stubbornly resisted any suggestion that he might be in the wrong. The problem was compounded by the fact that he was frequently surrounded by the obsequious, fearful, and awestruck. Only a handful of his friends and associates could confront him with candor. I was one, because we had a cordial, easygoing relationship. Among the others who spoke with honest conviction were Irving Hoffman, and Arnold Forster. Hoffman, in particular, offered no-nonsense opinions; and Irving was the only

one who would dare interrupt a Winchell monologue and tell him to
"shut up and stop being a bore."

Forster was on the West Coast when the Josephine Baker ruckus
kicked up. On his return to New York, he dictated a memo to
Winchell:

> Got back to New York this morning to feel the heat of the
> Stork Club teapot-tempest. Just finished reading all the clips. . . .
>
> If the Stork Club was not guilty of discriminating against
> Josephine Baker—and it appears that a good case can be made
> out for that position—the best public relations would have
> been (and may still be) for Sherman Billingsley to give you
> a simple one-paragraph letter in which he states the policy of
> no discrimination by the Stork Club, and adds to it an expres-
> sion of regret for the discomfort caused Miss Baker from the
> combination of accidental circumstances. Had Billingsley given
> you such a letter to read along with the Walter White letter,
> it would successfully have choked off any further ado. . . .
>
> The reason this thing continues to grow hotter is that Billings-
> ley has thus far failed to make a clean-cut simple statement that
> the Stork Club does not and will not discriminate. That will
> also get you off the hook on which you have been so wrongly
> hung.
>
> If this thing continues to get worse, it will not be too late to
> do it next Sunday night on your newscast. A forthright statement
> by Billingsley, I think, will satisfy troublemakers.

Winchell returned the memo to Forster with the reply "I told
this to Sherman and I agree with him that nothing you can say will
please them. This is their party line and racket. I have been accused,
indicted, convicted and almost lynched by the very people who have
asked and gotten me to fight such things. W.W" It was obvious
that Winchell had wrapped himself in the cloak of martyrdom and
voices of reason would be unheard.

Nonetheless, I made another attempt. I wrote an editorial noting
the folly of becoming disenchanted with the struggle for the rights
of minority groups simply because some members of the groups are
foolish, vicious, or ungrateful. People, I stressed, are never as flawless
or steadfast as principles. In addition, I emphasized the absurdity of
using the Stork as a symbol of the struggle for equality. I concluded
with Booker T. Washington's observation that the right to stand

at a workbench is more important than the right to purchase a seat at the opera—or, I added, "wine at the Stork Club." Winchell returned the editorial with a two-word comment: "Forget it!"

Attack was more congenial to him than conciliation. The Winchell column, in common with many others during that period, was peppered with items relating to the fracas. He obtained a translation of Josephine Baker's autobiography, in which she devoted several pages to attacking Jewish landlords in Harlem and Jews in general, and published her bigoted remarks in a full column entitled "In Black and White."

On October 24, 1951, he reprinted a 1935 story from the Associated Press reporting Miss Baker's announcement that she "would campaign to get Negro help for Premier Mussolini against Ethiopia." Another column said, "Newspapermen are checking the tip that one of the complainants against the Stork Club (and her husband) helped incite and participated in the Paul Robeson Peekskill riots."

On October 26, Billingsley called Winchell's office to report a tip that *Stars and Stripes* in late 1944 or early 1945 had carried a story reporting that Josephine Baker had refused to entertain an army company when she found out that the troops were black. Winchell asked Arnold Forster to check the story out. It proved to be phony.

The November 5 Winchell column carried the following: "Gov't people interested in the Josephine Baker thing are keeping tabs on her for use if she tries to enter the U.S. again." Several days later, his report was denied in a *New York Post* story.

Subsequently, Winchell received a wire from Walter White, the NAACP chief, quoting Assistant Attorney General James M. McInerney as follows:

> Responsive to your telegram relative to the Stork Club incident involving Josephine Baker, no investigation has been authorized by the Department [of Justice], the Federal Bureau of Investigation, or the Immigration and Naturalization Service. . . . We trust that in the interest of fair play to Miss Josephine Baker as well as journalistic accuracy, you will print the refutation by the Departments of Justice and State in your column to the end that the truth may be known.

Winchell's response was brief and barbed: "This shmuck expects me to repeat the *Post*'s skewp! The denial was published in the *Post* over a week ago. Shtick opp tookiss!"

Many newspaper and magazine editorials commented on the controversy. The majority blasted Winchell, though a Negro newspaper in Pittsburgh defended him.

Winchell remained insufferably self-righteous, condemning his critics as "professional troublemakers." As the criticism mounted, he became increasingly irascible and developed symptoms of paranoia. He believed the Baker case was part of a Red conspiracy directed against him. When the NAACP threw a four-man picket line in front of the Stork, the Winchell column accused three of the pickets of being Communists.

Early in November he rejected an opportunity to extricate himself from the disaster. In Eustis, Florida, two young blacks, one dead, the other dying, were discovered handcuffed together in a roadside ditch. They had been struck by six bullets from the gun of a Lake County sheriff who had been transporting the prisoners from the Florida State Penitentiary to a nearby town for trial. Two years before, they had been convicted of rape and sentenced to death. The Supreme Court had reversed the conviction because there had been no blacks on the jury. The sheriff pleaded self-defense.

Here was an opportunity for Winchell to demonstrate his allegiance to justice. He mulled the idea over for a time, then decided to forgo the opportunity. He rationalized: "If I went to bat for these poor kids, I would be accused of making deals. I never make deals, you know. And I would be accused of seeking favors or publicity." He sighed and added, "I think you all have lost me."

It was clear that the nation's most powerful antibigot voice had withdrawn from the cause. In the end, the clash of viewpoints was irreconcilable. The Winchell diehards regretted that he had deserted the civil-rights battlefield. On the other hand, Winchell was convinced that the liberal army had deserted him.

Meanwhile, as the storm of abuse intensified, Billingsley's original obstinacy began weakening. The transformation was accelerated by a decline in business at the Stork as a result of the picketing as well as pressure from friends and customers. Thus, on November 27, more than a month after the Baker incident, the Stork Club host began discussing the possibility of writing a letter of apology and explanation. Sherman had previously refused to write anything or explain anything. Now, with the help of friends and his attorney, he composed several versions of a letter he planned to make public.

One version of the letter, addressed to the Anti-Defamation League, read as follows:

> Gentlemen:
> The interest of your organization in human relations prompts me to write you and present the facts concerning the Josephine Baker visit to the Stork Club, and our guest policy.
>
> Miss Baker made a reservation one afternoon. That night with three other people she came to the Club. She was seated at an excellent table in the crowded Cub Room—where world celebrities gather. For an hour or more she and her friends were served drinks of their choice and seemed to be enjoying themselves.
>
> Because of an unusual food order for that time of the night— it was after the theatre—there was an unusual service delay. Unfortunately this sometimes happens—even to our best customers.
>
> It is the policy of the Stork Club—as it always has been— to cater to a clientele made up of peoples of the world, naturally giving preference to those who have been our constant patrons over the years. This seems broad enough—and understandable enough—to explain our joy at serving ladies and gentlemen from the four corners of the earth without discrimination—as we have for twenty years, and always will.
>
> Very truly yours,
> SHERMAN BILLINGSLEY

Obviously, the letter was too late, too little, and too self-serving. When it was read to Winchell, he said, "Forget it." It was filed and forgotten—until now.

That year Winchell departed for his favorite sunny playground, Miami Beach, in late October, somewhat earlier than usual because a barber strike in New York had interrupted his daily barbering ritual. About the time Winchell arrived in Miami, Ed Sullivan appeared on Barry Gray's midnight radio talkfest. For more than an hour, Sullivan delivered a tirade against his rival:

> I came here tonight particularly to discuss Josephine Baker. I'd like to start off by saying, if I may, that I, as an American, despise Communism. As an American, I despise anything that is contrary to old-fashioned Americanism. No liberal conception of Americanism—I'm talking about old-fashioned Ameri-

canism where you get a great thrill in your heart when the Star Spangled Banner goes by in a parade and you take off your hat. . . . Of all the things that are un-American to me, the gravest affront is character assassination. So I despise Walter Winchell for what he has done to Josephine Baker. . . .

Walter Winchell was one of the originators of character assassination. Now, you'd think that this former small-time vaudeville hoofer would have been content—and a real small-time vaudeville hoofer—never got to the Palace, and that is the dividing line between great hoofing and inferior hoofing. He never got to the Palace. He was a small-time vaudeville hoofer, then went to work on the *Vaudeville News*, and then down the years in the most amazing story in American newspaper work, he became a very powerful writer. . . . Winchell has developed into a small-time Hitler, and he has made the practice and capitalized on the big lie. . . .

I say that what Winchell did to Josephine Baker is an insult to the United States and the American newspapermen who don't pursue the racket that he pursues. . . .

I despise him as a very dangerous influence on American journalism and American communications. . . . Now, Barry, I want to tell you that Winchell is going to smear you. But, Barry, when you are smeared, I want you to know that a lot of us are in your corner—a lot of us. A lot of us who've demonstrated that we can take care of him.

The next day Winchell received a wire at the Roney-Plaza:

Within the last five days Josephine Baker, Arthur Garfield Hays, and Ed Sullivan have all appeared at my microphone with comments regarding the attack made by you against Miss Baker. In accordance with the policy of my program, you, or an accredited representative, are herewith invited to use my microphone and broadcast to present any facts that you wish made public at any time any night. Please acknowledge.

BARRY GRAY

After Walter read the wire, he commented, "It reads like the legal department wrote it and is worried." Only one aspect of Sullivan's diatribe disturbed Winchell: Mrs. Winchell had heard it, and it had upset her. Nevertheless, Winchell shrugged, saying, "I'll get around to all the ingrates."

In time, he got around to Barry Gray. In column after column,

Winchell damned him as "Borey Pink" or "Borey Fink," suggesting that he was pro-Communist, as well as an all-around louse. And Ed Sullivan, who had vowed to protect Gray, stayed on the sidelines. Nineteen years later, in a *New York Times* interview, Gray said:

> I never heard from Sullivan again. . . . Winchell had the power to kill someone professionally. How I managed to live through those years is a miracle. I lost two television shows. I lost my sponsor list. Actors stopped coming on the program. I was a pariah. A week before, I had gone into Lindy's and it was "Hi, how are you?" I walked into Lindy's then, and there was a silence; I felt like I was in *High Noon*. I was ostracized.

Some of Gray's associates and fickle friends curried favor with Winchell. One provided Walter with a daily, detailed diary of Barry Gray's activities. Another former Gray pal, comic Jack E. Leonard, rushed over to Walter one evening in Lindy's and shook his hand: "I want to congratulate you, Walter. You're making Barry sick. He can't sleep! He can't eat! He can't shit!"

During that period, Gray was severely beaten twice. A *Journal-American* editor sent Winchell a photo of Gray's mashed face. Walter examined it and smiled. "He never looked more beautiful." Then he sighed. "Some people will probably think that Winchell's attacks inspired the beatings, or I had something to do with it. Bullshit! That kind of face comes from fooling around with another man's wife!"

Exactly a year after the Baker incident at the Stork, the wire services carried a story from Buenos Aires:

> Josephine Baker, who opens a singing engagement here tomorrow, already has starred in a loud display of anti-American propaganda patterned right after Argentine President Juan Perón's own heart. Miss Baker waged her fight against the United States in a six-article series in the Perón newspaper, *Crítica,* in an audience with Perón himself and in a press conference. While denouncing the United States as a "barbarous land living in a false Nazi-style democracy," she praised God "because He makes men like Perón."

Columnist Robert Ruark commented:

> It's very likely that even the most dedicated protagonists of racial equality will now give up on Miss Josephine Baker, the hand-

some colored lady who stirred up such a ruckus here a year or
so back and who became a somewhat clouded *cause célèbre* in
the more hysterical press over the fancied slight of receiving lousy
service in a posh ginmill.

Ruark was mistaken. Miss Baker's outburst in Buenos Aires had no
effect on the newspapers, radio commentators, and human-rights organizations that had given her their blessings a year earlier.

Winchell gleefully reprinted the tale of Baker's eruption in Argen-
tina. That also had little effect. Everyone's opinion on the controversy
seemed to have settled in cement.

Years later, in a book published in 1973, Hollywood columnist
Shirley Eder reported an interview in which Miss Baker had said
that she was very sorry about the whole affair. She had come to realize
"that she had been used as a pawn in the matter, and Walter had
done nothing to hurt her." Indeed, she insisted she had sent letters of
apology to Winchell. But according to Winchell's office, such letters
were never received.

In retrospect, the historic impact of the incident was probably
overshadowed by its effects on the various individuals involved. It
was a pioneer civil-rights case, a controversy deliberately provoked and
designed to magnify the problem and thus arouse the public conscience
to press for alleviation of an injustice. But Winchell was oblivious
to the historical implications. Years later he observed, "The Baker story
was my most frustrating experience. The unfairness of the whole
thing was sickening. I had the same feeling when I was a kid in
Harlem and was left back in school. I couldn't understand why the
teacher had been so cruel."

=14=
The New York Post vs. WW

In the Josephine Baker affair, Winchell embodied the saying of the Supreme Court's Chief Justice Hughes that every man's virtues are also his limitations. Walter excused in his friends acts that he would not tolerate in his enemies or himself. His misplaced loyalty led him to defend his friends from just punishment long overdue by pointing out worse behavior in others that had gone unpunished. Yet he was often the victim of monumental ingratitude. Some of those whom he protected recognized his efforts in their behalf only by kicking him in the groin.

In his other fights he had emerged vindicated or victorious, at least in his own mind. This time, he came out of prolonged struggle embittered, shaken, chagrined, and with a noticeable lack of his characteristic resiliency. He felt that the Baker case had brought him a bum rap, and he was shocked to discover his vulnerability.

For the first time the Winchell structure trembled. And I had the disconcerting sense of something ticking, something that might detonate at any time.

Within months the ticking became louder. Walter learned he was to be the subject of a *New York Post* series. His informant, one of the paper's executives, added, "It will be a hatchet job."

At first, Walter was unconcerned. After all, some of his best friends and allies were on the *Post*. Leonard Lyons, the paper's Broadway columnist, had been a Winchell contributor, was vice-president of the Runyon Fund, and as recently as March 22, 1950, had sent Walter a warmly supportive missive.

Post columnist Earl Wilson and his wife were also ardent Winchell fans. Earl had written a flattering magazine piece about Walter. And when Winchell plugged his book, Wilson excitedly called and said, "Thanks a million copies." The paper's political columnists Max Lerner and Murray Kempton often sent Winchell friendly, chatty letters. Paul Sann, the executive editor, once told friends, "Winchell writes the only column in town." Publisher Dorothy Schiff had often tried to lure Winchell from the *Mirror* to the *Post* with generous financial offers. Besides, the *Post* and Winchell had been liberal allies during the Roosevelt years, and both opposed Truman in the 1948 campaign. Remember, too, that Walter's dislike for Truman began with the President's crude reference to Mrs. Schiff. And James Wechsler, the *Post*'s editor, had once written a kindly essay about Winchell.

In addition, his professed indifference to the upcoming profile was fortified by experience. Years before, a scathing six-part profile in the *New Yorker* had failed to impede his ascending career. Incidentally, on December 16, 1950, the author of that profile, St. Clair McKelway, had wired Winchell:

> Having read, in the course of my researches, so many of your columns in the dead past, I haven't read many of them in the live present. But I would like to convey to you my congratulations on your Sunday column. This message being from your severest critic, who is not your best friend, I hope it will give you a moment of satisfaction before the retroactive anger in you sets in, and before I reconsider the words I am putting down here. Anyway, you seem to me to be on the ball politically and patriotically if I may say so. But let's not terminate, for that or any other reason, the cold war or wholehearted hostility or, to coin a phrase, the feud that has given the two of us so much satisfaction and fun all these years. With vast and opprobrious regards, and in the spirit of a time that, as Lincoln said, tries men's souls, I am faithfully yours,
>
> ST. CLAIR MCKELWAY

Winchell circled the name "Lincoln" and wrote on the wire, "Haw! Tom Paine said it!"

Years later, in *Variety*'s February 3, 1971, issue, McKelway went still farther: "Maybe I did him wrong because Walter was long in advance of history with warnings of the Nazi danger, the Bundists, his

FBI inside stuff, as a pal of J. Edgar Hoover, not to mention his influence on American journalism."

Walter generally dismissed his enemies as envious, un-American, or otherwise disreputable. Even friends who wrote about him cordially invited his resentment. When Ed Weiner, a press agent, who had been a member of the Winchell circle for many years wrote a flattering Winchell biography, it ended their friendship. He considered such acts to be violations of his privacy. When it was argued that his success was based on revealing other people's private affairs, Walter insisted, "That's different; that's business."

Another Winchell biographer, after completing his work, took his manuscript to Winchell in his penthouse in Miami Beach. Eager to unveil his literary creation, he said, "I want to show you something."

Winchell asked, "What is it?"

"A book about your life."

"Where did you get it?"

"I wrote it."

"Who gave you permission?"

"You did."

"Let me see it."

Without a word, Winchell took the typed manuscript, briskly walked to an open window and threw it out. The horrified author watched as his pages fluttered down over the Atlantic. Yet another Winchell friendship literally had flown out the window.

His irritation in such cases stemmed in part from his hostility toward people who exploited his name.

One of Walter's caustic biographers had a criminal record. But Winchell was more concerned with the fact that he had changed his name. Privately he damned him "as a Jew who changed his name. So what can you expect?" Similarly, in 1951, he fumed at the idea of the *Post*'s using his "name as a box office attraction because their own columnists are without marquee value." His assumption proved correct. It was estimated that the *Post*'s series on Winchell added about forty thousand readers. In fact, the *Post* followed a deliberate policy of using sensationalism and exaggeration as circulation-building gimmicks. Wechsler had transformed a money-losing liberal paper into a gaudy money-maker. The paper lured readers with front-page promises of "exposés" of prostitutes, abortion, and homosexuality, not to mention "The Life and Loves of Franchot Tone."

About a month before the series was published, Winchell's inform- ant reported that it would be "primarily about Winchell but will also deal with Sherman Billingsley." The *Post,* it seemed, had "uncovered the Stork Club proprietor's serious criminal record." Moreover, the paper would use the Josephine Baker incident to demonstrate Billings- ley's "bigotry."

It was true that Billingsley had a criminal record, but it could not be classified as serious. During Prohibition he had been convicted of bootlegging.

(Later Billingsley visited the *Post*'s offices and pleaded with Dorothy Schiff, "as a parent," not to expose his past. He said that his two children by his second wife were unaware of his criminal record. Mrs. Schiff suggested that he see Wechsler, but Billingsley said he had been advised by his attorneys not to talk to newspapermen. To which Mrs. Schiff is said to have replied, "How about Mr. Winchell? Isn't he a newspaperman?")

Walter learned, too, that the *Post* would charge him with defection from the liberal line by being pro-McCarthy and anti-Truman.

Wechsler and seven reporters—almost the entire reportorial force— were feverishly planning the 24-part series. They scurried around the city gathering information. A *Post* team flew to Miami to interview Winchell, who refused to cooperate.

The *Post* reporters were asking questions about me as well. One day I learned that they were about to descend on my home. My wife offered a frivolous suggestion: "Why don't you just tell them you're in the shoe business? Make it a farce interview." I thought it was a fine idea and called Winchell in Miami Beach. "I think it's a cute approach," he said, "but I am not as concerned with what the *Post* will write as I am about what kind of column you will write for me tomorrow." Winchell, incidentally, never instructed me either to cooperate with or to refuse to answer the *Post* interviewers. He never offered any advice on the subject. I presume he trusted my discretion.

That evening *Post* reporters Alvin Davis and Irving Lieberman visited me. At first they offered flattering comments about my reputa- tion and writing talents, but their faces hardened when they spoke about Winchell's refusal to cooperate and his McCarthyism. When they inquired, "What do you do for Winchell," I deadpanned the story about being a simple shoe salesman. They were annoyed by my flippancy. "We know what you do for Winchell!" one of the reporters exclaimed impatiently, displaying a column I had written. At this point

I terminated the five-minute interview and ushered them out the door. Later Davis phoned with several perfunctory questions.

The *Post* subsequently interviewed my mailman and the proprietor of the candy store where I purchased my newspapers. Its reporters made phone calls to my mother, asking such questions as "How often does he visit you?" and "How much does he contribute to your support?" Dirty pool, I thought. In fact, the reporters muffed an opportunity for a "scoop." My mother knew exactly what I wrote for Winchell, was proud of every word, and believed I deserved public recognition as well as a higher salary. If they had only asked the right questions, she would have told all.

Gradually, Winchell's unconcern changed to anxiety. Although he never mentioned it to me, I later learned that he exerted every form of pressure on fellow journalists, politicians, lawyers, and public-relations men in an effort to stifle the series. He was unsuccessful, though *Post* reporter Lieberman conceded, "Winchell's heat made the *Post* brass uncomfortable for a while."

Winchell was prepared for a drubbing, but the opening flurry of articles in January 1952 jolted him with the realization that the series would be bloodier than he had expected. It's destructiveness imposed unaccustomed silence and timidity on Winchell. He not only refrained from commenting on the articles while they were being published but even refused—or was unable—to read them. Like a man facing a firing squad, he chose to wear a blindfold.

The *Post* biographers exaggerated his worst side. Winchell was pictured as perverse, coarse, an unmitigated liar, an utterly contemptible egotist with an iron necessity to be right, a plagiarist, a demagogue whose cynicism put him on the right side for the wrong reasons, an unethical newspaperman who violated the principles as well as the amenities of his craft—in brief, as an all-around monster.

At first, readers probably took some pleasure in the dismemberment of a famous and powerful man. But as the harsh metronome clicked on day after day, the nature of the attacks inspired comforting letters to Winchell, including several from *Post* columnist Murray Kempton.

It was a classic case of overkill. Walter, the "overdog," had become the underdog and reaped both sympathy and rare support from the Hearst organization. His name was bannered on *Mirror* trucks, headlined on the paper's front pages, and hailed in its editorials. Not one paper dropped his column as a consequence of the series. Moreover, his lofty radio rating remained secure. Only an infinitesimal few of his enormous radio-column audience were influenced by the *Post* story.

While the series was running, columnist Robert Ruark asked me how Winchell was reacting. "Very badly, I'm afraid," I said. Ruark replied, "He's silly. Those pieces are great publicity. I wish they would write about me."

I shared Ruark's view. Winchell's brooding silence was self-inflicted torture. But one couldn't discuss it with him. He isolated himself and sulked. Although the *Post* installments failed to dent his career, they did damage his psyche.

On January 10, 1952, I picked up the *Post* and was shocked to see a front-page three-inch headline in color, "Winchell's No. 1 Ghost," accompanied by the large photo of myself in buttoned overcoat. The caption under my photo on an inside page read, "The Winchell You Never Knew Till Now." The next day, the *Mirror* countered with a clever page-one banner: "THERE IS ONLY ONE WALTER WINCH-ELL." But the Winchell column in that issue was written by The Winchell You Never Knew Till Now.

The *Post* story became more amusing as it went on. Darned if they didn't treat my flippancy about being a shoe salesman as a nefarious attempt to mislead the vigilant *Post* reporters, who, of course, were not fooled. Moreover, the *Post* reporters treated the salesman-strawman as a tragic figure, comparable to Arthur Miller's Willy Loman.

The *Post*'s revelations merely revealed the tip of the iceberg as far as my Winchell contributions were concerned. The front-page explosion, however, gave me celebrity status with my family, friends, and neighbors for a whole week. Everybody inquired, "What'd Winchell say?" The fact is, he was almost a sphinx. Oh, he let loose a stream of profanity when his secretary read bits from the *Post* to him, but usually he maintained his eerie, hushed attitude, though he was inwardly stricken. Inevitably, the inner turmoil took its toll.

After the publication of the *Post*'s eighteenth article, the *Mirror* announced that Winchell was suspending his newspaper column and newscasts "to take a rest on doctor's orders." The next day, the *Post* graciously proclaimed: "In view of these developments, the *Post* is postponing publication of the last six installments. They will be published as soon as he resumes his column. We believe in the old journalistic principle that a newspaper should not argue with a man while he isn't in a position to answer back."

Winchell's previous emotional upsets had lasted two or three weeks, but this time he crumpled into a depression that lasted three months, most of that interval being spent at his home in Scottsdale, Arizona. For the first time in years, the Winchells were together for a lengthy period.

I was paid for eight of the thirteen weeks during which the Winchell mill no longer ground. Later he referred to this as my "severance pay." Walter, incidentally, was paid in full by both the *Mirror* and ABC throughout the period.

After being dropped from the payroll, I began job-hunting. Within three weeks, I received a message stating, "Winchell will resume columning if you agree to return to work." Loyal soldier that I was, I readily agreed. Ironically, it was Mrs. Winchell who had persuaded him to go back to work. She knew that without his work he was one of the living dead. "June finally got tired of seeing me sitting in my bathrobe staring at my feet," he said. "By the way," he added. "I finally read the *Post* series."

"What did you think of it?" I inquired.

He replied, "I laughed."

Winchell returned to his column but postponed resuming his broadcasts for a while. After Walter had taken up the column again, the *Post* published the final six installments of its series. Walter's perky personality had been restored, and I could almost see it rising to white-hot vitality. Now he talked about "doing something about the *Post* bastards" and began responding to his tormentors with barbed one-liners.

In Winchell's color scheme, red was a fitting hue for the New York *Post*. He discussed his upcoming special portrait with me in his ABC office a few weeks after returning from Arizona. By this time he had consented to make his re-entry into television newcasting with a "simulcast"—a combination radio and TV program.

Winchell had learned that a *Post* editor and several others on the paper had Communist backgrounds. "I have the ammunition," he said impatiently. "Let's go!"

I proposed another battle plan. Absurdity was the key to the strategy. "Ridicule their attacks, debunk their exaggerations, poke fun at the insinuations, and you'll make the *Post* mob look foolish." Walter promptly rejected the lampooning tactic. "You don't understand, Herman. Those sons of bitches tried to kill me! Kill me, you hear!"

He obviously had made an irrevocable choice of weaponry. In his view, the conflict was a deadly struggle, with survival his only goal.

This was the Winchell credo: Use your heaviest artillery and never stop fighting, even if the odds are you against the world.

He often described his fighting style as a "straight left to the balls" (He was left-handed) and frequently boasted, "I'm the man who invented the low blow." On occasion, he clawed those who deserved only a slap. In retaliating against the *Post*'s apparent malignity, he believed it was naive to observe rules of politeness or show pity.

Several days after our ABC newsroom meeting, he fired a merciless full-column salvo at the *Post* in general and James Wechsler and Dorothy Schiff in particular. Later, at the Stork, Winchell was in a good mood. Months of tension had evidently been relieved with a single retaliatory blow. He beamed. "I'll bet the *Post* executives are now holding a meeting about my column." When, a few minutes later, his *Post* informant called to report that a meeting was indeed planned, Winchell roared.

General Winchell had originally intended to crush the enemy with what he described as "one atomic column." The *Post* foolishly counterattacked, and Walter, the master of the jugular slash, the man who had vowed, "I want to get back at a lot of people. If I drop dead before I get to the Zs in the alphabet, you'll know how I hated to go," launched Operation Mayhem.

Within days, Winchell was joined by a host of mercenaries—an assortment of former as well as current *Post* staffers, friends and ex-friends of Schiff and Wechsler, Hearst executives, newsmen from other papers, and publicists—not to mention the inevitable crackpots. Some people Walter abhorred suddenly became his allies. For example, Lee Mortimer, the *Mirror*'s nightclub columnist, was the source for one anti-*Post* column.

The bare-bones facts about the *Post* and Communism: Years before, the *Post* editorials under editor Ted Thackray had followed the party line intermittently, and the paper still had its share of onetime Communists and fellow travelers. Under editor Wechsler the *Post* became consistently anti-Communist. However, during the 1930s, Wechsler himself had been a member of the Young Communist League.

With the foregoing ammunition, Winchell managed to arm a battery of more than thirty columns. Wechsler was kept busy responding to Winchell as well as enduring Senator McCarthy's inquisitions. The Senator joined Winchell in damning the paper along with other "left-wing smear sheets" for following "the Communist Party line, right down to the last period."

Unpredictably, Winchell included his friend Leonard Lyons in his scattershot offensive. "Lyons," he said, "helped the *Post* people trying to destroy me." It wasn't true, but neither Arnold Forster nor I could change his mind. I did manage, however, to discourage him from publishing a malicious column about Lyons. This incident was one of the most melancholy aspects of the incessant mayhem. It would be years before Winchell and Lyons became reconciled.

In the beginning, the *Post* responded to Winchell's furious fusillade by debunking his pro-Red charges. Then the paper threatened to publish another series called "Winchell Revisited." Nothing diminished Walter's firepower. Finally, the *Post* sought refuge in the courts. Late in December 1952, the *Post* and editor James Wechsler filed libel suits for $1,525,000 against Winchell and the Hearst Corporation, his radio and TV sponsor, and the American Broadcasting Company. Winchell smugly accepted the lawsuit as a flag of surrender. "Newspapermen," he argued, "are supposed to fight each other without running to lawyers for help."

Winchell's behavior in the *Post* matter was further evidence of a process of political change that began after World War II. His crowd-pleasing blasts at Soviet expansion and domestic Communists were the honest reactions of a supervigilant reporter. Unfortunately, they coincided with the spiral of McCarthyism and became entwined with it. Winchell's anti-Red crusade and the crooked lightning of McCarthyism, followed by the Josephine Baker affair in 1951—an experience that haunted him the rest of his days—eventually destroyed Winchell's link with the liberal alliance of FDR's devotees and champions of human rights.

In the magic mirror of egomania, Winchell could see only the changes in his former supporters, not those in himself. Certainly he had been maligned in the Baker affair, but his self-righteousness was so pervasive that it made reconciliation impossible. The others involved were also envenomed. The purists and the do-gooders had become stern-eyed zealots, forever locked in certitudes. Even after Miss Baker died, in April 1975, the misconceptions persisted.

Embittered and enraged, Winchell turned increasingly to the right, though he privately believed that the change was for mere expediency and that he would soon be restored as a powerful liberal voice. His hopes were never realized. The transformation had become evident to me within a year after the Baker incident. Arnold Forster exited from the Winchell scene. Another man had Winchell's ear. He was Roy

Cohn, who was at that time counsel to the McCarthy Committee.

While the *Post* vs. Winchell began its long journey through the courts, Winchell more and more became a McCarthy fan. He was constantly stunning the populace with forecasts of McCarthy's upcoming "bombshells," most of which turned out to be duds. Still, Winchell was not dismayed. McCarthy had fortified his position with the columnist by supporting his war against the *Post*. As Winchell's former liberal backers turned hostile, his uneasy alliance with McCarthy was strengthened and with it his zealous anti-Communism.

A story in his June 13, 1952, column, was typical:

> The House Un-American Activities Committee is editing new headlines. One is expected to be John Garfield's last long statement just before he passed away. When (and if) it appears there will be lusty howls from the Broadway and Hollywood Reds plus red faces along Lawyer's Row.

The inescapable implications were that the famous young actor had "confessed" 'to having been a Communist and that the admission would embarrass Hollywood notables and some attorneys. The facts, however, were that John Garfield had made no "last long statement" to the congressional committee. When he had died, he had been putting notes together, with Forster's help, for a letter to a West Coast producer who had offered him a starring role in a new movie. The letter, never sent, would have said that Garfield had never been a Communist or a Red sympathizer. Arnold Forster, who had been with Garfield day and night the last two days before his death, knew the true Garfield story. But Winchell was in no mood to listen.

Besides doing these unsavory errands for McCarthy, Winchell had become a drummer for an Eisenhower presidency. The "boom" began as early as 1948, when Eisenhower was the NATO chief, stationed in Paris. At that time, Chicago boss Jake Arvey and other Democratic leaders wanted Ike to run as their candidate instead of Truman. But he wasn't interested and, instead, accepted an appointment as president of Columbia University. At the time, Winchell ran a postcard presidential poll. It disclosed that Ike was the overwhelming popular choice. Before announcing the final tally, Winchell went to Columbia, told Eisenhower the results of the poll, and pleaded with him to run. Apparently, he helped convince him. Eisenhower became the Republican standard-bearer, and George E. Allen, Eisenhower's close friend, later wrote that Winchell had played a vital role in bringing about Ike's decision to run.

Although Eisenhower wasn't another FDR in Winchell's eyes, he was a reasonable facsimile. Accordingly, Walter displayed his "I Like Ike" banner in the column and particularly in his radio-TV newscast. And he remembered to leave a barbed farewell note for the departing President Truman: In October 1952, he released photostats of seven sworn affidavits allegedly made in 1944 by members of the Missouri Ku Klux Klan in support of the charge that Truman had once been a member of the Klan. The next day, Truman's press secretary denied the story.

Winchell's source was a Hearst executive. The Hearst papers had gathered the affidavits back in 1944, when Truman was running for Vice-President, and made a similar charge without releasing the affidavits. Winchell's release of the documents created an uproar. To this day, the truth or falsehood of the charge remains undetermined.

An enormously popular figure, Eisenhower easily defeated his Democratic opponent, Adlai Stevenson. Thus, Ike went to the White House —and so did Walter. At the inauguration, Winchell was on the White House steps broadcasting the event and greeting Ike and Mamie.

Eisenhower's administration began auspiciously with the settlement of the Korean War, but he was unable to halt McCarthy's guerrillas. At first, the President endeavored to appease McCarthy by outdoing him. The White House announced that 9,600 government employees had been dismissed or had resigned as a result of Eisenhower's security program. It turned out though that only 11 had been dismissed for loyalty reasons, and no active Communist had been detected.

The glaring failure of Eisenhower's attempt at appeasement became evident when Senator McCarthy charged that though "Eisenhower was doing more than Truman in ousting security risks, . . . too many cases were ignored by the White House." In addition, McCarthy hammered at the administration's foreign policy. The President's response was a long silence.

Some people are driven by conscience; McCarthy was driven by spleen. Eventually he was driven to attack the U.S. Army, castigating General Ralph W. Zwicker, commanding officer at Camp Kilmer, for "shielding traitors and Communist conspirators." The army countered with a series of charges against McCarthy, Roy Cohn, and another associate, G. David Schine. Their differences were settled by a senatorial investigation. For thirty-six days, millions of television viewers witnessed a remarkable spectacle. McCarthy's published comments had helped to build him up, but the menacing sight of McCarthyism in action helped to tear him down. The TV cameras were his firing squad. McCarthy started the hearings as a roaring bully and ended as a forlorn figure mumbling, "what did I do wrong?" Within two weeks after the hearings began, the Gallup Poll disclosed a sudden drop in McCarthy's popularity.

On December 12, 1954, Winchell wrote, "*Newsweek* revealed that 'the public is thoroughly bored with the McCarthy controversy.' . . . That will explain why this column has been giving it a minimum of space." He explained his position in an editorial planned for his February 28, 1954, newscast:

> Mr. and Mrs. United States:
> The raging argument over Senator McCarthy (and his methods) brought me a lot of mail from people who want to know where I stand . . . I attacked McCarthy when he forgave the Nazis in the Malmédy massacre and at other times. I am for him in his fight against Communists. Many who hate McCarthy hate J. Edgar Hoover too. . . .
> I agree with McCarthy when he says the State Department was fooled on Red China. I think he is ridiculous when he attacks the integrity of General George Marshall. I think McCarthy is right in getting to the bottom of the army scandals. I think he is dead wrong when he impugns the honor of General Zwicker. Most Americans hate Communism more than they like McCarthy. But that's where he gets his strength. They back up his punch mainly because they all saw Alger Hiss (and Judy Coplon) get off with a slight slap on the wrist. The most a Red gets if convicted is five years for plotting the overthrow of our government by violence. You get six years (and more) for a stickup. . . . Of the twenty-four Reds convicted in New York some are still on the lam. There are less than 100 convictions all over the land—and fewer than 50 Reds are in jail. They are out on appeal, and some are still teaching in New York schools.
> McCarthy once asked, "How would YOU fight Communism?" . . . I say, "There is no *wrong* way of fighting a fire—or your country's enemy. I am on no man's team or in anyone's hip pocket. When I can no longer stand alone and unassisted I will tell my wife to get the wheelchair ready. . . .
> I'll be back with some advance news . . . on an oil company.

As this editorial indicates, Winchell's attempt to justify his position on McCarthy merely recapitulated the senator's own deviousness, slyly worded rhetoric, and belief that the end justified the means. Winchell argued, "There is no *wrong* way of fighting a fire." He was wrong, of course, and McCarthy proved it by fighting a fire with gasoline.

Winchell and the liberals had parted company three years before. Editorials like the foregoing represented his farewell to the antiliberals. By the end of 1954 he was politically alone. He never again was anchored to a party or a philosophy, though he remained an Eisenhower supporter.

After the smoke had cleared, Winchell showed me a newspaper clipping that quoted Russia's Gromyko denouncing Winchell as a "menace second only to the atomic bomb." He sighed, "This is my only medal from the McCarthy wars."

Incidentally, Winchell's promise to present "some advance news . . . on an oil company" exemplified a type of reporting that initiated a controversy at the time and continues to confuse people today. In an interview in November 1973, Walter Cronkite said that he had been asked to promote a uranium stock but had refused. "It was," he commented, "the kind of thing that Walter Winchell was doing almost every Sunday on his broadcasts—he was floating stocks." Similarly, on January 21, 1975, Robert Metz, a *New York Times* financial columnist, wrote:

> In the 1950s Walter Winchell, the late Broadway columnist, began touting stocks on his broadcasts. His tips invariably proved to be winners—no doubt because he had a considerable following. Listeners would hear the show on Sunday night, buy the recommended stock the next morning and the stock would move up in extraordinarily active trading. Mr. Winchell tended to recommend speculative stocks—securities with relatively thin trading markets—and this further assured the success of his predictions.
> He was halted under pressure and his era passed.

The fact is that Winchell never touted stocks. He reported information of a type published in several business publications, including the *Wall Street Journal* and the financial section of the *New York Times*. Usually, however, he reported the news first. Furthermore, he was not "halted under pressure"; he continued to report financial items until the end of his column-writing and newscasting days.

Only once did Winchell purchase a small amount of stock—*after* making public news about the company—and he lost money on it. However, one of Howard Hughes's aides, who was a major source of Winchell's Wall Street reports, took full advantage of his position. It was said that he made more than $500,000 in the market before Walter discovered that he was being used. Winchell often cautioned those who read and listened to his Wall Street news, "All of those on Wall Street are blind, but those who truly lack vision are the ones who are convinced they can see."

A few weeks after the collapse of McCarthyism, the *Post* lawsuit was settled. An announcer read a statement on the Winchell program:

> Walter Winchell has authorized ABC to state that he never said or meant to say over the air or in his newspaper column that the *New York Post* or its publisher or Mr. James A. Wechsler are Communists or sympathetic to Communism. If anything Mr. Winchell said was so construed, he regrets and withdraws it. The American Broadcasting Company also retracts any statements which were subject to such construction.

The Hearst Corporation agreed to print a similar retraction in its syndicated papers.

The *Post* whooped about the "abject retraction," while Walter shrugged it off as a mere legalistic token. He derived satisfaction from the severe punishment he had inflicted on his opponent after being knocked to his knees in the first round. Laughing, he said, "The *Post* got it in the balls, and it didn't cost me anything. Not a bad bargain." Winchell's employers had agreed to pay $30,000 to the *Post* to cover the legal expenses of bringing the suit and taking depositions.

Several days later Winchell asked ABC to expand and strengthen his libel insurance. The next morning he arrived at his ABC office feeling chipper after a sexual conquest and was stunned to learn that ABC balked at his request. Impulsively, he wrote a letter of resignation. His attorney cautioned, "Don't leave one job until you have another one." Winchell laughed. He was confident that ABC would reject his resignation and provide the additional libel protection. Besides, he expected offers from other networks. "What have I got to lose?" he said. A minute after submitting his resignation, he phoned Ernest Cuneo and fired him.

To Winchell's surprise, the ABC Board accepted his resignation, and his lifetime contract ended after four years. It was the biggest mistake of his career.

The ABC brass allowed Winchell to abrogate his contract for two reasons. First, they found their abject apology to the *Post* humiliating. More decisive, however, were Winchell's disappointing TV ratings. Walter confessed, "I don't like myself on television." Too many others apparently agreed with him. Over the years, I thought his clickety-clackety radio newscast was a great show. Yet, when he faced the television cameras, something happened. He appeared uneasy, stiff, and grim. He came across as a disjointed mechanical man, and he looked old. Ironically, the whole Winchell failed to live up to his exciting voice.

Winchell publicly proclaimed that he expected to change to "another network, probably NBC, and may even produce my own radio-TV program through my own company." This was pure bravado. He sat back and waited for the flood of offers that never came, though he eventually received a radio proposal from the Mutual Broadcasting Company.

A meeting was arranged between Winchell and General David Sarnoff, chairman of the board of RCA. It was cordial, and Sarnoff presented him with an autographed copy of a book he had written. But it produced no offer.

Then one day Winchell received a call from Frank Stanton, president of CBS, the network where Walter's longtime foe Ed Sullivan was a prime TV attraction. When he met Stanton, Winchell said, "Frank, I turned you down to stay with ABC seven years ago. Now here's your chance to turn me down. Would you consider me for things other than commentating—panels, quizzes, variety? I don't want to be off television." The response was. "Don't worry about a thing."

"I never heard from Frank after that," said Winchell. "I subsequently heard that when Sullivan learned about the talk, he threw a tantrum. I guess Frank decided to leave well enough alone."

Ed Sullivan vehemently denied this charge. He told a magazine writer, "In the case of Winchell, once he started something I was eager to tangle with him because I've never liked the guy very much."

Walter replied, "Translation: In the case of Winchell, once Walter started something I immediately copied it. I took Walter's column format after I publicly announced that I would never resort to such gossip—blah, blah, blah—and I even tried to copy his radio newscasts, but I flopped at it. And what I have never made public before—in fact I have denied it—is that it was Walter Winchell who recommended me in the early thirties to take over his microphone at CBS when Walter had a better offer to go on NBC for Lucky Strike. I finally took Mr. Winchell's style of emceeing benefits—and when Walter made personal appearances at the Paramount, I just loved the way he introduced the various celebrities sitting out front. So I put it on television and made a lot of money."

After being rebuffed by CBS and NBC, Walter accepted Mutual's radio-only deal at less than half his ABC salary. His professional setback was followed by a shattering private calamity. Winchell's son had joined the U.S. Marine Corps after dropping out of school. Like many sons of famous fathers, he was obviously searching for an identity, a life of his own. Walter, Jr., was a handsome, bright, and energetic youngster. Yet he had a brooding, sometimes mercurial quality. He had been involved in a number of minor episodes that his parents dismissed as schoolboy pranks. Walter, Sr., loved his son but rarely had time for him. Eventually young Walter dropped out of the marines and went to Africa in an attempt to build a business career and work out his destiny. The boy returned from overseas showing a marked personality change. He spoke of having been tortured during his brief career in the marines, recounted wild experiences in Africa, and began making the rounds with a woman he described as the daughter of a Nazi general. The Winchells urged him to stop seeing her. He not only refused but threatened to marry her. Winchell responded by changing the locks on his doors and deciding to disown his son. The alienation was complete.

Winchell never understood how his benign neglect could have contributed to his children's difficulties. Nor did he understand that his rash decisions could have been damaging. Time and again, when the children were grown, he would stop handing out spending money and cancel their credit cards for wrongs real or imagined. Just as rashly, he would change his mind and reinstate the financial favors. In the end, his love for his children only intensified his bitter disappointment in them.

It was not long before the ratchets of reality stopped grinding for young Walter. He married the Nazi general's daughter and soon thereafter began appearing in public wearing a Nazi uniform. He would goosestep into a Third Avenue bar and shout, "Heil Hitler!" Inevitably, he was involved in brawls. One night he shoved the jagged edge of a broken beer bottle into someone's face. The victim lost the sight of one eye, and Winchell paid a substantial sum to settle the case.

One day Mrs. Winchell called Arnold Forster and urged him to come and see her as soon as possible. When Arnold arrived, her distress was obvious. "I want you to start a denaturalization proceeding against my son," she announced.

Forster was not sure he had heard her correctly. "I thought," he subsequently told me, "that she was out of her mind."

Mrs. Winchell continued, "He's a Nazi, an anti-American. He wears a Nazi uniform. I think his citizenship should be taken away."

Forster patiently sought to explain that it was legally impossible to denaturalize a native-born American. In retrospect, Arnold said, "I don't think I was able to convince her."

Walter was more grimly realistic. He wanted to commit his son to a mental institution. In time, Walter, Jr., did undergo psychiatric therapy, but to little apparent avail. Eventually he drifted out to the West Coast and spent the next few years in a series of odd jobs, including a column-writing stint, much to his father's displeasure. To my knowledge, Winchell never saw his son's two children, though he was a doting grandfather to the daughter born to Walda, who had remarried.

Winchell's panacea for private despair was work. This was one of the paradoxes of his existence because the ordeals of his work helped engender his personal misery. In 1956, he embarked on a campaign for Eisenhower's re-election, carried on a running feud with his syndicate, and openly broke with Sherman Billingsley, thereby exiling himself from the Stork Club.

The tiff with Billingsley was initiated when the Stork's cigarette girl placed two packs of Winchell's sponsor's cigarettes on his Stork Club table instead of the brand Billingsley was paid to plug by putting them on customers' tables. As a consequence, Billingsley fired her. Walter was furious. He spent the next day getting another job for the cigarette girl and boycotted the Stork. The *New York Post* gleefully headlined that Billingsley had taken down Winchell's photo from its position of honor in the Stork foyer. A few days later, the news was flashed that the photo was back on the wall, and Billingsley soothingly explained, "It's clear that Winchell is angry about something. But he's as welcome here as any customer." The spat was eventually patched up, but their friendship had been tarnished since the time of the Josephine Baker incident, and it remained less than idyllic.

At the same time, Winchell was feuding again with his syndicate for deleting certain items from his columns. As usual, he threatened to quit. He was especially disturbed by the blue-penciling of his description of the Duchess of Windsor, whom he disliked because of her rumored anti-Semitism. He called her the "Dookess of Tookis."

Walter not only snuggled up to Eisenhower but launched strident attacks against Adlai Stevenson, the other White House contender. When Winchell capriciously compared Stevenson to Christine Jorgenson, the transsexual, his infuriated radio sponsor, Seaboard Drug, decided to quit. Walter struck back by sniping at the defecting sponsor in his column. The president of the drug company that had bankrolled him finally exploded, "Malicious, libelous, and untrue. The man has gone mad." Walter's Mutual Broadcasting System newscast lingered for a while, then withered and vanished.

Winchell's pro-Eisenhower rampage trampled Drew Pearson for suggesting that Eisenhower, who had had a coronary, might be physically unable to survive another term. In a column entitled "The S.O.B.," Walter described Pearson as a son of a bitch in more than a thousand words.

At the autumnal age of fifty-nine, Winchell again sought a television news show. For the first time in his career, he allowed agents to represent him. They came up with an NBC-TV variety-show offer. Winchell resigned himself to the assignment primarily to obtain a television showcase for himself.

The advent of the new show started a progression of manic reactions. Unavailability had been part of the Winchell mystique. Now he suddenly became available for everything and everybody. Instead of merely presiding at the Stork, he rolled around town like the marble in a pinball machine, lighting things up here and there. At Lindy's he emitted a shrill fingers-in-mouth whistle to attract the attention of startled diners and suddenly began introducing celebrities. He walked uninvited onto the Paramount stage, where Sinatra was appearing to launch his new movie, and introduced several performers. He spoke to any newspaperman who would listen, even high school editors. Walter was both preparing himself for his TV emceeing chore and giving the show a promotional buildup, aided and abetted by his column.

Just before the show went on, Walter told the studio audience,

"After all these years, I'm back where I started from—vaudeville." The first show was a good one and attracted generally favorable reviews. At the postpremiere party, Winchell thanked me for carrying the burden of the column while he was busy with the variety show; then he added, "I'm going to prove something to that no-talent TV success, Ed Sullivan," pronouncing "success" as though the first letter were "f."

Judy Garland came to Walter's premiere party, as did Harry Cohn, president of Columbia Pictures, and several other luminaries. Winchell's daughter, Walda, was there, as well as Mrs. Winchell, who was making a rare public appearance. She sat quietly at her table, hardly uttering a word, and was obviously ill at ease when her husband introduced her to the assembled guests.

Incidentally, in a *Look*-magazine interview, Mrs. Winchell said, "Yes, I know Walter, but even after 33 years of marriage, I find him unpredictable," then offered a bittersweet comment: "I refuse to pose for pictures with him. Whenever I see a wife beside a notable man in a photograph, she always looks like The Wife. I want to look like his sweetheart."

The opening show had a high rating, and Winchell was once again a cockadoodling rooster. Unfortunately, the ratings dipped for the next two programs, and then dived. After the fourth show, the sponsor notified Walter that the program would be dropped when his option came up five weeks later. Winchell received $75,000 in severance pay.

Walter, who seemed to have trouble adjusting to reality, called a press conference to announce the news. He was quoted in *Time* magazine: "The sponsors love the show. I've never lost a sponsor in my life. I've been on the air 29 years. I said to Bobby Sarnoff, the president of NBC, 'Bobby, you knew from the beginning I didn't want to go back to small time. I never asked to do this show.'" Winchell also pledged a crusade to "expose the ratings system."

After the short-lived variety show, Walter bounced back with a third TV try, once again on ABC. It was a dramatic series called "The Walter Winchell File," purportedly based on his experiences but actually fictional. The show turned out to be another speedy disaster. Subsequently, his column raged against the tyranny of ratings, the same ratings he had quoted gleefully when he had been king of radio hill.

Privately, he was more subdued. He talked about retiring, confessed that he was becoming jaded with his work, and sighed, "Television has changed everything."

In time, Winchell scored his one and only TV hit in a minor role—as narrator for "The Untouchables" series, in which his contribution was confined to his voice.

The spring of 1958 was enlivened by an unexpected rumpus involving Jack Paar. I enjoyed the Paar show and plugged it in the column. One evening Paar showed up at the Stork Club and was disappointed to learn that Winchell wasn't there. He told Sherman Billingsley, "I'd like to shake hands with Winchell. You really do not appreciate him until you read his many imitators."

But a few evenings later, Elsa Maxwell, who made a business of giving parties, collecting celebrities, and attracting attention by needling famous people, appeared on the Paar show. Elsa, then seventy-four years of age, cackled a few cracks about Winchell. Because she got laughs, Paar was unable to resist and joined in tossing a string of firecrackers at Walter.

I wrote several frivolous paragraphs in reply to Paar and Maxwell. Winchell, who was in Hollywood, called after he read my comments and plaintively inquired, "Tell me, Herman, why am I mad at Jack Paar?" Apparently he had not seen or been told about the Paar and Maxwell carping. When I explained, he said, "Who really cares about an ingrate and a smelly old cunt?"

Soon after, Paar and Maxwell became nastier. She screamed, "He's never voted and never registered. Is that a good patriotic American or not?" Paar chimed in, "Walter is a has-been. Many Broadway people say Winchell is a heel. What worries me is the hole in his soul. His orchids are poison ivy in a crackpot. This type of guy wraps himself in the American flag. He wears it like a bathrobe."

At this point, the Winchell-Paar feud became front-page news. Winchell demanded a retraction and said he could prove he had voted by a 1956 *Mirror* photo showing him in a voting booth. Paar retracted, briefly flashed the *Mirror* photo to his TV audience, and continued his sniping at Walter.

Ironically, Paar later disclosed that he himself had never voted "until Bobby Kennedy told me to do so," and it also came out that Elsa Maxwell was another nonvoter.

After the demise of "The Walter Winchell File," Walter returned to vaudeville. He was signed for two weeks at Las Vegas's Hotel Tropicana at $35,000 a week. His opening was heralded by billboards for several hundred miles around Vegas, as well as by Winchell's commercials for himself on local radio stations. In the show, Winchell, the old-time hoofer, soft-shoed, mamboed, and even hazarded a buck-and-wing while nearly surrounded by showgirls showing their assets. His premiere attracted a full house and brought a shower of congratulatory wires from celebrities, including several from the underworld. But only three or four stars came to his opening, notably Milton Berle and George Raft. Frank Sinatra reserved three tables but failed to show up.

Walter was particularly disappointed by Sinatra's absence. At the time, he and Frank were spending a great deal of time together. When they were apart, they sent each other gag wires signed "Sam" and "Max." Winchell had helped to make Sinatra a star and later spurred his comeback. During this period, almost every Winchell column carried laudatory comments about Sinatra. Sometime later, Winchell heard that Sinatra had said Walter was "full of shit." "I don't believe Frank said that," Winchell commented, but they were never buddies again.

Soon after Winchell's opening, business slumped. Before long, he was playing to a half-empty club. It was an embarrassing, albeit well-paid, flop.

By the summer of 1959, the old Winchell fire was obviously burning low. He spent hours reminiscing about past triumphs and rarely appeared at his old haunts. With each passing month, the drive that had powered him diminished markedly. When he attended a Broadway show or restaurant, he was usually alone. And he looked older than his sixty-two years.

When *Time* magazine scornfully dismissed him as an "aging lion," Winchell flared up briefly and clawed at his tormentor. Years before, he would have left the weekly a bloody pulp. The aging lion was becoming a pussycat.

=15=
The Humpty Dumpty Giant

The rainbow world of Walter Winchell gradually began changing to a joyless gray in the mid-1950s. Its bleakness was clearly evident early in 1960. His once mighty thousand-newspaper syndicate had dwindled to fewer than 150 papers. At first he was bewildered, saying, "I'm still writing the same type of columns. I'm still doing what I have always done. I don't know what the editors want. I really don't know what's happening."

The relentless decline eventually had a numbing effect. Bored and indifferent, he made little effort to reverse the creeping paralysis.

At this time, Walter's star-making power had its last hurrah. And it was purely accidental. David Zaretsky, a friend, asked me to plug an unknown singer who had a minor role in a forthcoming musical, *I Can Get It for You Wholesale*. As a favor to Zaretsky, I gave Barbra Streisand a boost in the column. Neither I nor Walter had ever heard her sing. At any rate, after she became a star, Walter took credit for discovering her.

Privately, he wistfully discussed his fading career. "Television is destroying New York nightlife," he accurately noted, "and the talk shows are giving people the show-biz patter and prattle that belong in my column." Other career-depressing factors included the budding sexual revolution, which spawned publications offering names and details of the kind of scandals Winchell had reported as prim "blind" items. Then there was the wearing effect of time itself. "You can't be number one forever," Winchell would say with a shrug.

The major career depressant, however, was his inability to adapt his newscasting style to television. He had another brief fling as a TV commentator in 1960. An interview with presidential candidate Richard Nixon was a feature of the initial program.

The following week, candidate John F. Kennedy rejected an invitation to appear on his show. Walter did not forget the snub.

While rehearsing for the TV newscast, Winchell told reporters, "I'm happy to be back, but get this straight. I was never fired five years ago; I resigned. And what did it get me? Five years of not being on the air as a commentator. Actually, I was the most overpaid commentator on the air. . . . I've been looking at the boys on TV eating jelly beans. It's not their fault. The networks put on the handcuffs and everyone sounds alike. My sponsor wants me to be the old Winchell, and when you've got the sponsor in your corner, you can't help but go out and fight."

But bravado failed to prevent another quick flop. This one was his final appearance as a television commentator.

Nevertheless, the old Winchell flared again after John F. Kennedy's wafer-thin victory in 1960. The advent of the Kennedy Administration was the beginning of Winchell's last hurrah.

Articulate, witty, young, and handsome, President Kennedy was the perfect camera subject, and his televised news conferences enchanted the nation. He was a star as well as a President. Besides, Kennedy worked hard to befriend journalists. He socialized with them, sought their counsel, and was extremely cooperative. But as the President's involvement in controversial issues expanded, the romantic glow dimmed and he became the focus of criticism. Inexorably, when the Kennedy Administration clearly indicated it intended "to manage the news," all hell broke loose.

The *Herald Tribune*, for example, reported on its front page, "The Kennedy Administration has administered almost as many lumps to the Washington press corps in 19 months as did the three previous Administrations combined."

From the first, Winchell was not a Kennedy admirer. He privately scoffed, "How can I take this kid seriously? He was always a playboy. He spends half his time screwing every girl that comes around. I've seen lots of nothings like him around the Stork Club and other places where the sons of rich men go to waste their time and money."

Therefore, when Kennedy tried to escape the limits of normal political institutions by managing the news, Winchell pounced. The March

1962 column entitled "The Kennedys vs. the Press" reverberated with some of the old Winchell thunder:

I say the Administration's attempt to transform the American press into a propaganda weapon is as iniquitous as it is perilous. I say that the procedure by which this is being accomplished is contrary to the traditions of this democracy. And unchallenged, the liberties of the American people will be destroyed by default. All too often JFK has acted as if he were elected Publisher of the American Press.

We are told that modern warfare requires the manipulation of the news, but we are given no assurance that our democratic system of checks and balances will continue to control it.

It is important to note that the Administration's censorship has also extended to Congress. The historic fact is that Congress has the constitutionally guaranteed right to know anything about the Republic. Unless Congress has the facts it cannot pass intelligent laws. Yet the Administration has ordered the Department of Defense to present to Congress and the people only those facts it wishes Congress and the people to hear.

The stunning fact is that the Administration has made it clear it intends to shut down all sources of government information any time it decides there is an international crisis. Since we live in a time of constant global crisis it is sickening to think of the implications.

The President's power is all-pervasive, almost beyond the belief of the average citizen. There is hardly a single function of our national existence that is not touched by White House decisions. But the Bill of Rights made it clear that the press is not an extension of any politician's power. On the contrary, the press must serve as a watchdog against the abuse of power by politicians. There was no backdoor to Independence Hall, Philadelphia, in 1776 and there is no place for trap doors in the ramparts of our national defense today.

The Germans and the Italians once voted away their liberties —and the jagged wrecks of their public buildings eventually became monuments to that sorry day of their respective histories.

Over the years the free press has critically fought invaders. Lies and the arbitrary power of officials have been its foes. The challenge represented by such enemies is both formidable and perilous. And the soldiers engaged in the struggle are ordinary extraordinary newspapermen. For a newspaperman to report the truth is a public duty. For this government to withhold the truth is a crime.

If the American press ever becomes a weapon in the hands of government officials, then it will be a weapon aimed at the heads and hearts of the American people.

Winchell's ringing defense of freedom of the press was but one thrust in his assault against the Kennedy Administration in general. Other targets included pro-Kennedy papers and columnists, Bobby Kennedy, and several other JFK aides, especially Arthur Schlesinger, Jr. Schlesinger, Winchell claimed, was "haunted by intellectual snobbery, dominated by arrogance . . . as power-mad as he is venomous . . . a threat to fundamental American concepts." When Schlesinger offered his resignation as a result of the attacks, Kennedy reassured him, "Don't worry about it. All they are doing is shooting at me through you."

For the first time in years, the Kennedy controversy embroiled Winchell in a headline-making event. It attracted comments from editorialists and columnists around the country. *Time* and *Newsweek* devoted full pages to the dispute. Winchell told me, "Thanks, Herman, for making an old man a big shot again."

Some journalists contended that Winchell was miffed at the President because he wasn't invited to the White House. Columnist George Sokolsky wrote, "Winchell doesn't like Bobby Kennedy because Bobby went on the Jack Paar show."

Actually, Walter's anger at Bobby Kennedy was based on the fact that the nation's Attorney General had attempted to coerce Hearst executive Richard Berlin into suppressing anti-Kennedy comments in the Winchell column. Such pressure was not an unusual tactic for Bobby. Accompanied by two husky companions, he once appeared unannounced in the office of *Look*-magazine editor William B. Arthur and sought to suppress an upcoming article by making a series of threats. The editor listened, then ordered publication of the article.

On the day Kennedy was assassinated, Winchell called me. "I'd like a paragraph for tonight's column. You have fifteen minutes." Within the prescribed time, I called him and read:

Every President desires unity, but no Chief Executive worth his salt demands blind support. It is hardly news to note that this reporter disagreed politically with JFK. But our respect for the

Presidency remains constant. No American can contemplate the Presidency without a sense of solemnity and humility—solemnity for the proud inheritor of a noble tradition—humility in the thought that Presidents are the slaves of their responsibilities. We have often observed that in time of profound tragedy there are no words. For Mrs. Kennedy and her children there are no words—only the deep, deep silence that follows the bugler's notes—a silence that expresses reverence, faith and hope.

Winchell listened and then commented, "That's pretty, but it isn't the way I really feel. I don't want to be a hypocrite." He made no comment about the Kennedy tragedy.

His reaction to Kennedy's death depressed me. By this time, I was fully aware of his abysmal bitterness, not only against Kennedy but against the world in general. Winchell had cut himself adrift. The liberals had abandoned him years before. Eventually he became disenchanted with the right-wingers. Thus deprived of an ideological anchor, he became an island of one, with nothing left to fight for except his own professional survival.

And then the furies gathered.

After the 114-day printers' strike of 1962-63, the *Mirror* ceased publication on October 15, 1963. I was at the receptionist's desk when the staff learned that the paper had died. Shock and grief were the initial reactions. Not even Winchell had known about the collapse in advance.

One of the *Mirror*'s top executives was reportedly in bed with a famed movie star when he learned of the paper's expiration. "Well," he said, "I've been fucked twice in one hour. One good. One bad."

Winchell's private comment about the demise of the paper: "My flagship has been sunk." In the final edition, it was announced that some of the *Mirror*'s features, including Winchell's column, would be published in the *Journal-American*, the Hearst afternoon paper.

At the *Mirror*, the column had been edited with tender loving care. Winchell's new editors were careless and indifferent. They slashed his copy at random.

The departure of the *Mirror* was followed by the disappearance of another landmark in the Winchell landscape. Early in October 1965, a sign was posted at 3 East Fifty-third Street: "Stork Club closed. Will relocate." Only a few weeks before, Sherman Billingsley had undergone treatment for a heart ailment at Roosevelt Hospital. On the same floor, at the same time, Winchell was undergoing a checkup. It was Walter's first hospital visit as a patient. Neither man was aware that the other was a patient.

Walter never saw Sherman again. He was aware that Billingsley in his final desperate months, ailing and broke, was borrowing heavily. He never asked Walter for a penny. And Winchell never offered a penny.

A year after the Stork closed, Billingsley died. Winchell wrote, "Many who accepted his free victuals, perfume, gems, expensive clothing and other gifts forsook him. He lost the fortune he hoped would keep him and his family in his Sunset Years . . . $7,000,000."

Late in 1965 the struggling *Journal-American* instituted a drastic cost-cutting program. Winchell, along with Dorothy Kilgallen and other columnists, had his column and salary slashed. Walter was cut to three short columns weekly and was given less than half the space the column had occupied in the *Mirror*.

I learned that Winchell could no longer afford me several days before Thanksgiving in 1965. As usual, he relayed the bad news via his secretary. After twenty-seven years, the separation was as swift and as drastic as a surgical incision. The pain came afterward. When I asked about severance pay, I learned, again secondhand, that "he couldn't afford it," that I had "received severance pay twelve years ago," that he was "too upset to think straight," that he was "suffering from a gum infection."

I listened with disbelief, surprise mingling with bitterness. In retrospect, my surprise, under the circumstances, was surprising. After all, I was familiar with his rampant feelings of insecurity, his adherence to the primitive vaudeville financial code of "no play, no pay," and his niggardly attitude toward severance pay. One secretary, fired after seven years, had to threaten to sue before Winchell reluctantly gave her severance pay. Another was compelled to threaten legal action before he collected $900 from the all-cash millionaire. Once when he received $12,000 for a *Collier's* article written by Ernest Cuneo, he informed Cuneo that he was donating the $12,000 to the Runyon Fund; then he added, "Ernie, I bet you must hate me for this."

And yet, this unpredictable man was capable of generosity. Over the years I was well paid for a newspaperman, and now and then, he surprised me with a bonus or an impulsive raise.

Our working relationship was a good one. A prime factor was expediency: Winchell needed my typewriter. By and large, he was incurious about the state of my health or the vagaries of my personal life, but when I was bedded by the flu or some other ailment, he would call and express the hope that I would soon be well enough to resume working. In many ways he treated me with a tactful consideration generally foreign to his character. During my long association with Winchell, he never uttered a single harsh word to me in person. On the contrary, when we were together, he frequently praised something I had written. His editorial criticism was always relayed via his secretary.

Nevertheless, when a job is terminated after twenty-seven years, one has little inclination for psychological ruminations, and that is no time for healing memories. I felt like a crimeless victim and the logical target of my fury was Winchell. Time and again he had assured me, "Don't worry, kid, as long as I have it, you'll have it." Well, I was no longer a kid; I was the father of two children, one of whom was then attending college. Winchell had it—but I didn't. My only thought was "Where in hell is my kindly benefactor?"

My wife sarcastically observed: "I thought you were like a son to Winchell." And I replied: "And he was like a son of a bitch to me."

As the days passed, other emotions broke through the fury at Walter. I was staggered by a loss of self-esteem and consequent anger at myself for indulging in years of delusions about Winchell. I could hardly forgive myself for rejecting all the lush public-relations offers in the past. There were no such offers after leaving Winchell, only condolences.

The fury subsided within a few months as a promising new career opened up. An icy shot of hopeful reality provided a bracing contrast to my initial despair when I received a contract to write Drew Pearson's biography. Finally, I could reasonably answer the question of why had I remained with Winchell for twenty-seven years?

The plain and simple answer is that I *loved* my job. For the greater part of twenty-seven years, I relished the reflected glory and reveled in the power. I was as romantic about being a newspaperman as Winchell was. For me, it was a dream life. Writing something that would be read or heard by millions within twenty-four hours was a never ending thrill. And the exhilaration of participating in the anti-Nazi and other Winchell crusades was beyond monetary value. To this day, when I read or hear about some glaring injustice, I regret not having the Winchell column and broadcast with which to strike back.

After all these years, I even miss the throbbing tension of the daily deadline.

Oddly enough, I rarely regretted the lack of recognition. The most important people in my life knew what I was doing: my family, my friends, and myself. In common with aides to other prominent and powerful individuals, I knew enough of fame in the raw to welcome the warm and comfortable serenity of obscurity. The Winchell experience was exciting, and it was fun. Of course, if I had to do it all over again, I probably would make some changes. But I wouldn't have missed it for the world.

Christmas Day of 1965, however, was neither jolly nor thrilling. I called the Winchell office to convey holiday greetings to his secretary. She was distraught. "WW is so bored, he doesn't want to open his Christmas gifts. But he took a few handkerchiefs. The tension of having him around the office every day is making me sick. Mrs. Winchell called and offered her sympathy. I have very little to do, and the boss is probably thinking, 'What am I paying her for?' "

At the time, the New York newspapers were paralyzed by another strike, this one for 140 days. It eventually forced the *Herald Tribune,* the *World-Telegram and the Sun,* and the *Journal-American* to merge into the hybrid *World Journal Tribune.* For the new paper, Winchell was reduced to being a once-a-week columnist.

Before 1965 ended, I received a letter from Winchell.

To Whom it May Concern:
Herman Klurfeld of 331 Southwood Circle, Syosset, N.Y., has been in my employ for 27 years. During that time his duties consisted of research and in some instances help in the preparation of my radio and television broadcasts and newspaper themes.

I have always found him to be thoroughly honest, capable and reliable.

I have no hesitancy in recommending him.

Very truly yours,
WALTER WINCHELL

The superficial letter of reference was an unusual confession—for Winchell. He had never publicly admitted that I was an employee. Thus this admission in writing coupled with his concession that I helped write his columns and newscasts was a cataclysmic Winchell revelation. Presumably, he considered the letter my severance pay.

On November 6, 1966, the twentieth anniversary of the founding of the Runyon Fund was celebrated at the elegant Rainbow Room. It attracted well-groomed socialites as well as such celebrities as Bennett Cerf, Arthur Godfrey, and John Daly. Walter did not attend, but the bandstand was dominated by photographs of Runyon and Winchell flanked by flower-filled urns. It caused one reporter to remark, "It looks like a wake."

A wake *was* held for the *World Journal Tribune* several months after it had risen from the ashes. With the paper's death, Winchell's column, which had hung on by a once-a-week thread, disappeared from his hometown for the first time in forty years. A few days later, the *New York Times* carried a mournful essay about the "decline and fall of the gossip columnist." It quoted a top executive of the deceased paper: "Frankly, our general feeling is that Winchell was passé. In his genre I think he was the best but I don't think he has substantial reader appeal any more."

When Walter learned that the Hearst management was planning to drop his column, he promptly arranged a meeting with Hearst executives, including one of the Hearst's sons. Walter abjectly pleaded for his job, and once he actually broke down and wept. After some discussion, he won a reprieve.

From that time on, the man who had defied and defeated his publisher during his glory years enshrined William Randolph Hearst in his column. He published fond anecdotes about him and publicly revered Hearst as "A beautiful boss. A beautiful boss."

When, early in March 1967, Arnold Forster visited Winchell, Walter admitted that he was "shopping frantically for papers to print my stuff." At least a dozen times during the conversation, he mentioned that he was approaching his seventieth birthday. At one point he lowered his voice and gravely confided, "Did you know I recently had several polyps removed from my rectum? I thought I had cancer. In the hospital, I was ready to meet my maker. No one was with me. I was alone. All alone." Before Forster left, Walter begged him "Help me land a TV job." Several days later, he sent a note thanking Arnold for trying to help.

"For the first time," Forster later said, "he seemed human."

At about the same time, Walter wrote to publicist Ade Kahn:

My new contract which was suggested by the *Journal* publisher, was signed last winter. I get a hefty severance pay ($35,000) if terminated. I didn't know until J. Kingsbury Smith informed me that as an independent contractor I DID NOT RATE SEVERANCE PAY! (OY!). . . . Trying to sell a movie and am set for a few TV pilot narration jobs. I forgot to add: also a $35,000 life insurance policy. A gift from my bosses.   WW

The pathetic letter was among the last-gasp brags of a dying man, personally and professionally.

Beginning in 1966, the Winchell output was reminiscent in style and content of the *Vaudeville News* and *Daily Graphic*. In doing this exercise in self-travesty, he ignored the world around him, writing about himself and the past as well as the show-business inanities that had captivated readers in the 1920s.

In April 1967, a seventieth-birthday party was tendered to Walter by two press agents. Many old friends and associates who were invited didn't bother to attend. Some guests found the affair embarrassing. "His party was pathetic," a press agent recalled. "He didn't stop gabbing. Still believes his own lies. Bob Sylvester, the official host, came late. Darryl Zanuck was there and some of his columnar cronies: Louis Sobol, Earl Wilson, Jack O'Brian. Walter was so grateful, it made me sick."

During the party, Winchell was surprised by a congratulatory wire from the Ed Sullivans. Winchell wired back his thanks.

Finally he gained a New York outlet in *Variety*. The young staffers with whom he exchanged cordial greetings on his visits to the weekly's midtown office derided him as a senile has-been after he had left.

"Winchell's office," Ernest Cuneo told me, "has become like something out of *Sunset Boulevard*. For no reason, a state of euphoria exists. He thinks nothing has changed. When he was in Chicago, he confided to me, 'Nobody has my phone number.' Well, who in hell wants it?"

Cuneo added, "Herman, you did the right thing. Both of us are better off without him. I don't even miss the $100,000 a year—or his vile language. Winchell owes me $900. He promised to pay me $300 a week to help him write a TV show. Hasn't paid me. He says, "When I'll get it, you'll get it.' "

The stench of rotting pride was evident in Winchell's full-page ad in *Variety* pleading with any New York newspaper, including the *New York Post,* to publish his column.

Shortly after Walter had received his birthday wire from the Sullivans, the *Ladies' Home Journal* published an interview with Ed Sullivan wherein he confessed:

> During my years on the *New York Daily News*, I continued my rivalry with Winchell. I wore myself out trying to catch and surpass him. No matter which way I turned, there was Winchell in my way. He invented the Broadway column and wrote it better than anybody. His sources of information were fantastic. You must remember there was a time when he could move governments. Any columnist had to run in his shadow. Me included. Winchell and I haven't spoken to each other in years. But I wish we'd continued to be friends. He's the best columnist of his kind who ever lived.

When, a few months later, Walter spotted Sullivan and his wife in a restaurant, he walked over to greet them. Sullivan rose and returned the cordiality with a handshake. Mrs. Sullivan smiled and said to him, "You look great. What's all this bunk about you being seventy?"

"Sylvia," Walter laughed, "you are now looking at the worst advertisement for clean living you ever did see."

"Seventy-shmeventy," Mrs. Sullivan cracked. "You're not seventy. You're two thirty-fives."

They exchanged snapshots of grandchildren and reminisced.

As Walter departed, he said to Ed, "Let's not be separated for thirty-five years again."

The following week, Sullivan introduced Walter on his popular television show.

Two days after his Sullivan-show appearance, I was startled to get a call from Winchell. We had not seen or spoken to each other for two years, but he launched into a monologue as if time and circumstances never existed. I had an eerie feeling that the clocks had been turned back as he yammered, "Arthur Godfrey tried to take the Runyon Fund from me, but I beat him. He's just another ingrate, Herman. I hear you're doing great. How's your family? I got a press card from the *Daily News*. I'm doing the town with Jimmy Breslin. I'm on my way back. They want my column regularly for a new paper. It will feature all the displaced columnists. I'm coming back, kid, just as if nothing had happened. Can you help me?"

His voice had some of its old frenzy, but it was sending echoes around an empty, illusory world. Sadly, it was not the old Winchell. It was an old man named Winchell. I said I would try to help, but I never could bring myself to do it.

Winchell was one of Johnny Carson's guests on Carson's October 25, 1967, show. Backstage he talked incessantly. Finally, after the appearances of Dick Cavett, Tammy Grimes, and Aretha Franklin interspersed with fifteen commercials, Winchell was introduced at 12:40. He appeared in his special uniform: blue suit, blue shirt, blue tie, gray fedora. During the eight-minute interview, he praised a new Broadway show, called producer David Merrick cowardly for criticizing critics, damned union leaders for killing several New York newspapers, said he was writing a book that would reveal why Dorothy Kilgallen died, attacked Bobby Kennedy, blamed the Lindsay Administration for preventing New York City's police from cracking down on criminals in various minority groups, said that the Runyon Fund had raised more than $30 million, handed Carson a $10,000 donation from the Runyon Fund to Carson's alma mater, the University of Nebraska, for the university's cancer-research program, and finished with a creaky ten second soft shoe routine to the tune of "Tea for Two."

Carson handled him beautifully and appeared respectful before the "grand old man." How Winchell must hate that image, I thought. He had built his career on being the "bad little boy."

Several weeks later he appeared on another NBC television show, "Stagedoor Johnny," a nostalgic throwback to the 1920s. Walter's bit consisted of singing the oldie "Makin' Whoopee," of all things. It was embarrassing. Still another embarrassing incident happened at the Palace, where day after day Walter intruded on the Eddie Fisher-Buddy Hackett act. Finally, the manager of the theater ordered him to stop the interruptions after Buddy Hackett humiliated him onstage. "He used to be the Lion of Broadway," Hackett said, "now he's a pussycat. Here pussy! Here pussy!" The same Buddy Hackett used to call the Winchell office pleading for plugs when he was a struggling comic.

On November 22, 1967, *Variety* carried a social note:

> Walter Winchell's daughter, Walda, will be married, probably in New York, to Texas insurance man L. E. Gilbert. They met in Arizona only six weeks ago. She was previously married to hotel man Hyatt von Dehn and has a daughter from that marriage.

Walter wanted the income from his memoirs to go to his grand-daughter, Mary Elizabeth Faith. Doubleday was supposed to be his publisher, but it dropped the project. Years ago, when I urged Walter to write a book, he chuckled, "I can't write a book. I can't write the truth about myself." He was right.

When I mentioned Winchell's comment to Ernest Cuneo, he observed, "Walter doesn't *know* the truth about himself." That was true enough. So much of the Winchell story is based on what he wrote and said—and what he said and wrote was so often written by others—that it was impossible for him to tell the truth about himself.

Besides, Walter was never a listener. Leonard Lyons once cracked, "He hasn't hea:d a human voice in thirty years." Nor was he interested in other people, except as they related to his career. Consequently, a Winchell self-portrait must be a sketch of his illusions.

As it turned out, in his autobiography, Winchell makes a vain effort to define and justify himself.

Alone, anguished, confused, he pursues the demon of self-scrutiny by denying his McCarthyism, rationalizing other blunders, and losing himself in a maze of self-deceptions and omissions. He forgets salient features of his prime stories: Lepke, the *New York Post*, Jack Paar, Cissy Patterson, President Kennedy, Josephine Baker, the anti-Nazi crusade, the Runyon Fund, and many others.

Incredibly, he neglects to mention his son and daughter Walda, Variety's Sime Silverman, who was central to the early Winchell career, Irving Hoffman, his closest friend for many years. Ed Weiner, who made the rounds with him for over a quarter-century, Arnold Forster, who marshalled his campaign against Nazism here and abroad—and Herman Klurfeld, All in all, a melancholy exercise.

While Winchell soared with the fantasy of a resurgent career, his estranged son, in his own flight from reality, attempted suicide on Christmas in 1967. If Walter was aware of the tragic incident, he did not mention it to his friends. After the suicide attempt, young Walter underwent therapy for about four months at a California institution.

Early in 1968, Walter's Hearst reprieve ran out and he began shopping around for another syndicate. He approached John Osenenko, then president of the Bell Syndicate, and was turned down. Osenenko later told me, "Winchell's more trouble than he's worth. Why doesn't he quit?" Eventually, Walter signed with the McNaught Syndicate.

Later that year, he secured a daily New York outlet in the *Daily*

Column, a newspaper that provided a haven for columnists rendered homeless in New York by the death of four dailies. Winchell received $24 a week for his column and was delighted with the opportunity. Many of his columns, however, were repeats of old ones. He played reporter by covering student riots at Columbia University, where he was knocked down, and race riots in Washington, D.C. While visiting the nation's capital, he spent a few hours with Drew Pearson. Pearson later recalled the meeting: "Winchell was so forlorn. He was eager for friends, anyone who could help him. I felt sorry for him."

One summer weekend in 1968, Arnold Forster and I walked into the Montauk Manor hotel on Long Island to meet a friend. As we strolled through the lobby, I noticed someone who looked familiar. At first, I was not certain that the puffy-faced old man sitting there was Winchell. As we approached, he lowered the *New York Times* and without rising from his chair, extended his hand. He appeared slightly bewildered, and his voice was heavy with weariness. After a few clumsy pleasantries, we walked away. Old age hadn't crept up on him; it had pounced with a flying leap. For days afterward, the memory of him sitting there disturbed me. I had seen so many like him in Miami Beach and other havens for retirees—sitting, snoozing, waiting for the next meal, or for death.

Early in October Winchell began complaining about abdominal pains. He had the typical hypochondriac's fear of a doctor, but the pain persisted, so he checked into Roosevelt Hospital for tests to determine whether he had cancer. The results were negative. Apparently, the pains were psychosomatic.

Much relieved, Walter resumed his work. Less than two months later, on Christmas of 1968, he was staggered by the suicide of his son. After some years as an itinerant dishwasher, a quondam newspaperman, and a sometime welfare recipient, young Walter, aged thirty-five, had shot himself at his home in Santa Ana, California. He left a widow and two childern.

The crushing blow plunged Winchell into sleepless nights and nightmare days. A week after his son's death, it was announced that he was going to his Scottsdale, Arizona, home "to get his bearings." He was quoted: "I'm so upset, so distraught. I've got to go away and rest, got to calm ›down." His syndicate stated that he would resume his column "after taking a vacation."

On February 5, 1968, Winchell announced his retirement. "This is the time for me to step down," he said. "We've had a lot of heartaches. It's too much of a load to pick up again. I'm also worried about Mrs. Winchell. She is a sick woman." Exactly one year after the day he retired, his long-ailing wife, who had been in and out of hospitals for years, died of a heart attack in a Phoenix, Arizona, hosptial. She was sixty-four.

Several months later, Walter began having difficulty urinating. The problem was diagnosed as an enlarged prostate, not uncommon in men of his age. Further tests revealed a malignancy. It is not clear whether or not he was told the grim facts. In any event, at his daughter's insistence, he decided to undergo surgery. In November, the tumor was removed, and several weeks later he was discharged from the Los Angeles Medical Center twenty-five pounds lighter.

He regained the weight during a lengthy recuperative period. At the time, Arnold Forster met him at the Ambassador Hotel in Los Angeles. "Walter," Forster said, "seemed to have a little of his old zip. He had all kinds of big plans. Television ideas, television shows, writing a column or a book."

Late in 1970, Robert Farrell, a wealthy optimist, decided to revive the *Daily Mirror*. He offered Winchell his old spot on page ten, and Walter grabbed it. He was scheduled for three columns a week.

Winchell came to New York to launch the paper with a press conference at the Overseas Press Club. He drew a substantial number of newsmen, including radio and TV reporters. His once vibrant voice, which had seemed raspy and tired at Montauk, had now faded to a whisper. Despite the microphone, he couldn't be heard around the room. He answered a flurry of questions. He said he had had a tumor removed and that it had not been malignant, but he would not be more specific. Further, he explained he "was getting bored with putting around the putting green" and planned to write his column "just as if nothing had happened." He did not recommend retirement for anyone and announced that the Runyon Fund donations had topped $35 million.

The *Daily Mirror,* a typographical twin of the original, began publication early in 1971. After several months, Winchell returned to Los Angeles for medical treatments. By May 7, 1971, when the Runyon Fund's silver jubilee was celebrated in the Grand Ballroom of the Waldorf Astoria, Winchell was too ill to attend. Only one major star showed up—Jimmy Durante.

On November 19, 1971, Winchell entered the University of California Medical Center in Los Angeles. He suffered for four months while old as well as new and revolutionary forms of cancer therapy were employed in an effort to stop the spreading killer. The nurses considered him a docile, cooperative patient. Toward the end, his intense pain required heavy sedation. His lone regular visitor during his terrible final ordeal was his daughter, Walda. Winchell died on February 20, 1972, at the age of seventy-four.

The next day, a white hearse carried his body to Greenwood Memorial Park in Phoenix, Arizona. Three pallbearers took the simple cedar coffin to the burial site, near the graves of his wife and son, then left Walda Winchell and Rabbi Albert Plotkin alone for the ten-minute ceremony. Miss Winchell asked three bystanders to leave. "I would rather not have to control my emotions in front of the public," she said. "My entire family is here now. I have wanted it this way. Will you please forgive me?" Then she knelt beside her father's coffin. Later she said he had died "technically of cancer, but actually of a broken heart."

The most read and listened to newsman in the history of the printed and spoken word was buried with only a single mourner and a rabbi present. The kid from Harlem, the guy from vaudeville, the man from Broadway, Hollywood, and Miami Beach ended up in Phoenix.

After learning of his death, I recalled a conversation we had had more than twenty years earlier. "Never forget, Herm," he gloated, "Winchell begins with *win*." "And it ends with *hell*," I replied. At the time, Winchell laughed loud.

Winchell left the bulk of his more than $750,000 estate in trust for his daughter. There were several bequests, including $500 for each of his son's children. Their mother received nothing under the terms of the will.

On April 14, 1972, the *New York Times* reported:

> Walda Winchell, Walter's daughter, miffed over the famed columnist's legacy, has filed suit to upset his will, contending that her father was 'not competent.' The plaintiff, Mrs. Walda Winchell von Dehn, opposed a will giving her $400-a-week benefit of a trust, preferring instead an earlier will leaving her outright the bulk of his $750,000 estate."

The suit was eventually resolved with Walda gaining a generally favorable settlement.

Winchell's death was front-page news in the *New York Times* and countless other newspapers. I believe he would have savored the page-one banners. The *Times* obituary ran to approximtely ten thousand words.

I read about fifty Winchell obituaries. Generally, they were a surprising potpourri of misinformation, misconception, and misinterpretation. Many were rewritten articles by old Winchell critics who had, in turn, rewritten the work of older Winchell detractors. For example, numerous obituaries echoed the hoary canard that Walter had approved of discrimination against Josephine Baker. As someone once observed, "A lie travels around the world while the truth is trying to get its pants on."

Some painfully depicted his work as a mass of misrepresentation. Actually, a single Winchell news column encapsulated about a hundred stories from several hundred sources. He packed more stories into one column than many papers have on thirty pages. Almost every item was a potential headline. Given the number of his stories and sources and the incidence of human error, his right-wrong ratio probably paralleled that of the more reputable news services and dailies. Winchell's problem was simply that his audience was so vast and his critics so numerous that every fumble was magnified nationally, sometimes internationally. Some of his defamers, in addition, were incredibly picayune. If Walter reported that a criminal was driving a Buick, the nit-pickers could be counted on to point out that it was a Pontiac, even if the car was irrelevant to the story.

Many categorized him as a failure by focusing on the final despairing decade of his life. Time and human weakness take their inexorable toll, of course. Often the price of great success is to be broken by it. When a longtime champion loses a fight, he instantly becomes an ex-champion, and there is nothing "exer." Thus, when Winchell's syndication shriveled from 1,000 papers to 150—a total most columnists might envy—he was considered a failure, a has-been. The fact is that he was the nation's most popular columnist from the early 1930s until 1963, when the *Mirror* folded. Moreover, until the mid-1950s— for approximately two decades—he reigned supreme as a newscaster. Actually Winchell wielded more power longer than any other person in American history, with the possible exception of J. Edgar Hoover.

A number of writers brandished "gossipmonger" like a bludgeon. It was a catchword used to berate Winchell as a purveyor of malicious or trivial fabricated tidbits about the private lives of Broadway and Hollywood personalities. In the real world of journalism, one man's gossip is another man's news. No newspaperman worth his salt would deny the existence of a gray area between news and gossip. If it's in the *Times,* a wise man once said, it's sociology, but if it's in the Winchell column, it's gossip. It should be noted that for almost a quarter of a century, Winchell devoted the bulk of his columns to political controversies, investigative reports, poetry, philosophic musings, and an abundance of wit and humor. More than 90 percent of his broadcasts were devoted to political and international news, editorial commentary, and exposes of pro-Nazis and other lunatics, plus a bright or sentimental punch line. In brief, for many years his "gossip" was a sideshow. The world was his three-ring circus.

Although his public hosannas were constantly shadowed by private heartbreak, on the whole his life was not tragic. Yes, he wandered sadly through the wasteland of the final ten years of his life, but during the greater part of his career he had fun. And what fun! He reveled in his work and in his power, loved to laugh, relished every possible material comfort and sexual joy, and derived intense delight from the excitement of functioning as a reporter, whether he was breathlessly following police calls in his car or interviewing presidents.

As late as December 1974, dramatist Arthur Miller wrote that Winchell was one of those "semiliterate sentimentalists [who] bestrode the world as powerful as Popes before the Reformation." At times Winchell was sentimental, but more often he was tough and cynical. At times he acted like a semiliterate but more often he was smart, shrewd, and possessed of a knowledge of human nature that few scholars can emulate. Winchell could never have achieved his media pinnacle without intellect, application—and *chutzpah.*

A few writers have attributed to him the worst features of Ivan the Terrible, Machiavelli, Judas Iscariot, Henry VIII, Jesse James, and Scrooge. And they were not totally wrong; he did have some monstrous characteristics. But they were merely fragments of a jigsaw personality. The trouble with most of his biographers and obituarists is that they failed to appreciate the complexity of the man. If they had known Winchell, they would have realized that he was not a man who could be hastily sketched. In fact, he was a collage of contradictions, so intensely singular and unpredictable that almost anything one wrote about him would have a certain degree of truth and falsity.

He was niggardly—and generously distributed his power to enrich people. He was rude, crude, and imperial—and a champion of the underdog, whether it was a waiter or a chorine, a small-time performer or a victim of bigotry. He battled and overcame editors and publishers in the name of independence—and sacrificed principles by catering to the emotions of a mass audience. He was vindictive—and on occasion compassionate. He was a cynic who never lost his little-boy innocence and enthusiasm.

He was Napoleonic in defense of his media empire—and often exhibited a democratic informality. He never stopped expecting gratitude—and rarely gave it. He was an egomaniac who could privately laugh at himself. He was a loner who functioned brilliantly in the public arena. His triumphs were unparalleled—and his failures were magnificent. He was selfish—and raised more money for cancer research than any other individual. He never feared enemies—and often dodged responsibilities.

He believed in "being nice to people on the way up—because you meet the same people on the way down" and was a vigorous proponent of the low blow. He was a libertine who primly said that "nudity on the stage and screen sickens me." He was venomous and milk-pure, depending on whether he was pilloried or pampered.

He was a shrewd roughneck who was easily fooled by flattery, a rich man obsessed with chimeras of poverty. He frequently infuriated associates, yet he retained their loyalty with his undeniable charisma. He refused to give his writers public recognition, yet he entrusted them with considerable power.

As a newspaperman, he believed in getting the news out to the people and raising hell. And that commitment made him an important natural resource. As a reporter, he was innately curious and fascinated by the sensational. Moreover, he was a fine dramatist. He cared nothing whatsoever about abstractions of any sort—economic, scientific, theological, artistic, philosophic, or even literary theories and dogmas. On occasion his judgment was distorted by self-importance and his unbridled success drive. With Winchell, almost everything was Here and Now, Black and White. He was compulsive about getting the news—and getting it first.

Furthermore, as a newspaperman, Winchell was representative of that most endangered journalistic species, the nonacademic wise man. The unremitting vigor he brought to any subject that interested him was no less remarkable than the lucid, sharp prose in which he expressed that interest.

But, like the classic comic mime who longs to play Hamlet, Winchell yearned throughout his career for acclaim from the so-called intellectuals who unfailingly put him down during his lifetime and ignored him after his death.

Did he have any relatively consistent characteristics? Yes, I think so. He had a greater interest in people than in ideas, an abhorrence of totalitarianism in any form, an allegiance to the traditional tenets of Americanism, Yankee Doodle style, an insatiable desire for money, a love of brightly minted phrases and witty lines, and a passion for journalism.

It was his incongruous and demonic personality that powered his success, and helped transform him into a major, undeniable force with an enormous influence on contemporary history in general and journalism in particular.

As early as 1933, Alexander Woollcott described him in *Cosmopolitan* magazine as "that celebrated, most debatable, most enterprising, and most intrusive journalist of our time. I suppose it would be easy to assemble evidence in support of the contention that Winchell is lacking in taste. He has a more valuable asset. For want of a better term, let us call it zest."

Ernest Hemingway described him as "a terrible little pro, a roughhouse artist, maybe the only newspaperman in the world who would last three rounds with the Zeitgeist."

Stanley Walker, once city editor at the *Herald Tribune,* noted, "Winchell did much for journalism, for which journalism has been slow to thank him. He helped change the dreary, ponderous impersonality which was pervading the whole press. Do newspapers today print twice, or ten times, as many items about people—what they are like, what their crotchets are, what they eat and drink and wear— as they did ten years ago? Some of the credit belongs to Winchell."

After Winchell died, Jim Bishop wrote that he "was never winsome, nor winning. He was a snitch hated by every kid in the block. But they were afraid of him, so they conformed." In the same column, Bishop conceded, "No one ignored Walter Winchell. What he wrote, they ate. City editors became accustomed to marking Monday-morning items and sending reporters out to get the story Winchell had handed them. . . . He was truly a phenomenon in journalism—one of a kind."

Oliver Pilat, the veteran journalist and author, wrote that Winchell was one of the "most influential, innovative and historically important newspapermen in the twentieth century. . . . Winchell may have left the largest legacy, by adding more words to the English language than Henry L. Mencken and by teaching the world that gossip was an electric and enduring kind of news."

Heywood Broun once said, "If there never was a Walter Winchell, somebody would have had to invent him."

J. P. McEvoy wrote in the *Saturday Evening Post,* "Walter Winchell belongs in that illustrious company of Greeley, Dana and Pulitzer and Medill if for no other reason than that he resurrected personal journalism, which had been interred with their bones."

John Gould wrote in the *Atlantic Monthly,* "Editors who consider Walter Winchell a big-shot Broadway columnist need to realize that he is actually one of the best small-town item writers in the business; his births, marriages, deaths, gossip are exactly what rural weekly editors have lived on these many years. So how do you tell if something is local or foreign, regional or national?"

When Neil MacNeil was an editor of the *New York Times,* he wrote, "Winchell still sets the pace. It is a poor town that cannot boast of its own little Winchell. Even the colleges and schools have them. Few of them have Winchell's talent and almost none his adroitness."

He left his imprint on every media form. Newspapers, today offer New York Winchells, Hollywood Winchells, Miami Winchells, Chicago Winchells, San Francisco Winchells, Washington Winchells, as well as small-town and high school Winchells. "Notes on People" is the *New York Times*'s daily Winchell. There are radio and television Winchells. As a matter of fact, in the July 21, 1969, *New York Magazine*, the American Broadcasting Company ran a boastful full-page ad—"Winchell: The Man Who Captured The Notorious Lepke Inspired Our Newsconcept."

There are magazine Winchells too. *Newsweek* does its Winchelling with several pages devoted to notes on celebrities, as does *Time* magazine in its "People" pages. *New York Magazine* publishes a one-page Winchell, and the most successful new Luce periodical, *People,* is practically all Winchell.

Was he more devil than angel?

Was he a rigorous truth-hunter or simply a headhunter?

Was he more often right than self-righteous?

Was he essentially a democrat or a demagogue?

We he a quixotic crusader or a cynical con man?

Or was he a combination of all these things?

In this writer's judgment, the balance is tipped in his favor by the Runyon Fund and his finest testimonial, presented in 1949 by two historians: Louis L. Snyder, professor of history at the College of the City of New York, and Richard B. Morris, professor of history at Columbia University. They wrote, "He has done more to rouse the conscience of America against intolerance and totalitarianism than any other journalist of his time."

He tilted at windmills and he fought dragons.

He was both a windmill and a dragon.

Index

209